Psychoanalytic Theories of Affect

PSYCHOANALYTIC THEORIES OF AFFECT

by

Ruth Stein

Foreword by

Joseph Sandler

KARNAC BOOKS

London

First published in 1991 by Praeger Publishers
This edition published in 1999 by
H. Karnac (Books) Ltd.
58 Gloucester Road
London SW7 4QY
by arrangement with Ruth Stein

British Library cataloguing in Publication Data

A C.I.P. record for this book is available from the British Library.

ISBN 1 85575 231 X

10 9 8 7 6 5 4 3 2 1

Contents

Foreword

The role of affect is becoming increasingly important in psychoanalytic theory. Freud's theories of affect, in which affects were seen as derivatives of the instinctual drives, have proved to be inadequate, yet the different theories on the role and nature of affect put forward by psychoanalysis have proved equally unsatisfactory so far. The present book, which is based on a project carried out under my supervision, attempts to address the essence of these problems. Dr. Stein achieved the rare cum laude for her doctorate.

Ruth Stein has considered the history of psychoanalytic theories of affect and has undertaken a comparative study of these theories as they have appeared in the analytic literature. In my opinion, this book is by far the best review of the psychoanalytic theories of affect so far available. It includes a consideration of the work of British and French analysts, normally neglected by the significant writers in this area in the United States. It takes into account the work of such nonanalytic writers as Tomkins, Lazarus, and Mandler, and teases out the implicit theory of affect embedded in the writings of Melanie Klein and her followers. This review has enabled Dr. Stein to put forward a number of formulations in regard to the requirements for developing a suitable and appropriate psychoanalytic theory of affect. In doing this work, Dr. Stein has drawn on relevant work in adjacent areas of psychology.

Ruth Stein has a brilliant academic mind, which she has been applying in the psychoanalytic field for many years. She has been involved in the practice of psychoanalytic psychotherapy, as well as conducting supervised cases at the Israel Institute of Psychoanalysis over the past few years. She is also interested in the integration of the knowledge accumulated in experimental and cognitive psychology with psychoanalytic knowledge. She has an excellent background in philosophy and has conducted experimental work in psychology in collaboration with Daniel Kahneman.

Her comprehensive analysis charts and clarifies the complex domain of affect theory, cutting across different theoretical streams and disciplines. Dr. Stein succeeds in reaching a series of conclusions that, though not comprising a definitive new theory, certainly lays much of the groundwork for a future theory that will, of necessity, have to be close to clinical experience. At the same time she cautions us against possible pitfalls in further theoretical development in the area of affect. She sketches the central themes of a future theory, e.g., the so-called self-generation of affects, their intricate links with cognition and motivation, changing concepts of emotional maturation, and the role of affects in shaping self and object relationships. In this regard her work is not only an excellent piece of historical research but also a significant conceptual study.

The range and depth of the discussion of the problem involved in the psychoanalytic theory of affect, the eminently readable style, and the fresh critical thought manifested in this study make it a recommended book for psychoanalysts, psychotherapists, psychologists, and indeed all those interested in the history of ideas.

Joseph Sandler

Acknowledgments

First and foremost, I wish to thank Joseph Sandler for his great help, steady encouragement, and intellectual stimulation during the years of research and writing of my doctoral thesis, on which this book is based.

During the years 1982–1984, in which he was professor at the Freud Centre at the Hebrew University of Jerusalem, I was granted a scholarship by the Freud Centre, which helped me to start the work.

Professor Sandler guided me toward thinking in terms of psychoanalytic theory. I enjoyed the savor of his immense knowledge, his love for clear and precise formulations, and his dislike of half-baked ideas posing as complete and self-evident.

For two years I participated in an unforgettable seminar at the Freud Centre. Every week, Itamar Levy, Meir Perlov, Carlo Strenger, some others, and I presented the work we were doing, while Joseph Sandler would listen, comment, pose intriguing questions, and share with us some of his latest ideas as they were ripening in his mind. We continued this small group for years afterward; we described to each other our work in progress, debated, criticized, and helped with suggestions. Theories, philosophies, and conceptualizations came alive during those intense discussions.

I also wish to thank analysts Jacob Arlow, André Green, Otto Kernberg, and Pinchas Noy and philosopher Eddy Zemach for the stimulating talks we had on affects, either personally, by letter, or both. Each from his own perspective illuminated for me some central issues with which I had been grappling at that time.

Naomi Goldblum has not only been a good friend, responding to the vicissitudes of the work with compassion and understanding, but also edited most of the text.

I am also gratefully indebted to my patients, whose vacations from analysis and therapy had to coincide with the time I could find for writing, and I thank my children, Dolli, Bitti, and Yoav, who encouraged me and filled me with hope that one day the work would be finished.

Introduction

This book deals with one of the most difficult, problematic, and haunting areas in psychoanalysis—the affects. Affects have been at the focus of psychoanalysis from the moment of its inception, and clinical work has never proceeded and cannot conceivably take place without them. The literature is strewn with remarks indicating that a general theory of psychoanalysis cannot be constructed until there is some progress in affect theory. Similarly, on the clinical level, there is almost no text without mention of affects, a fact that is reflected in the words of André Green, who wrote in 1977: "It is no exaggeration to say that, in psychoanalysis as it is practiced today, work on the affects commands a large part of our efforts. There is no favorable outcome which does not involve an affective change" (p. 129). Bion, in an address delivered to the British Society, touched upon the special status of affects when he remarked that "feelings are the few things which analysts have the luxury of being able to regard as facts" (unpublished address to the British Society, 1976, quoted by Limentani, 1977, p. 171).

There is widespread agreement in psychoanalysis as to the constitutive role of affects in the clinical process. On a recent panel in which several clinicians of different theoretical persuasions made their comments on the same clinical material, it was found that therapists with different ideas about dynamics and treatment agree as to what makes good clinical work, even if it is conducted according to theoretical perspectives different from their own. Sydney Pulver, the chairman of this study, suggested that the nonspecific curative factors common to all therapies have to do with affects. He mentioned the finding that analysts of various persuasions are all working out the same unconscious affects and fantasies in the transference, even when they approach them from different

levels of development or with different metaphors, since all these levels reverberate with one another (Pulver, 1987, p. 298).

Yet until recently a coherent and updated affect theory has been conspicuously
lacking in psychoanalysis, and more than one article has been written deploring
this state of affairs. Today, the situation has changed; many serious theoretical
and empirical studies on affects have appeared in the last few years, and the
task now is rather that of organizing, selecting, and further articulating the many
ideas on affects prevalent today.

Some ideas and conceptions engendered by recent theoretical work on affects,
such as the close link of affects with object relations and with the self, as well
as conceptions of emotional development, have extensively permeated clinical
thinking without being sufficiently appreciated by theoreticians. The constant
searching of the analyst after what lies behind the patient's feelings and affect
states may be construed as indicating an awareness of the fact that affects have
representations of their own and comprise important cognitive aspects. These
clinical insights need to be taken into consideration in the theoretical work on
affects, or emotions.

To effect this rapprochement between theory and practice, the new ideas about
affects must be brought together under a common roof, so that analysts may
acquire a clearer overview of what has been done so far and thus make better
use of the ideas in the future. At the same time, the vast material that has
accumulated from clinical work, which harbors new and perhaps unexpected
wisdom about affects and feelings, needs to be tapped and transformed from its
tacit, 'practical' state to articulation and public knowledge.

The tremendous task of extracting ideas about how affects work and how they
interact with other dimensions of mental life must await future work. The present
study focuses on the project of sketching the outlines of the most important
affect theories that have been articulated in the last hundred years, interpreting
them, and making them more intelligible. I select the best substantiated ideas
wherever possible, and I point out future directions to which these ideas might
lead, so as to envision some fragments, or perhaps even an outline, of a future,
more advanced, and updated theory of affect that will have greater relevance to
clinical knowledge and practice. In the process of this study, I point out the
theories and hypotheses that have been found to be grounded in outdated conceptions or have been refuted or made improbable by empirical evidence.

Some remarks are in order on the complicated issue of definition of terms.
Having in mind the endless endeavors to define affect and to differentiate affect,
emotion, feeling, and related terms from one another, and given their changing
usage at different times and in different places, I make little effort to distinguish
among feelings as awareness of affect, affect as a more comprehensive term
including all the thinkable components belonging to this domain, and emotion
as the complex mixture of affect and our previous experience with a particular
affect, as a rather strongly felt feeling, or as just a feeling (see Basch, 1976a;
Laplanche & Pontalis, 1973).

My close reading of Freud on affects was extremely rewarding. Going beyond the trodden path of some of Freud's conventional and widely known models of affects, my reading uncovered many ideas, some of which look surprisingly compatible with modern sensibility, whereas others fit older notions of mechanics, humors, energies, and drives. This reading also unraveled the clear interdigitation of general psychoanalytic theory and more specific conceptions of affect. This ground is covered by the first chapter.

The second chapter deals with a group of thinkers who, in my view, have received too little recognition. These theorists, who were Freud's immediate successors but were much less known than the ego psychologists, struggled to continue psychoanalytic thinking on affects by building more so-called personal theories, which would come closer to clinical practice. I describe some of their successes and failures in the development of their outlook. The third chapter presents the inherent difficulties facing ego psychology when approaching the affects, difficulties arising from its very definition as a natural science model. These two chapters provide an opportunity for observing to what extent different theories satisfactorily accommodate the various manifestations of affects.

The fourth chapter deals with the implicit affect theory embedded in the writings of Melanie Klein and Wilfred Bion, who are altogether different from their American counterparts in ego psychology. For example, the Kleinian and Bionian core distinction is between violent affects that defy psychic reality and truth, as opposed to modulated (contained, 'depressive') emotions. In contrast, ego psychology distinguishes between id-spawned, potentially traumatic affects and ego-dominated, signal affects. Both types of theory distinguish between manageable and unmanageable emotions, but they do so very differently.

The fifth, sixth, and seventh chapters describe the thinking of three important contemporary contributors to affect theory, Joseph Sandler, Otto Kernberg, and André Green, who represent the most advanced work on affects in British, American, and French thinking, respectively. Of the three, Sandler is the most concerned with the experiential side of the affects, and he considers it the only means the mental apparatus has of knowing anything about itself and the world. Kernberg has tried to synthesize ego psychology, object relations theory, Kleinian theory, and ethological thinking on affects. Like Sandler, he postulates that affects are basic. But he does not address the epistemological level, as does Sandler, who speaks of affects as being the basic data of knowledge. Kernberg deals rather with the ontological dimension and talks of the affects as being, together with self- and object representations, the building blocks of psychic structures. Green, who broke with Lacan precisely on account of the latter's refusal to refer to affect in his theory, is concerned with putting the non-neurotic pathologies with their specific affective dimensions into the first and second topographical theories and in generalizing affects as phenomena with representations of their own.

In chapter 8 I deal with recent theories of emotion in academic, experimental psychology and distinguish some historical trends in this area that closely parallel developments in psychoanalytic thinking about affects. This experience has been pleasantly surprising to me; I realized that, with all their differences, both domains progressed along a common evolutionary line, in accord with the present zeitgeist. I look at some similarities, mutual influences and points of contact between these two adjacent disciplines in chapter 9.

The tenth chapter is a recapitulation of the work done so far; I extract the main points and ideas relevant for contemporary theoretical and clinical notions of affect and point out some new trends. I hardly touch upon the very important infant studies on affects, as they are outside the scope of this book.

The philosophical and methodological background of this study draws on many sources, of which I wish to mention the two most direct influences: some of George S. Klein's ideas, as present in his book, *Psychoanalytic Theory* (1976), and Joseph Sandler's views on theory development in psychoanalysis, particularly as they were presented in his 1983 paper, "Reflections on Some Relations Between Psychoanalytic Concepts and Psychoanalytic Practice." Klein believed that psychoanalytic theory is a theory of motivation, that it has to provide an account of experience and behavior in terms of reasons and origins, significance and meaning, and that its formulations should potentially connect with clinical experience. He also believed that the principles of psychoanalytic theory should be formulated in a fashion consistent with contemporary psychology and be responsive to changes in the latter. The present work is aligned with the views of both Klein and Sandler that psychoanalysis can be considered a part of psychology. Like Sandler and in contrast to Klein, however, I believe that the idea that psychoanalytic theory should be reformulated as an exclusively clinical theory is untenable. Through the study of the nature of emotions—their being sometimes both compelling and passive experiences—one arrives at the conclusion that there must be a metaclinical theory that will go beyond all conscious experience and will provide explanatory constructs for certain affective phenomena. The ideas of Sandler, who wrote in 1983 that "psychoanalysis as a theory encompasses more than the clinical and the pathological" (p. 37), are germane to the outlook I offer here. Consequently, I also review some of the newest ideas developed in general and experimental psychology on affects in order to make them more accessible to potential theoretical work in psychoanalysis.

Another line that guided this study is the view that conceptual terms in psychoanalysis often have multiple meanings, which vary according to the context in which the term is used; each concept thus possesses elasticity and pliability in its usage and contains a whole spectrum of context-dependent meanings, some of them tacit (Kaplan, 1958; Polanyi, 1958; Sandler, 1983). Thus, dimensions of meaning and various uses of the concept of affect are explored as we take a historical journey into psychoanalytic thinking on the subject. A historical approach enables us to understand better the intellectual climate and soil in which the different ideas grew and in terms of which the most absorbing questions were put and are still being asked.

Psychoanalytic Theories of Affect

1

Freud's Writings on Affect

HISTORICAL AND CONCEPTUAL BACKGROUND

In the earliest days of psychoanalysis, several disparate streams of thought converged that, if looked at from today's perspective, enable us to draw the general picture of affects in those days.

First, there was so-called commonsense knowledge. It can easily be observed that strong emotional experiences usually elicit motor responses that involve expending of muscular energy. It is a truism that fright may 'make' a person scream, run away, or do other things, and there is usually some correspondence between the power of the experience and the intensity of the reaction to it. Anna O. spontaneously knew that after she had given utterance to her hallucinations, she would "lose all her obstinacy" and what she described as her 'energy' (Freud, 1893, p. 301).

A second source was clinical observations. From its ancient usage onward, catharsis, or abreaction, as Breuer called it, was known to have a dramatically liberating effect on its subject. Freud spoke in an approving tone of catharsis as late as 1930 and described it as "a passionate outburst of feeling under the beneficent influence of loving sympathy" (p. 210). In addition, clinical observations showed the existence of a partial hallucinatory reliving of emotional experiences at the moments of catharsis. Hence, it was reasoned that if such 'cleansing' discharge failed to occur, chronic symptoms were liable to appear. Furthermore, Freud and Breuer noticed that in their patients the events surrounding the initial appearance of the symptoms were uniformly frightful and highly emotional. They consequently argued (following other authorities, such as Ellenberger, 1984), using the then prevalent model of psychic trauma, which asserted that the effects of railway accidents are identical to those of physical lesions, and that these events (which had occurred concomitantly with the initial appearance of the symptoms) should be regarded as constituting the psychical trauma, in which fright and other intense emotions are active. Thus, *any* experience calling up a distressing affect was by definition considered a trauma.

A third source leading to the initial psychoanalytic conception of affect was derived from contemporaneous medical psychiatric conceptions. The ideas in psychiatry related to affects may be divided into three:

1. Freud accepted Charcot's explanation of hysteria as a functional illness that comprises a physiological abnormality but no anatomical lesion. Freud thus chose an intermediate position, lying halfway between pathoanatomical models such as Meynert's and strictly psychological ones such as Bernheim's, who claimed that "everything is suggestion". This position made it necessary for Freud to coin an 'intermediate concept' that would denote some flexible, transposable quantity and whose attributes would fit observations and theory alike, rather than a local lesion, i.e., an irreversible anatomical and structural change, or a purely psychological effect, such as transient suggestion. The concept of affect as Freud developed it fitted these requirements perfectly.

2. Another idea reigning in psychiatry at that time was abreaction theory, which postulated affects as the 'stuff' that had to be abreacted, that is, to be let out and then vanish. Abreaction theory made desirable a conception in which affect assumed no discernible form or existence after it had been released.

3. As was mentioned, Freud and Breuer accepted Charcot's idea of hysteria, according to which trauma in predisposed individuals induces hypnotic states in which autosuggestion occurs, which in turn leads to symptoms. Thus affect came to possess the characteristics of a negative quality. On the whole, affect theory was conceived in a matrix of distressing and morbid or exceptional and abnormal states. The idea that hypnoid states are a sine qua non of hysteria (and hysteria was in those days paradigmatic of neurosis) was taken over by Breuer from Moebius, who had regarded the operation of affects as analogous to that of hypnosis, in which the generating of somatic phenomena by ideas is facilitated and occurs easily.

However, the method of treatment implied by this model, namely, hypnotic countersuggestion (trying to bring the sequestered, pathogenic idea into association with the ideas of normal consciousness), failed to resolve the symptoms. It soon became clear that it was necessary to relive, to reexperience, the emotional events that accompanied the pathogenic event. This realization, based on clinical evidence, led Freud and Breuer to develop an alternative therapeutic model, built on affective elements, in which the same emotional configuration that was assumed to have led to the initial trauma was reinstated in order to resolve the trauma. The emotional event was then eventually explained in terms of psychic energy.

All these developments in medical thinking helped to constitute affect as a recurring observational phenomenon and to position it as the central notion in explaining trauma, then to be elevated into a hypothetical construct. This state of affairs, accompanied by accumulating clinical observation and theoretical hypotheses, led to a change in the theory of hysteria in particular and in the theory of neurosis in general. Theory shifted from concern with hypnotic, sometimes autosuggestive, states of consciousness toward vicissitudes of energy distributions that were said to be governed by certain regulative principles.

The fourth cardinal source for the evolution of the Freudian conception of affect was the philosophical zeitgeist. Freud was a Helmholtzian, subscribing to physicalistic physiology, which was based on the doctrine of scientific materialism. This school maintained that no forces other than the known and basic physical and chemical forces are active in an organism (cited in Bernfeld, 1944). Organisms were seen as systems of atoms moved by forces according to the principle of conservation of energy as formulated by Helmholtz, a principle that maintained that the sum of forces (motive forces and potential forces) remains constant in every isolated system. Within this framework, 'forces' stood for the real causes in science, and scientific progress at that time accordingly meant the reduction of the numerous forces found in an organism into two: attraction and repulsion. Freud (as Bernfeld, 1944; Levin, 1978; and others noted), saw neuroanatomy and clinical neurology as only a part of 'physicalistic psychology.' Some investigators of Freud's thinking of that period (see Levin, 1978, p. 92; Solomon & Corbit, 1974, pp. 34–35) even maintain that Freud undertook the investigations of the psychological aspect of the neuroses on extrinsic, purely tactical grounds. The neuroses were believed by Freud at that time (and perhaps to a certain extent all along) to be basically physiological and, until 1894, hereditary abnormalities, in which some basic energy-regulating mechanism had gone astray. What Helmholtz had called the constancy of the 'sum of forces' was assumed to have been made inoperative in the neurotic, who then failed to react to stimuli. This seems to be Freud's basic position, influenced by the neurophysiological frames of reference regnant at this time (see Amacher, 1964; Holt, 1965). Although the influence of Herbart, who spoke about conflict between psychic entities and about the importance of psychological motives, was also discernible in Freud's thought at that period, as we shall see, it was to assert itself only later (see Fonagy, 1982).

These introductory remarks will hopefully suffice as background for the following detailed examination of Freud's early theories of affect that are explicitly or implicitly found in his writings.

INITIAL MENTIONS OF AFFECTS IN FREUD'S WRITINGS

The first time Freud mentions affect is in 1892 (p. 121; the term 'emotions' is mentioned earlier, in 1888, p. 50). Freud speaks of an 'affect of expectancy' attached to certain ideas, assuming the form of active intentions that are bound to fail, or of passive, unshakable, negative expectations concerning the outcome of an event. Expectations of failure are called by Freud 'Kontrastvorstellungen' (translated by Strachey as 'antithetical ideas'). These are assumed to be given excessive attention by the neurotic or to fit in with the neurotic's "characteristic lack of healthy self-confidence." Such antithetical ideas then become inhibited, removed from association with the intention or the expectation, and become established as so-called counterwill, which has now acquired the power to influence action as easily as does an intentional idea.

Freud (1892) seems to speak of a primary, generalized low mood, an affective state in which gloomy, pessimistic thoughts about the self and about the future become established in the 'executive sphere of the psyche' and thereby form a volitional center of their own.

In a letter to Breuer (1892, pp. 147, 150), Freud lists affects among the dispositional origins of hysterical symptoms (as contrasted with the etiological factor), in juxtaposition to dreams and autohypnosis. Here again, Freud seems to regard affects as states of mind and, in particular, as altered states of consciousness. Freud considers affect, like dreams and self-hypnosis, to cause a splitting of the mind, a state in which every impression, while it lasts, is turned into a potential trauma.

At that time, at the end of 1892, Freud differentiated two circumstances in which an experience is taken up into the 'second consciousness' (the abnormal center of will, as opposed to primary, normal waking consciousness). The first is the willful, determined pushing away from normal consciousness of an idea or intention that arises from within; the second is the reception of stimuli coming from the outside while the person is in an altered state of consciousness. Both circumstances reflect Freud's conception of an affective state as something unusual and traumatogenic, a state that has the power to change the impact and meaning of stimuli by letting the so-called secondary consciousness gain ascendancy over the 'primary consciousness.' At this very early period of Freud's thinking he uses the concept of affect to denote a state of mind or a disposition that can change ideas conceived and impressions received while it lasts and sometimes afterward too.

Then, in 1894, another basic notion about the concept of affect was introduced. Until that time, Freud had been speaking of the power of an affect. Now he inquires about the extent of an affect. He terms it 'quota of affect' (1894, p. 60). The precise meaning of this term is not defined here, but in the context in which it appears it can be understood as referring to the extent, the span of an associative network, or the conception that persons have of some part of their body. The greater the quota of affect attached to such a bodily conception, the less accessible it is to the free play of associations, and as long as it persists it will cause the 'paralysis' of the conception of the relevant body part (not the body part itself). The passage where Freud describes this process presents us with the picture of an organ enclosed within a quota of affect so that it cannot function normally; it is hysterically paralyzed. Freud assumes that the conception (could we here speak of a representation?) of that bodily part, although it is not wiped out by some organic lesion, is nonetheless inaccessible to fresh conscious associations, that is, to correction by some sort of cognitive assimilation.

The quota of affect is considered by Freud a dimension of every psychological event (p. 171). To disperse it, the ego has to discharge it by motor action or reconnect it to the network of other ideas and memories through 'associative psychological activity,' i.e., thinking. This activity seems to be the counterpart of associative processes that occur when the ego is too weak to bind events together psychically and thereby prevent the dissociation, or splitting, of consciousness.

As a next step, Freud deals with the question of quantity. Considering the various routes an affect can take while at the same time preserving its identity, i.e., its functional equivalence (e.g., abreaction, thought activity, symptom formation, or conversion into the body), made it necessary for Freud to introduce the idea of quantity (see also 1894, pp. 62–68). If it can be shown that something can undergo different processes and yet attain one and the same goal, then it follows that the different processes are functionally equivalent and a certain constant quantity is preserved throughout all the transformations. In line with this reasoning, Freud assumes that when physical tension (which he equates with energy) surpasses a certain threshold value, the tension becomes transformed into 'psychical affect' (1894, pp. 192, 193). Furthermore, if the transformation fails, the physical tension is transformed into anxiety, which in this period he regarded as physical (1894, p. 190). Freud considers the transformation from the physical to the psychical the counterpart of the process of conversion from the psychical to the somatic.

Freud argues that since the process of conversion is rarely complete, some part of the affect "persists in consciousness as a compound of the subject's state of feeling—mood" (p. 180). Mood is here seen as a residue of the conversion process, as that which remains in consciousness after the main part of the quota of affect has gone into the body.

The issue of transformation touches not only on the bidirectional transformation of psychical and somatic energies, which are mostly synonymous with affects, but also on the transformation of pleasure into unpleasure. Both usages of transformation are couched in this period in energic terms. The second usage, that of transformation of pleasure into unpleasure, is important to the extent that the issue of unpleasure is critical for understanding the significance of the concept of affect in this as in later periods of Freud's thinking. As mentioned, in this period (and generally also later on), Freud discusses mainly the negative affects, such as affects involved in unusual states or in the accumulation and blocking of some tension, or affects that denote suffering, distress, or anxiety.

We see here a double usage of the concept of affect, as a body state and as an 'experiential state,' a usage that continued throughout Freud's writings and that essentially reflected the difficult problems Freud encountered in conceptualizing and explaining affects and their vicissitudes. Freud asks in this context whether unpleasure is the result of a merely quantitative disequilibrium (or distortion) or whether unpleasure should be seen as a qualitatively different (subjective) state. I shall come back to this question after reviewing two major works of Freud from this period, *Studies on Hysteria* (Breuer & Freud) and *Project for a Scientific Psychology*, in which he further elaborates these issues.

Meanwhile, in 1894 and in 1896, in *The Neuropsychoses of Defense*, Freud details the neurotic mechanisms that serve the transformation of affects. The basic situation depicted here is an overwhelming experience that arouses an intolerably distressing affect; such an affect cannot be solved by thought activity but can be dealt with only by forgetting it completely, by eradicating both its memory and the affect attached to it. In cases where this is not possible, attempts are made to weaken this so-called psychical group in order not to feel its distressing affect. These attempts, are the defenses. Freud details how different defenses are employed in paranoia, obsessional neurosis, and hysteria, in which reality, ideas, and affects are differently manipulated.

Freud considers hysterical conversion to be superior to the obsessional solution, because "the former deals better with affect" (1894, p. 52), in that the affect in hysteria is expelled from the 'psychical sphere,' i.e., out of consciousness altogether. This illustrates the prevalent conception that affect is a quantity and that the more definitely one gets rid of it, the better.

The notions here are quite simple. Freud works with two dimensions of an experience, idea and affect, which are assumed to travel from body to consciousness and vice versa. These movements, or transformations, afford a tolerable solution to an intolerably painful experience. By this time, the notion of secondary consciousness has disappeared; Freud feels that he is better served by notions of defensive and transformative processes. We see here some preliminary formulations around the different vicissitudes of ideas and affects (sometimes called by Freud 'psychical groups') under defensive processes. These formulations are further developed in *The Interpretation of Dreams* (1900) and in Freud's papers on metapsychology in 1915, in which both components of an experience, affect and idea, are given a common source: the instinctual drive. Meanwhile, affect is used here in two senses: as bodily sensations (1893, p. 179; 1896, p. 220) and as feelings, i.e., subjective, psychical states (1894, p. 193). An important shift is made here concerning defense, which is seen as an affective force, itself serving to defend against affects, although Freud later fell back on discussing only the defenses against instinctual drives and impulses.

At that period, Freud came upon a finding that, he believed, challenged his conceptions of repression and defense, which until this point had been conceptualized as the psychological binding of somatic excitation or of affect beyond a certain intensity. Freud found that anxiety in hysteria must be considered psychical rather than somatic (1894, p. 193). The hypothesis of psychical anxiety is very different from the one advanced in *The Neuropsychoses of Defense*, where somatic anxiety is seen as the transformed product of psychical libido. Freud now considered anxiety as psychic energy; because psychic energy had already been denoted by the term 'libido,' it followed that anxiety and libido as psychic entities could not be synonymous with 'sum of excitation,' which was regarded by Freud as somatic. This distinction notwithstanding, there are several places in Freud's writings of this period where sum of excitation is synonymous with quota of affect (1894, p. 60; 1895, p. 102). Are these two terms identical?

If they are, and if quota of affect is a physical, somatic quantity, would this fact contradict its conception as psychic energy? It seems that within Freud's perspective, adopted from Bruecke and Helmholtz, there is no contradiction. In this framework, the human organism is regarded as a phenomenon of the physical world, and physiology is an extension of physics; hence, saying that anxiety is psychical energy does not necessarily clash with its being regarded at the same time as physiological and, by extension, as physical.

A further terminological complication is the indiscriminate use Freud makes of the term 'quota of affect' and of the term 'affect' itself. The editors of the Standard Edition of Freud's writings, who investigated this problem, conclude, after a careful perusal of all the mentions of these two terms, that, although it looks as if affects are equivalent to psychic energy itself, in fact they signify for Freud the processes of discharge of that energy, rather than the energy itself (which is the quota, or the charge). In any case, it is obvious that Freud does not clearly distinguish between somatic and psychic quantities or between quantities, or charges, and their discharges; this lack of clarity is sometimes very convenient, enabling Freud to move freely between the somatic and the psychic and to attempt to explain tremendously complex phenomena with such umbrella terms as energy and affect. In the following discussion of Freud's work, I shall try to show how this is done.

STUDIES ON HYSTERIA (1893–1895)

This work, coauthored by Freud and Breuer, opens with the troublesome story of experiences and memories that, because of their "freshness and affective strength" (p. 11), cannot be left to fade away and die normally and peacefully.

Freud and Breuer maintain in this monograph that affect may occur in three forms: (1) a spontaneous reaction to an event; (2) a transformed reaction to an event, i.e., a symptom, which hides a memory; and (3) an induced abreaction from the outside, intended to achieve a spontaneous reaction, as in the first case, or to change the transformed reaction in the second case. The overall notion of affect is clearly energic. According to this notion, accumulated affect can be disposed of by direct, real action, by indirect, verbal action, or by cognitive elaboration—that is, by connection and comparison of an 'affected' idea with other regular, normal ideas. Affect here is a quantity and a force; that is, it has direction. It is assumed that if it is not reacted with, through an immediate behavioral response to an event, or if it is not acted upon, by associative 'absorption,' it has, alas, to be abreacted (the Latin prefix 'ab' means down, downward, off, away from; this easily calls to mind the image of induced birth). This concrete, materialistic conception of affect raises the question of whether there is a difference in the nature of affect when it is normally and spontaneously discharged and when it is artificially abreacted or, alternately, hysterically let out: Is the 'substance' or the 'conduct' of affect in all these eventualities the same? (Later, a completely different conception of affect made such a question meaningless.)

In this study, it is in fact Breuer who uses an affect theory to explain the working of the brain, psychopathology, and other phenomena. According to him, affects are disturbances of the dynamic equilibrium within the brain, which involve increases in excitation (p. 201). The brain is conceived by Breuer as a self-regulating mechanism that has two functions: restoration of lost energy (which is effected by the brain during sleep) and equalization of energy potentials (done during regular psychic work). During sleep, the brain produces and releases energy up to a certain level; when this level is surpassed, the organism wakes up, ready for psychical work (such as perceiving, thinking, producing motor innervations, and so on). This work consumes the potential energy that lies in store, because the brain itself, in order to function, requires, like a dynamo, a certain amount of tension even during rest; this tension is called by Breuer 'intracerebral tension.'

When potentials increase in some part of the brain, the brain works to equalize them by repeatedly activating the potential until it is leveled down. When this is not possible or not sufficient, and an energy potential builds up somewhere in the brain, a group of 'affective ideas' accumulates as an obstacle that hinders the passage of emotions from one sector of the brain to another. Thus, affects are essentially produced by a failure of equalization of potentials. An affective idea is consequently a state of a high level of intracerebral excitation that disturbs the flow of ideas and alters their relative values. The mental activity aroused by this disturbance is called by Breuer 'excitement,' and it forms, in his view, the basis of affects. Affects change the whole state of the brain, restricting all ongoing associative activity except for the affective group that persists in the brain with extreme intensity. Like the suggested idea in hypnosis, this affective idea is active, salient, and focused upon. This creates a discrepancy, a potential, between the focused idea and the vague, rapidly changing flow of the rest of the ideas in the brain. Phenomenologically, persons experiencing this state are focusing attention on one affective group of ideas, while their overall thinking stops and the environment grows dim around them; they are in a hypnoid state, in a 'rapt state of mind,' as Breuer calls it.[1]

Breuer explains this state of mind as a hypnoid state that arouses an 'abnormal psychical reflex,' in which the intensity of the affective idea becomes translated into bodily sensations and movements. The abnormal 'reflex' functions analogously to a short circuit in an electric network, where high tension breaks the insulation of the wire at some point, so that the lamp at the end of it does not receive light (p. 207); in much the same way the affective idea is divested of its affect, which has disappeared into the body. For Breuer, the affective intensity of an idea or of its recollection depends more on the amount of 'wearing away' or abreaction it has undergone than on the original amount of its affect (p. 205). Breuer equates 'psychical' with 'cerebral,' and the general conception here, although carried a step further from prevalent notions of trauma as physical injury into the domain of emotional phenomena proper, is still physicalistic and mechanistic. Emotion experienced through some meaningful event is considered to linger as a material 'foreign body,' which must be let out and drained away. On the whole, the purely quantitative factor remains the explanatory basis for Breuer throughout his theoretical exposition. He says that repetition of an 'ideogenic event' "stamps it into the body," and from that point on it is based not on a psychical process but on modifications in the nervous system; at this point, the symptoms become genuinely somatic (p. 220).

Breuer's predilection for a quantitative account of affect brings him into difficulties when he puzzles over an unconscious idea's being "sufficiently intense to provoke a lively motor act, and at the same time not intense enough to become conscious" (p. 223). This observation defeats his attempt to base all explanation of psychopathological phenomena on the factor of quantity or intensity alone. He then introduces notions of subjective quality: "The clarity of our ideas, and consequently, their capacity . . . for being conscious, is determined . . . by the feelings of pleasure and unpleasure which they arouse, by the quota of affect" (p. 225).

This passage would be clarifying, were it not for the last three words, 'quota of affect,' which seem to contradict the subjectivistic explanation of emotion preceding them. We can only guess either that Breuer fell back (perhaps carelessly) on some habitual expression of his or that the term 'quota of affect,' in addition to its denoting an unspecified, pure energic quantity, is also used to denote the subjective, experiential quality of an idea along the pleasure-unpleasure dimension, where this quality is a specific feeling. Here we clearly witness Breuer struggling with a difficulty he is unable to resolve: the quantitative hypothesis is not sufficient to serve as the sole basis of explanation for the power some ideas have to literally *move* the person (this is the etymological root of 'emotion') without entering consciousness. Breuer summons to his aid notions such as the clarity of an idea, which he equates with its capacity for being conscious, and assumes that this capacity is dependent on the degree of pleasantness of the feelings it arouses. Here a point is reached in Breuer's thinking where an integrated model cannot be put together. In spite of his considerable clarification of the concept of affect, Breuer seems to submit to his desire to prove the physiological, non-'ideogenic' nature of hysteria, and he thus repeatedly falls back on a quantitative, mechanistic account; on the whole, the usage of the term 'quota of affect' as a specific feeling dimension is exceptional in his framework (see also editor's footnote, p. 224).

On this point, and on some others, which will be brought up shortly, Freud, although borrowing some ideas from Breuer (notably the concept of discharge into the body), differs from Breuer in many ways in his thinking on affects and 'psychical mechanisms.' This seems to be the case, although Freud, in contrast to Breuer, who is concerned with affects, says little about affect per se, being drawn more to notions of incompatible ideas, willful resistances, counterwill, and cognitive weighing of possibilities and expectations. Freud, in line with

Herbart's thought, sees pathogenicity in the conflict of ideas or meanings, rather than (as did his teacher Charcot) in an overwhelming outer occurrence. Freud does not, however, consider psychical conflict a mere contradiction of alternatives; he believes that what makes the conflict poignant and personally significant is the affect that is attached differently to both sides. This conflict theory competes in his thought with trauma theory.

Thus, the trauma model asserts that undigested affect, which is neither metabolized (to the inside of the body) nor let out (outside of it), generates symptoms or causes illness (this hypothesis was common to Freud and Breuer). The conflict model, on the other hand, states that unpleasure generated at the point of incompatibility between contradictory ideas leads to repression of the weaker idea, which becomes transferred to the soma; the 'mnemic symbol' thereby becomes a bodily phenomenon. What causes affect in the trauma model is an altered state of consciousness, which lends the affect its specific status and coloring, whereas in the conflict model a feeling of unpleasure motivates the suppression of the idea (p. 116).

Thus, from the beginning of the *Studies* and throughout this monograph, the concept of affect has two functions and appears in two roles: (a) the affect (e.g., fright) is the psychical trauma, the foreign body, which, produced and provoked by some external events, immobilizes and traumatizes the person (here affect is synonymous with trauma) and (b) the affect "plants the pathogenic memory with its consequent somatic phenomena . . . on the soil provided by the hypnoid states" (p. 12). Here affect works to consolidate a pathogenic complex of memory and body state while the person is in a special facilitating (hypnoid) state of mind. While the first description deals with trauma as excessive experience, the second explanation considers traumatogenicity as a consolidated pathological structure, a memory implanted into the brain and body.

The problem of experience or perception versus memory seems to be another of the issues that Freud repeatedly refers to in his writings. Both authors of the *Studies* realize that not only fresh impressions but also—or rather?—memories create symptoms or conversions (p. 203). Breuer saw symptoms 'imprinted' by repetition as no longer ideogenic, but the observation that symptoms disappeared after the memories of the provoking event were described in detail and the accompanying affect was given words could no longer support this hypothesis, so that he now adopted the view that the recollection acts directly as a cause; i.e., it itself arouses symptoms, in analogy with psychical pain, which releases tears when remembered. Thus the memory of a psychical trauma operates as a contemporary agent, without the patient's being conscious of such memories (p. 213). In this way (and when no verbalization is made to another, to a listener), conversion is maintained by the renewal of affect in memory; there is no need for an external event to arouse fresh affect (the conception of affect as linked to memory is found in Freud's other theoretical work of that period, the *Project* [1895]).

The *Studies on Hysteria* is the story of two diligent and patient 'chimney sweepers' (p. 30) going about their Sisyphean task of trying to cure patients with unrelenting goodwill. But then comes the moment when one of them realizes that the chimney is in fact the top of a whole world full of seething forces and counterforces, and that the things emerging from there not only have to do with quantities but express staggeringly complex processes hidden deep down. The recognition and acknowledgment of the patient's conscious and unconscious feelings, his resistances to them, and the affective relation developing between him and the therapist, the transference—all these guided Freud's evolving technique of psychoanalysis. The personal affective and motivational variables opened a whole new area of psychotherapy, leaving catharsis and hypnosis far behind.

The multiple aspects that the concept of affect had already absorbed into its domain continued to coexist. Affect, at this stage of psychoanalysis, was not differentiated from cathexis (p. 89), from 'sum of excitation' (p. xxi), from feelings (p. 6), or from emotions (p. 224). It was also used to denote the more durable moods (p. 250), as well as sensations of pleasure and unpleasure (p. 250). Obviously, Freud and Breuer felt the need to explain the theoretical terms associated with the concept but not the concept itself; they left the usage of the term 'feeling' to tacit, conventional understanding. Thus, the objective aspect of the phenomenon of affect gained much attention, at the price of conceptually ignoring the subjective, feeling aspect of it.

In a way, Freud's and Breuer's visions of affective phenomena are diametrically opposed. Breuer speaks of an acute and active ('sthenic') affect as attached to an idea, or group of ideas, and as seizing all mental activity, to the exclusion of everything else. Such an extremely strong affect then ascends and expands in all directions, with nothing except motor discharge to stop its excited activity, to 'level down' this abnormal peak or halt this frenzy. When there is an overflow of this excessive excitation, and when there is a weak spot in the paths of conduction, affect spills through it to the peripheral organs, to evoke the so-called abnormal expression of emotions (Oppenheim, 1890, quoted by Breuer, p. 203). In Breuer's view, these expressions are hysterical only if they have no objective basis, i.e., only if they appear with apparent spontaneity as manifestations of an illness based on recollections that revive the original affect.

Freud chose a different angle to look at hysteria; he spoke of a disturbing idea as having a peremptory, disequilibrating effect precisely because it is suppressed, submerged, for reasons of defense against incompatibility with other, more acceptable ideas. This view of a forcefully suppressed subterranean idea, seething in the depths of the psyche, is very different from Breuer's overflowing 'peak phenomenon.' According to Freud, the idea is 'exiled,' so to speak, to these depths because of the unpleasure it might have given rise to, had it remained on the surface.

PROJECT FOR A SCIENTIFIC PSYCHOLOGY (1895)

Freud's *Project* is a work of considerable interest for affect theory in psychoanalysis, although it is obscure, has not withstood the test of empirical knowledge, and was eventually discarded by its author. This monograph contains numerous direct references to affect and introduces many theoretical terms that were to serve Freud for the next twenty years or so. Among the issues discussed here are the relationship between quantity and quality, the distinction between mobile and bound energy, the economic hypothesis, a model of the experiences of pain and satisfaction, the binding function of the ego, and the relation of thought to language and consciousness, which, according to Freud, is the main domain in which the perturbing role of affect is manifest.

Affects are conceptualized in the *Project* as residues of painful experiences (1895 [1950], p. 321). Pain is defined here as the breaking of the screening contrivances in the organism's systems of perception (ϕ) and memory (ψ) by excessive quantities of excitation. Pain is said to produce permanent facilitations in the memory system and to establish pathways of conduction in memory (ψ), a rise in the energy level, and a concomitant tendency to discharge this quantity by investing the image of the pain-provoking object. This quantity of energy, with which the pain-producing and therefore hostile object is invested, is discharged into the interior of the body by so-called secretory neurons, commissioned with inner discharge (in the same way as the motor neurons are responsible for discharge from the body outward).

Affect is thus the reproduction of the painful experience; it is not a direct emotional experience but rather the residue or trace of it. The reproduction itself, however, is not sufficient to produce affect. Affect is not just a memory, but a memory facilitated by a surplus of energy, by cathexis. Here Freud sees affect as consisting of an increase in psychic energy within the memory system; it is the cathecting of that system. The perception of an affect is effected through the excitation of a third system, consciousness, or quality, which is equated by Freud with the system of inner perception. This system of consciousness had to be postulated by Freud in line with his opinion that reproduction (remembering) is without quality (p. 308). In Freud's view, memories are not conscious in themselves; only the quality of unpleasure that arises by the excitation of the system of consciousness can make them conscious. An affect is therefore a kind of energy increase, which can be perceived or felt as pleasure or unpleasure. This formulation seems to put affects on a par with sensations, the only difference being, according to Freud, that in contrast to sensations, the excitation leading to affect is endogenous rather than external. Accordingly, the perception of the object is an inner perception, sometimes of a hallucinatory nature, rather than an outer perception, which occurs through sensations.

The central point to note here is that affect is said by Freud to be produced in the course of a repetition of an organic experience of pain. It is this reproductive quality which confers on it its psychic dimension; the inner reproduction of a passage of energy, accompanied by consciousness, is 'perceptualized,' so to speak, and thereby rendered into a kind of inner perception. The repetition of such an inner perception progressively weakens it; in the process of repetition, says Freud, the traces of the pain experience draw weaker and weaker investments of the mnemic image of the hostile object, so that they increasingly assume the role of signals for the production of defensive operations. According to this explanation, affect is the inner reproduction and occasionally the perception of a painful experience. Affect, in contrast to ideas, is not generated by external perception but is the re-emergence of a memory accompanied by body sensations. (We find this idea at several points in Freud's later writings.) Affects become increasingly 'interiorized', compared to the view of them as reactions to external stimuli.

Freud contends that whereas affects are the traces of experiences of pain, wishes are the traces of experiences of satisfaction. Both affect and wish involve a rise in tension level, but whereas the wish is seen as a rise in energy level by accumulation, which stimulates the hallucination of the wish-fulfilling object, in the case of affect the rise comes about by a sudden discharge of energy. Seen from another angle, the difference between affect and wish is that in the case of a wish, i.e., of accumulated energy, the psychic apparatus can allow itself to be deceived through the creation of a representation that satisfies the wish (hallucination), whereas affect, whose role is to provide information about the internal state of the body, cannot use the device of hallucination. On the other hand, whereas wishes will later lead, via hallucination, to thinking, affects are considered by Freud as disturbers of thinking.

Another important issue concerning the concept of affect is the relationship between quantity and quality. The whole *Project* is dominated by its author's effort to solve the relation of quality and quantity and their transformations into each other. Freud attempts to solve the problem of how a quantity of excitation, i.e., energy, becomes a quality of perception and sensation (which to Freud are synonymous with consciousness) by tracing quality back to vicissitudes of quantity. This is in line with the declared aim of the *Project*, namely, to consider psychic processes as quantitatively determined states of material particles. Freud denotes quantity by the sign $Q\eta$, and assumes that it appears under two forms, as a flow between neurons and as the charge that loads the neurons (see Breuer's 'brain energics,' 1895, p. 205). At no point does Freud specify the nature of $Q\eta$ or say whether it is physical or psychical energy. $Q\eta$ seems to denote an undifferentiated energy that invests all the systems, its attributes deriving from Freud's so-called quantitative hypothesis (see 1894, p. 60). As to quality, Freud maintains that the structure of the nervous system includes a system for transforming external quantity into quality (1895 [1950], p. 308). This system is linked with perception, and when it discharges energy, it produces consciousness by allowing the neuronal apparatus to perceive quality of impressions coming from the external world.

Freud thus postulated a system of consciousness (ω) between the perceptual system (ϕ) and memory (ψ), which receives quantity from the perceptual system. This system of consciousness, however, transfers neither quality nor quantity to the memory system but merely excites it (p. 388). In this way, the inner, mainly memory processes are assumed to be unconscious and can only secondarily acquire consciousness through being linked with processes of discharge and perception (p. 389). The model presented here assumes that whereas memory is in itself unconscious (it can acquire consciousness secondarily, through ω), a perception is as a rule linked with consciousness (and with indications of quantity). As Basch (1976b, p. 391) writes, the *Project* foundered on Freud's view of perception; having postulated that all sensory perception automatically commands attention and consciousness, Freud could not explain perception without consciousness, i.e., how, for example, potentially painful sensory impressions could be diverted before their effect was consciously felt (this is known in psychology as the 'pre-perceiver's paradox'). In Freud's view, quantity and quality are relatively independent, but not until 1920 did he fully realize what is implied in this view.

In the five years between the *Project* and *The Interpretation of Dreams*, the perceptual and memory systems φ and ψ were condensed into the system Pcs, while the system ω retained its function of consciousness. To these systems a new dimension was now added: the 'psychological,' i.e., dynamic unconscious. This momentous step abolished the synonymity of unconscious and nonpsychic and was another move toward forming a conception of dynamically unconscious affects, to which we shall return later.

Another important change at this time is Freud's discovery of infantile sexuality, which also contributed to loosening the exclusive link between affects and memories postulated in the *Project*. Affects are now no longer equated solely with the reproduction or re-enactment of (mostly painful) memories but are seen as also being linked with fantasies and wishes through their postulated common source, the instinctual drives.

These changes resulted in a double shift: On the one hand, the concept of the drives replaced to a great extent that of memories as the source of affects, a change that had not very fortunate consequences in subsequent thinking on affects, as we shall see. On the other hand, a gradual move occurred in Freud's thinking from viewing affects as a mechanistically determined discharge of memories to seeing them in motivational terms. This change is also apparent in some of his letters to Fliess and in his drafts. In 1896 (letter 52), Freud writes that he considers a hysterical attack not as a discharge but as an action, which, like every action, is a "means of reproduction of pleasure" (p. 233); it is not just an "intensified expression of emotions" (as he had thought in 1894; see e.g., p. 73), but a motivated act. He also writes that "the psychical structures affected by repression are not . . . memories, since no one indulges in mnemic activity without a motive, but impulses" (1897, p. 247, letter 61), and "symptoms, like dreams, are the fulfilment of a wish" (ibid.). These passages indicate that the view of affect as a mechanical accumulation of energy 'secreted' with memories and seeking discharge recedes considerably and gives way to more psychological, motivational explanation of affects.

THE INTERPRETATION OF DREAMS (1900) AND LATER

In *The Interpretation of Dreams* affects occupy a pivotal role, perhaps more than is immediately apparent, both in the explanation of the process of dreaming and in the conceptualization of dreams themselves. Freud contends in this work that affects permeate the raw material that serves for the dream thoughts and dream construction. He writes: "It is never possible to enter into the dream thoughts without being deeply moved" (1900, p. 247), and hence, "the affects felt in dreams belong to its latent content" (p. 248). He also says that, in contradistinction to ideas, affects in dreams remain untouched by distortion (p. 507) and are the least influenced by censorship; they are always appropriate (see Sachs, 1974, p. 92), at least in their quality (while their quantity may be increased by displacement and the additional affective quantity accruing from the idea that they are displaced onto). In many of his statements about affects in dreams, it is either explicitly asserted or indirectly implied that in order to understand a dream one must first understand the affects and then find the ideas originally 'belonging' to them.

Freud argues that affects are not distorted in dreams; rather, they are either suppressed or detached from their accompanying ideas. The issue of the suppression or transformation of affects in dreams appears several times throughout this work, although Freud's main interest here lies in dream symbolism and in the elaboration of the concept of a mental apparatus that came to replace the neuronal apparatus postulated in the *Project*.

Freud maintains that the issue of the suppression of affects in dreams would require "a painstaking investigation of a theory of affects" (p. 604); meanwhile, he lists two factors that may effect this suppression: (a) the very state of sleep, which is understood by Freud to interfere with the ability of unconscious thinking to call up affects, so that only the strongest affective impulses find their way into the dream and (b) psychic conflict, of which the dream is the structured compromise. Conflicting thoughts carry contradictory affects; these thoughts inhibit and partially cancel each other out, and when the suppressing and suppressed affects work together, they result in various compromises. These formulations reveal two assumptions, used in a sense as working hypotheses by Freud: (a) the constant presence in the dream of suppressed or attenuated affects and (b) the pairing of contradictory trains of thought, involving combinations of their accompanying affects. The well-known 'dream work' is defined by Freud as the agency that deals with affects in the dream, organizing them according to the wishes of the dreamer. To Freud, the most striking fact about affects in dreams is that the dream work is free to detach an affect from its links to certain dream thoughts and to introduce it at any point it chooses in the manifest dream. The detachability and fluidity of affects make them exert a constant influence on the association of ideas, so that the trains of thought in the dream are never free from purpose or meaning. This is so even though the ideational material, which has been changed by dream distortion, is no longer compatible with the affect, which is retained unmodified, so that the task of analysis is to "put the right material into its former position" (p. 461).

This relocation or redistribution of affects in different places in the dream can occur in three ways, in Freud's view: affects are 'allowed through' to the manifest content, they are reduced to nothing, i.e., suppressed, or they are turned into their opposite through the intensification of contrary affects. Thus, a dream thought, which is pleasurable in itself, may produce unpleasure (through the censorship; the phenomenon of the reversal of affect in dreams served Freud as a first hint to the postulation of a dream censorship).

Obviously, Freud gives affects in the dream an unusually significant role. In this context, two points are pertinent. First, the affect experienced in dreams is no less significant than any other affect of equal intensity experienced in waking life, and second, affects have, in a sense, a more stable and less dismissible role than the manifest content of the dream. Thus, Freud writes: "If I'm afraid of robbers in the dream, the robbers . . . are imaginary . . . but the fear is real" (p. 460). Affects are thus pointers to missing thoughts: "The ideational material has undergone displacements and substitutions, whereas the affects have remained unaltered" (p. 460). Freud deems affects absolutely necessary for understanding the dream experience, and he considers them reliable indicators of what the dream is about, more than any other dream element. Nevertheless, he believes that there has to be an ideational counterpart to the affect in order for the affect to be understood. Although affects are regarded by Freud as the most valid element in the dream, he still maintains that he cannot "assess psychically an affect unless it is linked to a piece of ideational material" (p. 460).

The ideas or dream thoughts are incorporated into the wishes, the exclusive "psychical motive forces for the dream." Thus, in the *Interpretation*, the roles of wish and affect are reversed, as compared to their role in the *Project*, where the wish was said by its nature to permit indulgence in hallucinations, whereas the affect was assumed to remain closer to reality and to the body. In the *Interpretation*, by contrast, affect is conceived as a structureless entity that cannot even be repressed, whereas the wish plays the central role in the play of the dream. The wish seeks to re-establish the original situation of satisfaction by recathecting the mnemic image of the perception of satisfaction and establishing 'perceptual identity' between need and satisfaction (p. 565). This is so because the internal need perpetuating the wish exerts a continuous impact, while affect, which is defined as a transitory phenomenon, is unable to maintain and sustain a stable perception, or perceptual identity. Thus, the wish, as the psychic product and elaboration of a need, is assumed to have movement and direction of its own and to be of a higher order than affect, conceived as energic expression; affect can at most serve as an initiator for the wish.

Another important issue at this stage of Freud's theory is whether affects are pure psychic energy or motor and secretory discharge processes controlled from the unconscious (1900, p. 52; see also Kulovesi, 1931; Rapaport, 1953). Rapaport (1953) maintains that the year 1900 signaled a sharp break in affect theory, when Freud espoused the view of affects as discharge processes from the unconscious, rather than psychic drive energy proper. It seems, however, that even the newer conception of affects as discharge processes proved insufficient, for if affects are discharge processes that are centrifugally directed, that is, tending away from the psychic apparatus, then they would necessarily be evanescent and self-exhaustive, tending to run their course until they ceased to exist. This is in marked contrast to the important, persistent role affects have in dream theory. There is an inherent contradiction between seeing affects as fluid discharge processes and seeing them as relatively stable indicators of meaning or of missing thoughts. Rapaport explains this contradiction as due to Freud's failing to assume the existence of discharge thresholds for drives and/or affects that arrest the leaking of affects and thereby give them substance and persistence. This contradiction will be taken up later in this study, in the discussion of the relationship between tension and discharge, as dealt with by Brierley (1937) and later by Jacobson (1971).

Let us go a step further, to the year 1905. Freud, having written *The Interpretation of Dreams* and having achieved some deep personal insights in his self-analysis, now defines psychic trauma as a conflict of affects (1904, p. 24). During all this time, the conception of trauma as caused by retention of affects is not discarded by him altogether, although he seems to use it mostly in discussions intended for laymen (e.g., 1904, p. 257). By this time, however, Freud's perspective in discussing his theories has changed from the general-scientific (see the *Project*), through the theoretical-clinical (see *The Interpretation of Dreams*), to the empirical-clinical level (see *Fragments of an Analysis of a Case of Hysteria* [1905a], and *Three Essays on the Theory of Sexuality* [1905b]), which now implicitly includes the self-analytic viewpoint as well. This may be an additional reason that Freud, when discussing the genesis of Dora's neurosis, lengthily describes the course and vicissitudes of conflicted feelings, of having feelings of one kind as a reaction to other feelings or as a buffer against experiencing other feelings (1905a, pp. 56, 58, 62, passim), and tells us how he explained to Dora "that the expression of emotion and the play of features obey the unconscious rather than the conscious, and are a means of betraying the former" (p. 59).

When it comes to conceptualizing feelings, however, Freud again resorts to economic, energic, and instinctual terms. Thus, he sees anxiety as a repressed sexual feeling (1907a, pp. 60–61), and while ideational pathogenic material can be variously remodeled and transposed in different people, the accompanying affects are "uniformly transformed into anxiety" (1909, p. 137). The hypothesis that all affects are transformable into anxiety is another version of the theory that all anxiety derives from 'strangulated' libido and is the energic discharge of it; subjective feelings have as yet no place in Freud's theory (as contrasted with his practice).

Thus, in the *Three Essays on the Theory of Sexuality* (1905b), affect is scarcely mentioned, while the concept of instinct is conceptually elaborated to a great extent. The phenomenon of sexuality, in which feelings play such an important part (see G. S. Klein, 1976), is considered exclusively from the instinctual and somatic angle, except for such short mentions as the "sexually exciting affect of many emotions" or the "erotogenic effect of . . . feelings" (1905b, p. 204). Freud considers feelings as having a sexually exciting effect, never the other way around, that sexuality arouses diverse feelings—except in the case of defensively unpleasurable affects, such as disgust or shame (1905b, pp. 151, 157, 159).

The five or six years around 1900 were tremendously fruitful years in Freud's evolving thought. He grasped and gave form to profound clinical insights of behaviors in which the personally meaningful, the subjective and private have the most basic and mutative power over one's life events and acts. At this time, he also articulated his idea of "an elemental psychology—*a metapsychology which ignores the difference between conscious and unconsciousness,*" a statement that foreshadows future developments in psychoanalytic theory (emphasis added). On the other hand, Freud declares in 1907 that "one would have to make a sharp distinction between instincts and emotions. First, one would have to establish that instinct is a concept, a term for the dynamic or disturbing influence which organic needs exercise on psychic processes. The instincts bridge over from the organic to the psychic. Emotions, however, belong entirely to the psychic realm" (1907, p. 138). This is a striking example of Freud's formulating an idea that was to disappear afterward, only to become a focus for future efforts at elaboration.

Although Freud came to realize that fantasies and memories of events rather than the actual occurrence of the events per se were the etiological factors in the neuroses, he still had to support his explanations with the concept of psychic energy. The concept of energy itself, however, had changed; from cerebral energy (in the *Project* and in the *Studies*), it became, from 1900 onward, instinctual energy. The great transition in this period concerning affects was that affects were no longer seen as cerebral energy stored in memories in the brain, but as drive derivatives, on a par with ideas. Affects are now no longer considered pure energic forces striving to emerge directly through some 'emotional' acts; neither are they initiators of wishes. At this stage of Freud's thinking they have become secondary surface manifestations, while priority is given now to the drives and impulses that inhabit the system Ucs (unconscious) in the recently conceptualized regions of the topographical model.

THE TOPOGRAPHICAL MODEL:
THE METAPSYCHOLOGICAL PAPERS (1915)

Freud's discovery of childhood sexuality and his articulation of its developmental stages (1905b), which led to his discarding of the seduction theory of the neuroses, also effected a shift from the fixated event-in-memory toward the fantasy-generating drive. The repressed pathogenic memory was now no longer seen as necessarily a memory of a real event, but more often as a memory of a wish-fulfilling sexual fantasy springing from libidinal drives. With this major shift in emphasis, the problem of how a memory can be as strong and influential as a current experience, which in Freud's terms of this period meant that it could involve as much psychic energy, appeared to be solved; the interplay between infantile sexual drives and the fantasies subserving their fulfillment was regarded as being no less powerful than a current reaction to a real external event.

The drive came to replace, in its power and immediacy, the vividness of a past or present experience. This shift made affect into a drive-derived phenomenon, instead of a lived and encapsulated experience. The concept of drive itself, however, was used by Freud in a deliberately ambiguous way (see 1915a, p. 12) as a concept at the 'frontier' between the psychic and the somatic, and as a phenomenon that must remain by definition unconscious in itself but that can be deduced from its manifestations, the idea and the affect. The introduction of the topographical model, which hinged on the differentiating axis of the existence or nonexistence of consciousness, helped to separate the fates of the two kinds of drive representations, affect and idea, thereby providing different accounts for the different neurotic manifestations (in which ideas and affects undergo different vicissitudes), although this model proved to have its drawbacks with respect to affects, as we shall see later.

The introduction of the concept of the instinctual drive now made possible a more complicated picture of mental functioning compared with the former reflex-discharge model, which had been more static and had assumed a short, automatic circulation of stimuli and responses (see Emde, 1980). By their increasing and decreasing demands for mental work, the drives assumedly hindered the nervous system from its perennial task of discharging stimuli. Freud saw the nervous system as mostly subject to the pleasure principle, which equated pleasure with tension reduction (e.g., 1915a, p. 120), and he pointed out that he still did not know the nature of the relations obtaining between pleasure and unpleasure, on the one hand, and fluctuations in the amount of stimulation, on the other; this issue was to be taken up by him in *Beyond the Pleasure Principle* in 1920. Even in 1915, however, Freud had doubts concerning the identity of the constancy principle and the pleasure principle, which he had equated in the *Project* (1895) and in *The Interpretation of Dreams* (1900). In *Beyond the Pleasure Principle* (1920) and in *The Economic Problem of Masochism* (1924) the two principles were to be to some extent differentiated.

We have seen that affect at this period of Freud's thinking was no longer considered a mere quantity, or a state of mind, but a drive-derived phenomenon. In further discussing affects in Freud's so-called Metapsychological Papers (1915a, 1915b, and 1915c), I have chosen to focus on three cardinal intertwined issues concerning the conception of affects: the issue of *quality* (with its complicated relation to quantity); the problem of *transformation* of affects, in the sense of transformation from pleasurable into unpleasurable affects; and the question of *unconscious affect*. These points, in the order presented here, follow

Freud's line of thought running through the three papers and express his attempt to deal with changes and developments in affects. In *Instincts and Their Vicissitudes* (1915a) Freud introduces the concept of the instinctual drive as being the quantitative root, which at the same time determines the quality of behavior, ideas, and affects. The instincts are understood by Freud to undergo various vicissitudes, the main one being repression, which is discussed in a paper bearing the same name (1915b). The concept of repression, as well as other transformations, leads to a topography of the mind in which there are unconscious, preconscious, and conscious regions or systems, and in which there may be unconscious affects too (1915c).

The paper on instincts (1915a) does not deal directly with affects, but in it Freud discusses the feelings of love and hate as springing from different sources, rather than being the opposite of each other. He ascribes love to pleasure and sexuality, and hate to the self-preservative instincts; however, he is mostly concerned with investigating the instincts as the unifying concept for mental phenomena, whereas affects are scarcely referred to in this work.

In the paper on repression (1915b), in which repression is considered one of the vicissitudes of the instincts (the other three being sublimation, reversal to the opposite instinct, and turning around upon the subject's own self), Freud introduces the concept of a quantity representing the instinct, called again (see 1894) 'quota of affect,' which is separate, to his mind, from that of the idea. Until this point, the psychical representative of the instinct was assumed to be an idea (or group of ideas) charged with psychic energy. But

clinical observation now obliges us to *divide* up what we have hitherto regarded as a single entity; for it shows us that besides an idea, some other element representing the instinct has to be taken into account. . . . [This element] undergoes vicissitudes of repression which may be quite different from those undergone by the idea. For this other element of the psychical representative the term quota of affect has been generally adopted (1915b, p. 152, emphasis added).

In this famous passage, Freud maintains that idea and instinctual energy, that is, idea and a specific quota of affect, have to be treated separately. Instinctual energies may be transformed into affect, particularly anxiety. In this paper, Freud also says that repression of affect is more important than repression of ideas. The true task of repression is to deal with the quota of affect, although the vanished affect comes back as social or moral anxiety and self-reproach (1915b, p. 157).

In *The Unconscious* (1915c) Freud posits that mental processes are inherently unconscious and can be perceived by means of consciousness similarly to the way in which the external world is perceived through the sense organs (see 1900, pp. 615–17). This formulation considers consciousness a separate dimension added to mental thought processes. *The Unconscious* contains also the first description of the unconscious in the systemic sense and a discussion of the three parts of the topographical system. Within this framework, affect is assumed to undergo three kinds of vicissitudes: the affect may remain as it is; it may be transformed into a qualitatively different affect, namely anxiety; or the affect may be suppressed and thus prevented from developing at all; in this way the instinctual impulse is prevented from turning into an affective manifestation. Freud believed that only in the latter case may affects be considered unconscious. The three vicissitudes of affect enumerated here bear a striking resemblance to the three main issues I have selected for discussion on affects in this period: affect remaining as it is opens up the question of its quality; affect transformed into anxiety bears on the problem of transformation; and affect suppressed is, in Freud's view at this time, unconscious affect.

Let us enlarge on these points, beginning with the issue of feeling quality. It can be seen that in Freud's writings, both quantitative and qualitative aspects of the instincts are given the name of affects. Thus, Freud writes that affect is "the quantitative aspect of the instinct detached from the idea, which finds expression, proportionate to its quantity, in processes which are sensed as affects" (1915b, p. 151; 1916–1917, p. 395). The term affect, however, is also used to denote the qualitative experience of the quantity of instinctual drives. More specifically, Freud says that the 'affective factor' is the quantitative one (see 1915a, p. 123; 1915c, p. 178), whereas the feelings in turn comprise the experiential or qualitative part of the affect. Feelings for Freud are essentially the perception of the affects generated by the body. Many of the complicated issues of quality and quantity are discussed in the first of the Metapsychological Papers, *Instincts and Their Vicissitudes* (1915a). As to the issue of transformation, the processes of transformation are described in the paper *Repression* (1915b); in fact, nothing substantially new is added to Freud's main idea that instinctual repression leads to anxiety.

The third question, whether in principle there can be unconscious affects, is crucial both for the concept of affect itself and for the theory within which it is embedded. Consequently, clarification of the question has to be approached according to how the concept is viewed and within what theoretical matrix the question is addressed, the two issues being mutually dependent. Since the metapsychological meaning of the concept of affect at this period refers to a drive derivative and a quantity of energy, part of it is unconscious in the sense of the nonpsychological and nondynamic unconscious. Occasionally, however, Freud separates the feeling aspect from the more general concept of affect and writes, on the one hand, that "it is the essence of a feeling to be felt," that is, to be experienced consciously; the notion of an unfelt feeling is inherently paradoxical. On the other hand, he takes into account the clinical phenomena of defended, displaced, or muted feelings, which are not available to their owner but may be apparent to or vicariously felt by an observer. Freud takes these facts as necessitating the assumption of the existence in the system Ucs of what he calls 'affective structures,' which, like other structures, can become conscious, but about which he does not go into any further details. At the same time, however, he adheres to the basic distinction of ideas as cathexes of memory traces and affects as processes of discharge, the final manifestations of which are perceived as feelings (1915c, p. 178).

All this is discussed again in chapter 2 of *The Ego and the Id* (1923), where Freud writes that all perceptions received from the outside (sense perceptions) and from within (sensations and feelings) are conscious from the start, and therefore, if affects are to include perceptions, they must be conscious to begin with and become repressed later. It is repression that inhibits an instinctual impulse from being turned into a manifestation of affect; repression thus means not only withholding things from consciousness but also preventing the development of affect and muscular activity. Freud sees a constant struggle going on for primacy over affectivity between the two systems, Cs (conscious) and Ucs. The system Cs, which controls motility, also controls affectivity, although not with the same success.

Thus, in Freud's thinking of this period, unconscious affects are basically suppressed affects, which, rather than being structures that continue to exist in the unconscious, are essentially a potential, a beginning, which is prevented from developing. The interesting point here is the theoretical question. From the perspective of clinical experience, there is no question that there *are* unconscious feelings. But in theory, the term 'unconscious affects' depends on the meaning of 'unconscious' and on its logical tie to the concept of affect in that theory. Therefore, a brief review of the historically changing conceptualization of 'unconscious' may help to clarify this subject.

At the beginning, on observing hysterias, Freud identified the conscious and unconscious as the repressing and the repressed forces of the mind, respectively. Later, on observing the resistances in analysis, Freud realized that 'unconscious' has two senses, which should be differentiated: the descriptive unconscious, which is a particular quality of a mental state, and the dynamic unconscious, which may be said to be a particular function of a mental state. At the same time, the notion of system gradually increased in importance and culminated in the topographical model, in which the two nondescriptive usages of the concept 'unconscious,' the dynamic and the systemic, were condensed into one, now called the Ucs, which now embraced the whole repressed portion of the mind, whereas the 'descriptive unconscious' was given the name Pcs (preconscious).

Thus, when Freud speaks in 1915 about unconscious affect, it is not clear whether he means (a) affect that is located in the system Ucs, (b) affect that is dynamically unconscious, i.e., repressed, or (c) affect that is simply latent, being only contingently in an unconscious state and liable to become conscious at any moment—i.e., preconscious affect. Logically, Freud should have adopted the third option, as in his view unconscious (in a dynamic or systemic sense) means existing and subsisting in a repressed state, in a stable form, embodied in memory structures, and potentially retrievable in its original form,[2] and this could not be said in this theory about affects, which are considered by him as essentially centrifugal movements from the nervous system outward to the interior of the body. According to this conception, affects in the dynamic and systemic sense are 'pre-affects,' a potential or source for the emergence of affects; the instinctual impulse is inhibited from turning into a manifestation of affect by repression. Moreover, affects cannot be preconscious, because the system Pcs involves, by definition, word presentations, which affects lack; Freud says about affects that they can be either in a potential state or conscious, but never preconscious. Thus, affect, in this framework, can only be suppressed (inhibited from developing at all), or else it becomes, almost by definition, anxiety. Unlike ideas, which may travel back and forth, becoming alternately conscious or repressed, affect, in Freud's theory of this period, seems to be unidirectional. Affects are either discharged, thereby becoming conscious, or, when they flow back to the body, are resomatized and become somatic anxiety (see Schur, 1953, 1966). Thus, we see that although feelings were said by Freud to be a kind of memory (see *Project* 1895 [1950]), they do not have the form of memory, and the nature of the 'affective structures' Freud mentions is never further elaborated.

As to the question how affect can become conscious, Freud at one point states that affect does not arise, as a rule, until the breakthrough to a new representation in the system Cs is achieved; that is, affect depends on a representation to carry it through to consciousness. At another point, however, Freud allows for the possibility that affect may emerge directly from the system Ucs, but only in the form of anxiety. In the case in which affects need a conscious representation to forward them to consciousness, affects are seen as dispositions, which are realized through the ideas that represent them and carry them through or that, alternatively, prevent them from surfacing to the system Cs, as the case may be. This rudimentary conception anticipates formulations to be established in the next phase of psychoanalytic theory, that of the structural model.

BEYOND THE PLEASURE PRINCIPLE (1920); THE EGO AND THE ID (1923)

Beyond the Pleasure Principle (1920) opened new horizons for the understanding of affects, and it too began with a problem, a difficulty. In 1897 and in 1900, the difficulty confronting Freud had been how to link traumatic feelings to certain external events, such as seduction by parenting figures, a difficulty whose resolution revolutionized Freud's thinking and culminated in the theoretical elaborations of 1915, in which topographical space was accorded to instinctual vicissitudes and unconscious impulses. By 1920, another problem had made itself felt, namely the untenability of assuming a direct and proportional relation between feelings and drives (1920, p. 8). In this paper Freud writes: "We would readily express our gratitude to any philosophical or psychological theory which was able to inform us of the meaning of the feelings of pleasure and unpleasure which act imperatively upon us. . . . This is the most obscure and inaccessible region of the mind" (p. 7). Many observations led Freud to realize that there is no direct correspondence between quantitative changes in tension or accumulation of excitation, on the one hand, and intensity and pleasurableness of feelings, on the other.

In this work Freud asks why, given the predominance of the pleasure principle, people may wish, or may even be compelled, to create and recreate painful situations and affects. The answer he attempts to give at this point in his theory is that the phenomenona beyond the pleasure principle are but illustrations of the conservative nature and activity of the drives, which impel things to return to their former state, and he postulates that the death instinct in particular operates to reintroduce the original state of inanimate matter, that is, death.

Thus, *Beyond the Pleasure Principle* is essentially a reconsideration of the rule of the pleasure principle over mental life; this principle and the economic principle were assumed to relate pleasure and unpleasure directly and proportionately to decreases and increases in quantities of excitation (see the beginning of this chapter). This point is of paramount importance to Freud's theory of affect, which was until then based on the assumption of direct proportionality between pleasurableness and degree of physical excitation. The observation, culled from diverse sources, that there does not exist any such simple relation between the strength of feelings of pleasure and unpleasure, and the corresponding changes in the quantity of excitation, led Freud to propose an additional factor that partakes in determining the feeling quality of an experience or an event: temporality, or, more precisely, rhythm, which is regarded as the increase or diminution in the quantity of excitation at a given period of time (p. 8; also 1924, p. 160; 1938, p. 146); this is called the 'modified' pleasure principle.

Other causes for the generation of unpleasure, in addition to the modified pleasure principle, are the phenomena of conflict and repression. Pleasurable feelings may become unpleasurable, says Freud, as a consequence of conflict, which may lead to the compulsion to repeat unpleasurable or painful experiences. This compulsion, found in traumatic neurosis and in children's play, can be explained by assuming that what is unpleasure for one mental system may at the same time be pleasure for another system in the mental apparatus.

There are also unpleasurable experiences that are totally unsatisfactory and have never brought pleasure in the first place. In some situations, such as in the transference, painful emotions are compulsively revived and repeated not as dreams or memories but as actual experiences, and not for active mastery but in a passive way (p. 21). This is the repetition compulsion, which Freud considered to be more primitive and instinctually rooted than the pleasure principle. The repetition compulsion is autonomous and is opposed not only to the pleasure principle but also to its derivative, the reality principle, which functions to anticipate and prevent unpleasure. The repetition compulsion, in Freud's view, operates under the sway of the ego instincts, which exercise a pressure toward death (while the sexual instincts aim at the prolongation of life). The functions of the ego instincts, of self-preservation, self-assertion, and mastery, are intended to assure, according to Freud, that the organism shall follow its own path to death, a course regarded by Freud as internal and natural to organic life (p. 39).

Thus, phenomena beyond the pale of the pleasure principle are those connected with a powerful instinct, which operates against the erotic, libidinal (sometimes narcissistic) instinct. Unpleasure is here seen not only as conflicted or aborted pleasure but as deriving inherently from deep, immanent instinctual sources, which, paradoxically but fatefully, are seen as assuming the fulfillment of the ultimate destiny of life: death.

One effect of this general, metapsychological idea was that Freud severed changes in affect from the strength of the drives (or excitation). This received further elaboration in *An Outline of Psychoanalysis* (1938 [1940], p. 146). As said, the realization that there is no direct, simple correlation between intensity of drives and pleasurableness of the affect marked a turning point in affect theory. First, Freud realized that there is no primordial quality of pleasure inherent in the instincts, of which unpleasure is a secondarily transformed product, but there also exist, in addition to primary pleasure, primary untransformed kinds of unpleasure, which generate negative feelings. Second, the idea that affects are not a direct, quantitatively proportionate derivative of the drives brought in its wake theoretical discussions of the vicissitudes, transformations, and combinations of affects. From now on, greater complexity colors the picture of affects, and the discourse on affects pays them greater tribute, as we shall see.

In addition, and perhaps as an aftermath to the separation of instinctual excitation and quality of feelings, another important development concerning affects took place at this time, namely the distinction made by Freud between two kinds of perception, external perceptions of stimuli and internal perceptions of sensations and feelings. In discussing these matters, I shall also refer here to passages dealing with these issues in a later work, *The Ego and the Id* (1923).

In 1920, Freud asserted that consciousness, far from being the most universal attribute of mental processes, is only a particular function of them. In his view, the role of consciousness is to yield perceptions of excitations coming from the external world and of feelings of pleasure and unpleasure that arise from within the mental apparatus.

In *The Ego and the Id* (1923, p. 19), even more clearly than in 1920, Freud subsumes feelings under the function or system of perception. Consistent with Freud's theory of perception, feelings are conscious from the start, in contrast to thoughts, which may be unconscious. Freud maintains that only something that has once been a conscious perception can become conscious again (1923, p. 20) and that therefore anything arising from within that seeks to become conscious—apart from feelings—must first be transformed into external perceptions (through memory traces, which are regarded as verbal residues derived primarily from auditory perceptions). On the other hand, Freud says at another point that feelings too (like sensations and like external sense perceptions) need the mediation of the system Pcpt (perception) in order to become conscious; otherwise, they are not sensed or experienced but remain totally unconscious (see 1915c, pp. 177–78). Later, in the *Outline*, Freud reiterated this view and gave feelings the status of fully conscious perceptions (1938, pp. 161–62).

In 1920 Freud wrote that internal perceptions yield sensations of processes arising in the most diverse areas and in the deepest strata of the mental apparatus (pp. 21–22); that very little is known about these sensations and feelings; that they are more primordial and more elementary than perceptions; that these sensations are multilocular, like external perceptions; and that they may come from different places simultaneously and may thus have different or even opposite qualities (p. 29).

In the context of unconscious affect, we see Freud vacillating between the view of affects as sensations and perceptions arising from the depths of the mind, a view in which feelings can become conscious directly, without having to become transformed into external perceptions first, and the opposite view, which assumes that feelings too need the mediation of the system Pcpt; that is, they need to become external perceptions in order to become conscious.

The issue of unconscious affects thus received a new dimension during this period. The conception of consciousness also changed several times in Freud's theories, parallel to the changes undergone by the concept of the unconscious in Freud's different theories. After being elevated to the status of a system, consciousness became a quality again. As the criterion of consciousness no longer proved helpful in building a satisfactory picture of the mind, Freud maintained that, rather than contrasting the conscious and the unconscious, we should contrast the coherent ego and the repressed. Since it was found that the ego is to a great extent unconscious itself, the metapsychological distinction between conscious and unconscious lost much of its theoretical primacy. The contrast between the ego and the repressed was to find an echo in the domain of affects through the conception of affects being divided between dischargeable, or potentially traumatic, massive affects, and signal affects stemming from and emitted by the ego. These two kinds of affect are therefore unconscious in different senses.

In addition to developments in the concept of unconscious affects, the subject of transformation received intensive treatment and, in a sense, resolution in *Beyond the Pleasure Principle*. In this work, feelings were seen as being transformed from pleasurable into unpleasurable—and vice versa—not only because of repression but also because of changes in the rhythm of tensions. Furthermore, Freud now believed that some unpleasurable feelings are not just pleasure that has been transformed into unpleasure but were unpleasurable to begin with. Another angle of this conception is revealed in his case studies, where Freud repeatedly poses the question of how, if both love and hate are instinct representatives, love changes into hate, and how they are transformed into each other. He attempts to answer this question by positing a neutral, displaceable energy, which is added, in his view, to a (qualitatively differentiated) erotic or destructive impulse, thereby amplifying and augmenting its total cathexis. Dual drive theory, which had served Freud until now, could not explain the direct transformation of feelings into each other, because of its assumption of a separate and opposite physiological process underlying each instinct. Thus, through the neutral, displaceable energy, love can change into hate when some cathexis from the loving impulse is withdrawn and is added to the destructive one. The concept of neutral energy may therefore have to do with the third problem, that of quality. A point related to the issue of the subjective quality of feelings concerns the relation of affects and sensations. Freud often gives the name of feelings to sensations, but the English translation (which does not distinguish feelings from emotions) often adds to the confusion. When Freud writes in 1915 that the affective structures in the Unconscious can become conscious as processes of discharge that are perceived as feelings (1915c, p. 178), he seems to have meant 'sensations.'[3]

The clearer distinction between energy (or drive intensity) and affects that was made possible in 1920, combined with the ego-id-superego model of 1923, permitted the redistribution of affects within the mental structures and the linking of affects to the ego as one of its functions. The proposition that part of the ego is unconscious, which was the main precursor of Freud's structural model of the mind, now created a new framework within which the concept of affect could be developed. Given the structural framework, a further elaboration of the concept of affect was to follow within the next three years.[4]

NEGATION (1925)

In 1925, another important development occurred concerning unconscious affect and its transformations, as the paper on negation shows. Freud speaks of negation as a partial lifting of repression, which occurs without the emotional acceptance of what has been repressed; the content of a repressed image or idea can make its way to consciousness on condition that it is negated. Thus, in a deep sense, negation is a way to take cognizance of what is repressed; intellectual judgment affirms or negates the content of thoughts. In the process of affirming or negating that something possesses a particular attribute or that a presentation exists in reality, the intellectual function is separated from the affective one (p. 239). The 'no' of negation is the product of the (unconscious) intellectual repudiation of an idea, which has to be negated in order that its emotional impact remain repressed, while its content appears in consciousness under the sign of negation or repudiation and is thus rendered innocuous.

This conceptualization marks an important shift in the status and vicissitudes of affects and ideas; here it is assumed that ideas are negated, while affects are repressed.[5] Until this time, it was only ideas that were considered to be repressible, whereas affects were seen as capable of being only suppressed, but not repressed (see 1915b). The suggestion that affects can be repressed entails that they can be dynamically unconscious.

The use of different terms to denote various defenses against idea or affect (repression, disavowal, negation, and suppression) implies that the censoring or suppressing of an impulse can occur at any point on the way to consciousness, possibly even after having reached the system Pcs or the system Cs, through the operation of late expulsion, or negation (see Sandler & Sandler, 1983). The distinction here, even if it later proved to be somewhat artificial, between defenses against ideas and defenses against affects, implies a greater autonomy of the affects; affects are now seen as being repressible even when the ideas are not. This conception is very different from the formulations of 1915, which, although assuming different movements of ideas and affects, nevertheless saw defense against affect in terms that presupposed the previous repression of the idea on which the defense against affect depended. In sum, Freud suggests in this paper, first, that affects can be dynamically unconscious and, second, that the concept of defenses against affects definitely has a place within the structural framework.

INHIBITIONS, SYMPTOMS AND ANXIETY (1926)

Inhibitions, Symptoms and Anxiety may be said to be Freud's last exposition on affect theory, although it specifically deals with anxiety and, to some extent, with unpleasure, pain, and longing; but this is only another instance of the fact that in Freud's writings there is no affect theory that is not a theory of anxiety. In *Inhibitions, Symptoms and Anxiety*, Freud states that he is looking for some criterion for distinguishing true statements about anxiety from false ones. As we shall see, Freud did not succeed in this task, and his contradictory views about anxiety remained.

Nevertheless, the great novelty in this paper lies in Freud's view of anxiety as the reaction of the ego to danger, despite the fact that he occasionally still referred to anxiety as deriving from accumulated libido or as a residue of primeval, prehistoric, or very early experiences such as birth, which are revived like mnemic symbols when a similar situation occurs (p. 93). Essentially, this paper tries to show how the ego, regarded here as an organization (p. 98), deals with the various forms of feelings in different situations through inhibitions, symptoms, or anxiety. As we have seen, the structural theory had attributed to the ego the control of affectivity and had regarded it as the sole seat of anxiety (1923, p. 57) and not only its perceiving organ (1923, p. 24). This clear assertion in the context of the structural theory contradicted Freud's earlier formulations of anxiety as transformed libido, a felt quantity, or a perceived discharge process. Anxiety is now liberated from its unequivocal connection with libido and is considered to be a function of the ego, a perceptual signal, the reaction of the ego to unpleasure. This view is a profoundly different conception of anxiety in particular and of affects in general.

Clearly, the role of affects changed significantly over the years of Freud's thinking, concomitantly with the theoretical and conceptual shifts he made. Affects were now seen as more functional and adaptive, and ceased to be regarded as only waste or discharge products. In 1926 affects become conceived as appropriate and adaptive responses to various stimuli and situations.

The structural theory, which covered a wider clinical range than previously, inevitably led Freud to a new theory of anxiety. The new theory takes account of the finer forms of anxiety, such as those of the transference neuroses, as well as the less circumscribed and more incapacitating forms, such as the acute repetitions of 'actual' and anxiety neuroses, and the processes where anxiety seems to have disappeared altogether, as in neutralization. The new theory of anxiety goes further in recognizing the diverse psychogeneses of anxiety: anxiety aroused by the threat of the loss of the object, the object's love, the approval of the superego, and so on. Qualitative considerations now become as important and articulate as quantitative ones.

The most important statements about anxiety made by Freud in this paper can be summarized as follows:

1. Anxiety "is something that is felt; an affective state, although we are ignorant of what an affect is. As a feeling, it has . . . the character of unpleasure" and "it is accompanied by fairly definite physical sensations . . . [from] the respiratory organs and the heart" (p. 132). Anxiety states are defined by Freud as comprising three elements: a quality, a specific character of unpleasure; a quantity, which is discharged; and perception, that is, awareness or consciousness of the act of discharge (a definition that was to appear again in 1933, p. 81). The first two aspects result, in Freud's view, from an increase in excitation, but he believes that a purely physiological account of them is not enough, and he invokes the assumption of a 'historical' reproduction of an experience that "contained the necessary conditions" for such an increase of excitation and discharge along particular paths. A prototypical experience of this kind is the experience of birth. Freud considers other affects as well to be reproductions of very early, perhaps even pre-individual, crucial experiences, and he considers them to have the character of universal and innate hysterical attacks (p. 133). Such an early event in an individual's history has, according to Freud, no psychical content yet; it is modeled upon the anxiety of the newborn baby and the anxiety of the infant who perceives the mother's absence. Both are conditioned by separation from the mother, and since they have no content or representation, they can be explained biologically. Freud has thus come full circle, and in this way he has bypassed the necessity of a psychological and psychodynamic explanation of primitive anxiety.

2. Anxiety produces repression; anxiety is the cause of repression and not its outcome. This is a new and radically different conception, compared to that of the first phase of psychoanalytic theory, in which the 'pent-upness' (of libido or strangulated affect) is considered to produce anxiety. In this revised conception, it is a (libidinally or aggressively determined, external or internal) threat that liberates anxiety, which in turn activates repression; in other words, an affect activates a defense.

3. Anxiety is no longer regarded as merely the way in which a threatening instinctual wish manifests itself in consciousness, but as an affective signal, a response of the ego to a renewed instinctual demand of a previous danger situation. The dangerousness of the instincts demands their repression. The ego accomplishes this by emitting a signal of unpleasure, which activates the process of repression; if repression fails, then, according to this theory, a symptom or character trait is formed.

4. The danger situation is not identical in all developmental stages, but the object of the anxiety is somehow linked with a traumatic factor that cannot be overcome and thereby be subjected to the pleasure principle. Each developmental state has its own characteristic danger situation (e.g., loss of the object, loss of the object's love, loss of the love of the superego, etc.).

5. There are, basically, two forms of anxiety. One is an alarm signal to a threat, and the other is the involuntary and automatic recapitulation of a traumatic situation. These two forms correspond to the roles played by the two mental agencies, the ego and the id, respectively.[6] Thus, anxiety may be activated by the ego to stimulate defensive operations against the impulses coming from the id, or anxiety may emerge from the id itself, invading and overwhelming the defensive resources of the ego and arousing a sense of panic and helplessness. In the latter case, the ego can only suffer the anxiety and submit to it, the ego's possibilities of response being paralyzed, in contrast to the case of signal anxiety, in which the defense mechanisms of the ego produce symbolic activity that functions analogously to thought, coping with the situation by mastering it symbolically. It is assumed here that anxiety can be variously located, but is experienced in the ego, there being no anxiety in the id or in the superego.

6. The new anxiety theory introduces the concept of object into the conceptual domain of anxiety, and this is of tremendous importance to affect theory. Freud's emphasis on the role of the mother in the generation of anxiety leads him to some important formulations linking anxiety, pain, and mourning (pp. 169–72). According to Freud, when an object is loved and longed for, the longing turns into anxiety when the hallucinatory cathecting of the object's mnemic image has no effect; anxiety is thus the reaction to the felt loss of the object. But until the loss is finally felt and realized, there is longing and pain. Freud says that an object presentation that is highly cathected by an instinctual need has the same role as a body part that is injured and therefore cathected by an increase in stimulation, which is accompanied by the unpleasurable feeling of pain.

7. Unpleasure is distinguished from anxiety and is considered as more basic and extensive than anxiety. According to Freud (see also later authors, e.g., Rangell, 1968), unpleasure is primary and includes other feelings such as tension, pain, and mourning (p. 132). The differentiation among these related affects is assumed to depend on the degree of structural development on the one hand and on the degree of 'objectlessness' (from tension through pain to mourning) on the other. Freud does not further develop these ideas; his concern is focused on economic considerations, such as magnitudes of excitation and issues of rhythm and time; ultimately, he explains the differences in these feelings through differences in energy investments in objects.

Relevant to the idea of unpleasure is the old issue of transformation, which at the beginning of Freud's theorizing had to do with the question of how an instinct, whose discharge is pleasurable by definition, becomes unpleasurable. Later, the question of transformation was asked in relation to affects, and at a later stage still it turned into the problem of how an unpleasurable feeling such as anxiety comes to regulate perception and behavior by functioning as a signal for the ego to instigate defensive measures. It should be noted that the ego is now considered the sole seat of anxiety, while it also has the power, through its connection with the perceptual system Pcpt (p. 91), to inhibit the whole excitatory process in the id. With the signal theory, the problem of transformation of affect in its old form (in the sense of the turning of pleasure into unpleasure under repression) virtually disappears, as Freud himself notes (p. 91). On another occasion too, Freud (1938, p. 198) writes that the id can generate the sensory elements of anxiety; that is, the id is capable of a preliminary secretion of unpleasure, which is subsequently registered in the ego as anxiety. Basically, it is the ego, with varying degrees of consciousness in its parts, which is now seen as the locus of affects. With the aid of its perceptual machinery, the ego decides (when it is not overwhelmed by traumatic anxiety) what to feel consciously on any occasion by giving itself a signal of unpleasure or pleasure. Freud now no longer considers (as he did in 1894) anxiety or reaction formations such as shame or disgust as derivations or transformations of the original instinctual drives. Rather, he regards them as the manifestations of direct ego responses to such drives. A further reference to signal theory is found in the *Outline* (1938), where Freud speaks of the signal of anxiety meeting an increase in unpleasure that is expected and foreseen (p. 146).

In *Inhibitions, Symptoms and Anxiety* the concept of anxiety is elaborated in a new way, and it becomes a radically more complex and multidimensional concept than before. Anxiety is also differentiated from unpleasure; whereas unpleasure is seen as a primary and diffuse sensation out of which other feelings develop, anxiety is seen as a psychologically more elaborate feeling, an experience with sometimes symbolic contents, rather than a mere sensation. Freud even says that anxiety "should not be explained from an economic point of view. It is not merely created in repression; it is reproduced as an affective state in accordance with an already existing mnemic image" (p. 93). Thus, the affect of anxiety, when prevented from discharge, not only is a 'potential' feeling but becomes or remains repressed in a structured state and can therefore be reproduced as a signal even without the 'economic basis,' that is, without discharge.

When Freud attempts, however, to get closer to the problem of the qualitative feel of anxiety and, by generalization, affect—that is, the subjective experience of feelings—he does not go beyond discussing pleasure and unpleasure. Having discontinued his search into the subjective experience of feelings, Freud fell back, it seems, on explaining the sources of feelings not only in terms of instinctual somatic zones, as he had done in the past, but also in terms of precipitates of primeval traumatic experiences, such as birth. His model does not deal with pleasurable feelings or enduring, continuous feeling states.

Nevertheless, there is a beginning, an opening, for an account of the function of feelings qua subjective experiences. Freud's new, more environmentalist, and less drive-oriented approach offers greater possibilities of conceptualizing various situations as meaning bearers. The central conception of affects now is neither that of strangulated drives, of energy (the 'toxic' or transformational theory), or of drive derivatives hindered from discharge in action ('conflict theory,' in which affects are the substitutes or alternatives to acts). The context for the discussion of affects is now in terms of situations. A shift is effected from a theory of the mechanistic mimicry of hysteria, and of energic disequilibria, to a theory taking account of the impact of the specific and personal, subjectively experienced situations themselves. Even the conception of danger has altered from an economic disturbance (birth) to object loss or absence, and this conception is enriched with a developmental dimension (p. 146).

The problem of transformation received a partial solution through the concept of signal, whereas the problem of quality versus quantity is now placed in the context created by Freud's distinction between signal anxiety and traumatic anxiety. The distinction between quality and quantity now refers to the contrast between a qualitative notifying function and a quantitative energy function. Thus, one may look at affect as comprising two systems, one dealing with meaning and the other with force (see Green, 1977; Ricoeur, 1970). The issue of unconscious affects now received a very important tool in the concept of signal, and later theories of affect generalized from signal anxiety to various signal affects, as we shall see.

With the signal theory of affect, Freud endowed affects with the freedom of functioning previously accorded only to thought. Thought was characterized as discharging small quantities of energy with which the mental apparatus tests the outside world; the description of how signal anxiety operates is very similar. The important point here is that in this way the gulf between affect and thought was considerably reduced, after they had been considered separate by Freud for many years. The fact of the indissoluble link between affect and thought tallies well with our daily and clinical experience, which shows that, far from being two discrete and impermeable categories, affects and cognitions coexist and interact in myriad complex ways (see chapters 8, 9, and 10).

SUMMARY

Freud worked clinically with neurotics who displayed all kinds of disturbed or troubled feelings. Theoretically, Freud came to consider feelings first as mostly traumatogenic physical energy products and later as (physiological) drive derivatives. Feelings were seen to gather in so-called psychical groups or in the so-called second consciousness in the *Studies*; as accumulated libido leading to anxiety in *The Neuropsychoses of Defense*; and as disturbances of functioning in the *Project*. The main thrust of Freud's therapeutic work was aimed at getting the affects out, preferably but not necessarily with the accompaniment of the verbalization of the events and experiences that had surrounded them.

In 1900, affects were already considered indicators of significant unconscious dream contents, but it was only in the so-called *Metapsychological Papers* (1915a, 1915b, and 1915c) that affects were considered significant meaning bearers, signifiers, in waking life as well. But Freud needed the conceptual underpinnings of the drives to explain neurotic phenomena.

In 1915 and in 1923, in the first and second topographical theories, affects were placed in a system and were seen not only as springing from the drives but as being activated by the ego as well, being regarded as inner perceptions, while the ego, both in its conscious and unconscious parts, was regarded as controlling affectivity (1923). Thus, affects, in contrast to other processes arising from within the body, were considered to be free of having to transform themselves into external perceptions in order to become conscious. They were seen as unmediated inner perceptions, more primordial and influential than external perceptions and more commensurate in intensity and quality to inner bodily processes, which could arise even when consciousness was clouded.

The view of affects as drive derivatives on the one hand, and inner perceptions on the other, left them as passive perceptions of bodily discharge processes assumedly coming from the drives. There was no articulated theory of affect yet. Then, in 1920 and in 1924, Freud arrived at the idea that pleasure is not proportional to instinctual, energic quantity but depends instead on feeling quality and patterns of excitation over time. These developments made affects relatively independent of the drives, and they could be seen as partaking in subtle inner changes. This was a tremendously important advance toward the construction of a theory of affect, in that affects could be theoretically elaborated as autonomous phenomena, linked to subjective experience, fantasy, and object relations, rather than as mechanical by-products of accumulated substances. Experiential quality no longer had to be explained in terms of quantities of excitation.

Thus, the fundamental psychoanalytic problems of affects—namely, the problem of transformation, the problem of quality and quantity, and the problem of unconscious affects—acquired more satisfactory solutions. The formula of transformation of pleasure into unpleasure was generally replaced by the understanding that unpleasure is caused by conflict. The attempt to explain quality in terms of changes in quantity of excitation was abandoned in favor of a more complex model of changes in rhythm. The problem of unconscious affects was addressed in terms of feelings being not the conscious perception of outflowing drive energy from the mind to the body or to the outside feelings but unconscious in themselves, that is, either repressible and/or appearing as (unconscious) signals (1926).

The concept of signal implied anticipation and symbolization, and, most importantly, it comprised the unconscious status of the signal. The concept of a signal affect implied the emotional significance of situations for the person who experiences them and, later, for the world of internalized object relations. The hormone model of affects (Basch, 1976c) as secretory processes partially gave way to the signal model, in which affects were seen as sensitive markers, as conveyers of knowledge, as signals of the meaning of a situation. It is for this reason that the real emancipation of the concept of feelings was achieved in 1920 and then in 1926 rather than in 1923, when affects were only further put into systems postulated by the structural theory. In retrospect, it is obvious that the question of whether feelings belong to the ego or to the id (or to the external environment) is less important than whether they are signals, antedating and influencing conscious and unconscious perceptions (and object relations), or just discharge products.

"Consciousness is a highly fugitive state," writes Freud in the *Outline* (1938,

p. 159); he argues that consciousness appears and surges only occasionally, while the main flux of mental life is unconscious. Consciousness is only a particular function, rather than the most universal attribute of the mental, according to Freud (see 1920, p. 22). In other words, Freud sees mental experience as being basically and continuously unconscious, enlivened only by short-lived episodes of consciousness. The perceptual system is described by him in a similar way, and perception is seen as a process that operates via occasional samplings of the external environment.

This reversal in the relation of consciousness and unconsciousness makes a tremendous difference for the intriguing question of unconscious feelings. If we adopt the view that sees consciousness as a partial and occasional phenomenon, combine it with the assumption of unconscious feelings, and add to it the re-placement of the equation of perception with external reality by the enlarged equation of perception with external *and* inner reality (Freud, 1923, 1938), we get a picture in which most of our experiencing occurs through feelings without consciousness. We shall have to postpone the discussion of these issues until later; meanwhile, let us turn to the work done by Freud's immediate followers.

2
Theories of Affect in the Last Years of Freud and after His Death: Jones, Brierley, Glover

Psychoanalytic theory in Freud's last years and after his death was in a state of fermenting diversity. Gradually, two main trends evolved, which carried psychoanalytic theorizing further. In Britain, efforts were focused on reconciling the 'dynamic' and 'experiential' dimensions of psychic reality (Brierley called them 'meta-psychology' and 'personology,' respectively), while in Vienna, and later in the United States, a large-scale attempt was launched to develop the scientific, protobiological aspect of psychoanalytic theory, to be known as ego psychology.

A common denominator of these two different streams is, surprisingly, a concern, at least at the beginnings, with what may be called psychobiological accounts of ego development. This may have been a continuation of Freud's persistent concern, in his last years, with notions such as the biological 'bedrock,' the innate, unyielding 'alteration of the ego,' and other biological factors that he had deemed the greatest obstacles to therapeutic change (1937, p. 221).

This common trend, however, should not obscure the far-reaching differences between the groups of thinkers in the two different intellectual milieus. In the United States, thinkers such as Hartmann and Rapaport, in their attempts to develop psychoanalytic theory, followed a biological model. In London, by contrast, theoreticians such as Brierley, Balint, Winnicott, and Fairbairn laid greater stress on the experiential and the interpersonal (object-related) aspect of theory. Thus, Brierley, one of the representatives of the latter stream, even though she spoke of herself and of her colleagues as scientists, whose approach to psychology is fundamentally biological and who, to her mind, should consider human beings as organisms whose mental functions are their chief instrument of adaptation (1951, p. 100), expresses herself at the same time in a different vein. Thus, she writes, for instance, that the dynamics of ego organization are those of "pleasure synthesis and pain dissociation" (p. 98), that "ego modification is therefore a consequence of feeling, rather than of knowing," and that "the difference between knowing and feeling is the difference between intellectual knowledge and character structure." The crucial importance attached by Brierley and by her colleagues to the experiential dimension in the modification of the ego (in development as well as in analysis) and in the building of character is very different from the view, espoused by ego psychologists of this period, that affects are regulators of drive discharge, or signals for biological or quasibiological danger and survival situations.

I have chosen to highlight certain aspects of psychoanalytic theory at this period from a standpoint that may provide rewarding for the study of the concept and theory of affect. This consideration led me to choose what I called Freud's 'biological pessimism' (see 1920, 1933, 1937) as the background for describing the kind of psychoanalytic thinking reigning after Freud's last works, because reading the psychoanalytic literature of that time shows that the issues around this so-called biological pessimism were an absorbing, even haunting problem for many thinkers after Freud, who dealt with it in their own different ways.

Thus, the Kleinians, who adhered to Freud's theory of the death instinct (a theory that is perhaps the most profound and theoretically consistent exposition of this pessimism), developed a theoretical framework in which the death instinct is the ultimate victor in different psychopathologies. In contrast, the 'Londoners' (not to be confused with the British object relation theorists) strove to find the biological bedrock in the psychic depths (e.g., Jones's 'aphanisis'). These two streams, in turn, differ from what American ego psychology suggests as solutions to the same problems in their framework, in which the ego is regarded as both the product and the master of biology.

The investigators who worked on affects in London at that time were concerned with the relationship between the biological and psychic dimensions of affects in their work. Three main themes are discernible here:

1. The relationship between affects and drives occupies a central place in the thinking at that time. On the one hand, different affects have been related to different instincts; on the other hand, the layering (Jones, 1929) and compounding (Glover, 1939; Landauer, 1938) of affects are discussed, and sometimes they are used to explain mental phenomena without recourse to the concept of drives.

2. In general, affects are looked at from a basically biological viewpoint; they are considered either as hereditary response potentialities to all kinds of demands (Landauer, 1938) or as classifiable into tension and into discharge affects (Brierley, 1937; Glover, 1939), that is, as biologically determined phenomena. On the other hand, affects are also seen as linked with objects (Brierley, 1937) and with the ego (Brierley, 1937; Glover, 1939) in attempts to account for developmental and clinical phenomena.

3. In line with the biological perspective, fear is regarded by some thinkers in this group (e.g., Brierley, 1937; Jones, 1929) as the primary emotion. Fear is seen as the most immediate response to physical, biological danger.

In what follows, the work will be presented of three major thinkers on affects—Ernest Jones, Marjorie Brierley, and Edward Glover. All of them worked in London in the 1930s and 1940s.

ERNEST JONES

Jones, Freud's disciple, interpreter, and coworker, contributed greatly to the explication and propagation of Freud's ideas. He emphasized the extensiveness of Freudian theory and the mutual confirmation obtaining between it and other fields of study. Jones used as his frame of reference Freud's earlier model of the mental apparatus as a reflex arc (1900), in which affects were regarded as psychic energy seeking discharge; they were seen by Jones as the motive force determining the flow of mental life.

His reflex arc metapsychology notwithstanding, Jones's 1929 paper, "Fear, Guilt and Hate," served for many years as an example of a brilliant study of the complex interrelations among affects. The intricate web of relations between affects is spun, according to Jones, by the working of a principle according to which an affect that causes another unpleasant affect can at the same time 'cure' the latter by 'more of itself,' so to speak. This apparent paradox—namely, that an affect can be relieved through the very affect that was the generating occasion for its occurrence—is explained by Jones through an idea borrowed from homeopathic notions, the so-called isopathic principle. This principle says that if a feeling (for instance, hate) causes another feeling (e.g., guilt), then only more of the first feeling (hate), or that same feeling (hate) differently displayed or employed, can remove the second feeling (guilt); guilt is relieved by hate. Jones draws a picture of very complex affect-structures that a person builds to achieve an emotional balance and to be protected against unbearable, unspeakable dread. He distinguishes three different negative affects that he thought were at the base of the psyche: fear, hate, and guilt.

In addition, Jones considered various layers of secondary defenses against the three basic affects. When one of the primary feelings becomes unendurable, says Jones, secondary defensive reactions, deriving from one of the other feelings, are used. These feelings may also become sexualized, in which case fear turns into masochism, guilt into moral masochism, and hate into sadism. The choice of defense is determined, in Jones's view, by the infant's initial reaction to his or her primal traumatic situation, which establishes whether he or she 'chooses' fear, hate, or guilt to cope with this situation. It should be remarked that Jones uses mostly 'attitudes,' 'groups,' or 'a sense of' (e.g., guilt), thus avoiding the problem of whether to use the term 'feeling' or 'affect.'

The primal traumatic situation is called by Jones 'aphanisis,' which refers to "the total annihilation of the capacity for sexual gratification" (1929, p. 391); by sexual gratification Jones seems to mean pleasure and the capacity for experiencing it. Aphanisis, in Jones's view, consists of total inhibition, the death of desire; it resembles, he writes, the experience of a hungry man who, deprived of food long enough, ceases to be hungry. It is total despair, losing one's 'appetite' permanently. One may defend against aphanisis by fear or primal anxiety. The main therapeutic task, according to Jones, is the enhancement of the patient's tolerance of guilt together with the hate and the fear that underlie it, so that the patient may be enabled to avoid this terrible experience.

With these formulations, Jones reaches back to the earliest developmental phases and experiences, where, to his mind, lie the most basic anxieties. Like Melanie Klein, Jones repudiated the view of the phallic phase as a separate, independent developmental stage, and he disagreed with Freud, who thought that castration fear is the most central fear, from which all other fears derive. Rather, he saw the phallic phase as a defensive structure against an earlier fear, a basic anxiety, which at one point he even considered calling an instinct of fear, of which castration anxiety is the more advanced, genital aspect.

Another important concept in Jones's thinking is the 'complex,' which is defined as a "group of connected ideas, invested with a strong body of emotion and having a definitive conative tendency (such as a wish, a longing, etc.)." A complex has the power to assimilate and group together ideas that belong even loosely together, depending on the intensity of the emotion investing the complex; the more superficial are the associations between two ideas that have been drawn together, the stronger must be the emotion that establishes the connection (1920, p. 37).

There is a certain feature in Jones's writing that lends his thought its particular character: his persistent distrust of appearances, his desire to go beyond the apparent and to dismantle and break up a phenomenon (including a complex of affects) into its constituent parts. Thus, in a similar manner to his triad of affects of 1929, Jones later deconstructs jealousy into suspicion, fear, grief, and shame. In his passion to divine the mysterious, he stood behind such statements as "Now what I have to say is something sad, and that is that there is much less love in the world than there appears to be" and "Investigation of the deeper layers of the mind teaches one that love and passion can fulfill many other functions than their own" (1948, p. 331) (and in fact, his three basic affects are all negative). He speaks of those layers of the mind that are so foreign to ordinary consciousness that one might well despair of being able to establish a common bond between it and the familiar everyday phenomenon.

Jones's penchant for the mysterious and occult, for the oneiric and symbolic, for that which is not quite what it appears to be, may be the source for his approach to affects as entities that cover up and disguise one another and build up into complex systems of camouflage. In a similar spirit, he views defenses against affects through the prism of their rationalizing function, or what he calls their 'over-affective,' that is, self-deceptive role.

Jones's approach to affects is, on the whole, on a level of clinical rather than metapsychological theory, and it contains many clinical and phenomenological insights as to the way affects work. His contribution to a theory of affects may be summarized as follows:

1. He provided a sophisticated view of affects and their defensive and adaptive layerings, thereby lending a dimension of depth and structuralization to various affects. Notably, he found empirically that affects often function to reduce or annul their own effects at a secondary stage of their emergence.

2. Jones coined and elaborated the term 'aphanisis' to denote the 'rock-bottom experience' against which other unpleasant affects form layered defenses. This term helped give more weight to earlier, preoedipal phenomena in subsequent discussions of the affects in other than the language of energy.

3. Developing a system of affective interrelationships and stressing the ubiquity of affects that function to 'glue' ideas into a 'complex' enabled Jones to proportionately reduce or limit the role of instincts to that of secondary phenomena in affective life, whose main function became that of tinging feelings with an erotic or aggressive color.

Jones may be regarded as an important and somewhat neglected precursor to a modern theory of affect. His approach is fresh and original, and his outdated official theoretical views did not obstruct his deep perceptiveness concerning affects. Although he did not possess a conceptual apparatus for developing the concept of affects, he has pushed their study forward through his sensitive phenomenological descriptions of deeply felt, mostly unpleasant feelings. Except for the term aphanisis, however, which has been carried into psychoanalytic thinking, he remains on the periphery of affect theory, overshadowed by other, more central figures in this domain.

MARJORIE BRIERLEY

In the 1930s and 1940s, Brierley was an important figure among psychoanaltyic thinkers in London. Her work represents one of the most sustained efforts to come to grips with the pressing problems exposed by the Controversial Discussions (1942–1945), by the beginnings of ego psychology, and by the growing realization of the intricate relation between theory and practice in psychoanalysis. Brierley may be regarded as a source of insights and ways of thinking, and her formulations on affects often herald what was to come later (sometimes much later), but the central position that she occupied some forty years ago is largely forgotten (see Hayman, 1986). Today she is mainly remembered as the exponent of the so-called tension theory of affects, while the other parts of her work are regarded as of merely historical interest. The reasons for this are complex and seem to derive from historical circumstances rather than from personal merit or flaw.

In her book, *Trends in Psychoanalysis* (1951), Brierley works out a profile of psychoanalytic theory, which she divides into three parts, the fourth part being dedicated to affects—a clear indication of the importance she accorded to this subject.

The reasons for the pivotal importance of affects in Brierley's thinking are several. Affects are seen by her as the expression of the experiential dimension in mental life and in theory (as contrasted with conceptual abstraction), a subject that most intensely occupied her mind. She considered affects, more than any other mental manifestation, to be at the crossroads between theory and practice, and between what she called 'objective theory' and 'subjective theory,' and at the same time to be the most potent factor obstructing psychoanalytic theorizing. A most important point in this context is her realization that the primacy of affects in the clinical situation must find an appropriate niche in general theory: Without a strong theory of affect, she asserted, psychoanalytic theory as a whole cannot develop.

The significance of Brierley's work for affect theory lies in two main areas: (1) she expanded and delineated more clearly and forcefully the area of affects and their importance in psychoanalysis and (2) she maintained and developed the idea that affects are essentially tension states of the ego, rather than drive discharge phenomena. This last thesis helped reinforce the tendency, which became clearer only much later, to divorce affects from drives in theory and in practice, and to subsequently link them with the ego and with objects. But let us begin where she began.

In her chapter on affects (which had appeared as a paper earlier, in 1937), Brierley traces the historical development of the concept. In her view, in the early days of psychoanalytic theory, affect played a leading role in theory and practice. Freud's first hypotheses were framed in terms of ideas rendered dynamic by their emotional charges. The formulation of instinct theory and the view of psychic conflict as the conflict between the ego and the sexual instincts (rather than between emotionally charged ideas) shifted the scene, and the earlier ideo-motor terminology lapsed into disuse. Brierely saw Freud's theoretical developments of 1915 as a temporary eclipse in affect theory, when ideas were conceptualized as memory traces, and affects were regarded as discharge processes potentially detached from ideas. Affects were now ranged by Freud on the efferent, outgoing side of the instinctual reflex arc and were marked by automatic, reflexlike responsivity and centrifugal (i.e., 'running outward,' from the central nervous system to the interior of the body) discharge tendencies.

According to Brierley, 1923 marked a new era for affects. Parallel to the acceptance of the discharge idea in 1923 and in 1926, there was a change in affect theory that was entailed, in Brierley's view, by changing conceptions of psychic development. After 1923, mental development was still regarded as the progressive organization and modification of instincts, but also as the progressive mastery of anxiety. The concept of defense was expanded to include defense against the emergence of intolerable affects. With this expansion, she writes, affect acquired the same theoretical status as instinct, and, being equipped with a better overall theory, she thought it was time to restore affects to a place in theory that would be more consonant with their tremendous importance in practice.

Brierley suggested that working out a satisfactory affect theory should precede the elaboration of instinct theory (which, she showed, was the theory with which

Freud had replaced affect theory), since the study of affect could also contribute, to her mind, to instinct theory.

The main difficulties in working out a theory of affect are seen by Brierley to lie in the fact that affects are essentially ego experiences, while they have at the same time an intimate relation with the instincts. Brierley believed that affects are tension phenomena rather than drive discharge products, a view that fitted well with the conception of affects as ego experiences. Affect should be seen, she thinks, as a tension phenomenon impelling to discharge, either in the inner or in the outer world, rather than discharge itself. Brierley contended that clinical and developmental evidence (such as the central role of anxiety in development) contradicts the idea of discharge. Affects fit more readily with what she calls 'nuclear' than with 'boundary' conceptions. Affects to her are 'central' phenomena, closely linked with the ego, rather than 'peripheral' discharge manifestations. Although the sensory aspects of the affects are linked with the instincts, these should be distinguished from the emotional and experiential aspects of affects, which, in her view, are inherently linked to the ego.

The link of the affects with the ego is elaborated by Brierley in her account of the parallel development of the ego and the affects, in the sense that affects play an important part in the progressive organization of the ego, and the ego in turn helps affects to develop. Each affective experience, writes Brierley, is a blend, a "fusion of impulse and variations of affect," which is lived in relation to an object and forms an ego element, and each such element, which is stamped in by repeated experiences, forms an 'ego nucleus.' Activation of different nuclei in relation to a common object establishes linkages between them. Affect then becomes "the index to the fate of the relevant instinctual impulses and to the nature of the budding psychic object formation" (1937, p. 262). Brierley posits a progressive integration of part-egos into a personal, integrated ego, and she divides this developmental process into two parts: the 'pre-personal' period of ego and affect development, in which ego nuclei become established and interconnected, and the 'post-personal' period, in which affects become linked to objects.

The above summarizing statements indicate Brierley's ambitious attempt to integrate many areas of psychic functioning, which are at the same time areas of psychoanalytic theory, in her account of affective development. Let me present some more details of this account of structural and affective development, which deserves to be better known.

In what Brierley calls the pre-personal period there exist different grades of a general, diffuse, undiluted affectivity, which is objectless in the adult sense and is closely interwoven with sensations. Awareness of feelings is the only sort of cognition at this stage. The baby lives in a state of consciousness in which every sporadic flash is an ego experience, and when such a flash of awareness leaves behind a memory trace, it becomes an ego element. An ego element then becomes an ego nucleus by repeated experience. Complex linkages spread between different ego nuclei; similar feelings and similar nuclei will tend to integrate and to blend. The first feelings, insofar as they are qualitatively distinct, are simple 'like' and 'dislike', or 'attraction' and 'repulsion' affects. The ego at this state is a series of sensation-egos, that is, part-body, part-object nuclei.

In the so-called post-personal period, affects become connected with objects. They arise in the ego nuclei, which are, at this stage, related to relatively simple part-object systems; these are the first emotions. In addition, says Brierley, there are early formed attitudes, which are not in themselves emotions but dispositions to experience emotions about certain objects. From this point in time, feelings can be mastered by manipulating their objects through projection and introjection. In this formulation, Brierley expressed one of the most seminal and momentous ideas in affect theory (see M. Klein, 1935; J. Riviere, 1936).

The post-personal period is succeeded, according to Brierley, by the period of ego integration and superego differentiation. Both processes hinge on repression (which comes later than projection and introjection). Brierley assumes that 'good' objects are assimilated into the ego, while hostile objects tend to gather in the superego. There are certain affects, in her view, that never become integrated with what she calls the 'definitive ego' but remain part of the unconscious ego, although such a repressed fragment of an ego experience may emerge into consciousness and then be felt and experienced.

Brierley's approach to affect theory in particular and to psychoanalytic theory in general was guided by her interest in making psychoanalysis a general theory. Accordingly, she set out to accommodate psychoanalysis with larger notions of psychology and the social sciences, ethics and religion. Brierley did not construct a theoretical model of her own, but she attempted to lodge important insights from early Kleinian theory, from ego psychology, and from object relations theory within an integrative Weltanschauung. On a more specific level, she also worked to dispel views that she judged erroneous, such as the view of objects as having formative power in themselves or of the ego as preceding experience. She maintained (1969) that psychoanalysis is not an object relations theory nor an ego psychology, but first and foremost a theory of experience and self-object relationships. She conceived the basic unit of experience as consisting in the relationship of impulse, affect, and representation, which are held together in a series of adaptive processes and are linked by their common relationship to an object.

Brierley's wish to include all of Freud's views on affects in her own framework seems to have been a mistake. In her desire to unite in one encompassing view all of Freud's different, and sometimes incompatible, conceptions of affect, as well as in her act of placing in one melting pot such diverse ingredients as feelings, objects, experiences, ego, and self, without explicitly spelling out the different presumptions underlying them, her paper on affects becomes too condensed, sometimes to the point of confusion. Her style of exposition becomes flighty at some points, and one has difficulty in mastering the great amount of information in this paper. An example showing how the need to do justice to all existing psychoanalytic knowledge rendered her a disservice is found in her discussion of the relationship between drives and affects. First, she attempts to break loose of the straitjacket of anxiety as *the* 'ur-affect' by postulating (like McDougall in his famous theory of 1929) a one-to-one relationship between instincts and affects. This attempt fails, however, and she acknowledges the common clinical observation that the same impulse may arouse a variety of feelings. She then immediately turns to another unifying concept, the object, which she later links with the concept of the ego, but in a manner that does not allow the reader to form a clear conception of the relation between the two.

On the other hand, this paper, with its integrative conceptualizations and the refined understanding of the analytic process it displays, could have been a significant groundbreaker, were it not prematurely conceived. The fact of its being ahead of its time seems to explain why it has not been sufficiently appreciated and used. After many years in which her thoughts were neglected, Brierley seems to have recently come back to the minds of many workers in the field of affects. At the International Congress in Jerusalem in 1977 dedicated to the subject of affects, she was mentioned as one of the important pioneers of affect theory (e.g., Abrams and Shengold; Green; see also Kernberg, 1988).

Brierley's great merit is her bold contention that affects are essentially tension phenomena and ego experiences. Today it may be difficult to grasp the extent to which such a contention was innovative. But in those early days it was inconceivable to place affect as experienced tension in theory (there were writers who discussed the experiential aspect of affects, but not on a theoretical level, e.g., Alexander, 1935; Jones, 1920, 1929, 1948; Landauer, 1938. Defining affects theoretically in terms of experience had been precluded by the axiomatic definition of affects as drive derivatives). Keeping in mind Brierley's historical context, we can appreciate the important step she made by linking affects to experiences, on the one hand, and to objects as their carriers, on the other. Brierley's upholding of the view that affects are tension phenomena made possible the hotly debated discussions (see Jacobson, 1971) of whether affects are discharge or tension phenomena and in what sense. This controversy further opened up discussions of concepts such as thresholds, signals, and structures in ego psychology. Only after her work had been done could clarification of these issues be initiated.

EDWARD GLOVER

Two years after Brierley's paper, Edward Glover presented his paper on affects, "The Psychoanalysis of Affects" (in his 1939 *On the Early Development of Mind*). Like Jones and Brierley, Glover attached great importance to affects in psychoanalytic theory. He attributed what he considered the recent fallow period in the development of psychoanalysis to the neglect of the problem of affects. He saw one source for this neglect in the "labile and impermanent nature" of affects, which makes them harder to grasp than ideational content. Another source, in his eyes, is the greater subjective resistance to the exploration of affects, as compared with the ideational or even the instinctual aspect of mental life. Another reason, in his view, for the standstill in theorizing on affects was the excessive concentration on the anxiety-hate-guilt triad, inspired by Jones's 1929 paper, which had impeded the understanding of other important affective reactions that are not necessarily pathogenic.

Throughout his paper, Glover persistently argues for studying affects in their own right. He was one of the first thinkers to realize that instincts are less important for the understanding of clinical phenomena than had been assumed until his time, and he tried to introduce a more refined version of the relationship between affects and instincts than had been used so far. According to his version, different affective experiences spring from variations in the distribution of libidinal or aggressive charges throughout the different body zones. Another distinction between affects is that between simple and compound or fused affects (the term 'fused affects' is an extension of Freud's 1915 concept of fusion of instincts). Glover thought that in order to isolate and identify specific fusion affects one must investigate a large mass of clinical material and submit them to what he saw as the most useful classification, namely, in terms of reactions to instinctual stress, which are of two types: tension and discharge affects.

Glover focuses mainly on tension affects, which, to judge from his formulations, are extreme and usually painful psychic and bodily states, varying with different pathological conditions and inducing very different feelings and behaviors (e.g., the same unpleasant feelings may arouse resistance and pain in the hysteric but are taken for granted by the depressive, who may eventually commit suicide to get relief from them). Glover considers physical and psychic instinctual tension to be the characteristic accompaniment and amplifier of the affects, so that the tension aspect is much more important than the discharge aspect of feelings. In his view, tension is due to what he called 'instinctual stress,' the nature of which can be gathered, he believed, from unconscious fantasies. He envisioned an attempt to analyze the somatic and experiential components of different anxieties and fears, to correlate somatic aspects with fantasy content, and, in addition, to situate these phenomena along a hypothetical excitation-discharge arc. To get a better understanding of the nature of these tensions and to make his point, Glover adduces some examples that rely heavily on energic explanations.

Though Glover took some steps to sever the exclusive linkage of affects and drives, it is clear that affect, in his view, is basically and exclusively an instinctual product, which is sexually or aggressively energized. His use of notions such as blocking, fear of the consequences of discharge, and elaboration of tensions through fantasies renders the picture of affects more dynamic and complex, but he lacks concepts of development and structure, including those of the ego or of the object. Glover's controversy with Jones also illustrates his belief that affect is first and foremost an instinct derivative. This controversy revolved about the nature of primary fear in mental life. Glover agreed with Jones that fear is the earliest psychic affect, but he thought that the earliest fear is not aphanisis, as

Jones had claimed, but that preceding it developmentally is the more basic fear of disruption, of bursting, a fear that is the result of accumulation of sadistic tension in the body.

Glover's strategy is to suggest first, that affects and instincts should be conceptually separated. As a next step, he discusses what he calls 'primary affects,' which he takes to be primitive affects existing in parallel to each other or conjointly with primitive ego nuclei. Glover was interested not in naming specific affects but in classifying affects along dimensions more useful than those offered in the literature so far, which had related affects to instincts and had made them dependent on the pleasure-pain dimension.

The main issues in Glover's paper on affects are the following:

1. Glover called for giving affects a place in their own right in theory. He claimed that affects are more than just explanations in terms of instincts and should therefore be studied separately.

2. He sought a classificatory scheme that would account for different affects in terms of the different reactions to instinctual frustration and would also separate compound affects into their simple affective components. Basically, Glover regarded affects as instinct derivatives, based on different bodily sensations arising from specific instinctual frustrations or stresses.

3. Glover saw the dimension of tension versus discharge as the most pertinent line of division and classification of affects and believed that the bodily location of the sensations on which the different affects are based determines the degree to which they are either tension or discharge phenomena.

4. In Glover's eyes, tension affects are more important and at the same time more difficult to study than discharge affects. He proposed investigating tension affects concomitantly with bodily and instinctual phenomena, because he assumed that the somatic component of these affects might shed light on their experiential quality and on the mental state involved in them. Glover believed that, clinically, each component of a compound affect should be separately analyzed through the unconscious fantasy accompanying it.

In his attempt to locate the tension and discharge phenomena in the body, Glover speculated about mechanisms of afferent excitation and efferent discharge in different bodily zones that take part in affects and in sensations. But, lacking a developmental model as well as an object relations theory, his assertions remained no more than speculations. It would perhaps have been more rewarding had Glover attempted not to find some vague neurophysiological correspondence but to develop the idea of the conjunction of what he called the primitive affects with his concept of ego nuclei.

GENERAL SUMMARY AND DISCUSSION

There are two main points to be made about the work done by this group of thinkers in London from the late 1930s to the 1960s: (a) the striving to return to Freud's original affect theory before the days of instinct theory, which they saw as a regression in the building of a psychoanalytic theory of affect, and (b) the crude conceptual tools available to them.

Each of these thinkers separately was concerned with the fact that, with the rise of instinct theory, affects became merely external, automatic discharge phenomena, while the role of affects as tension phenomena, as ego experiences with a specific developmental history and object relatedness, was only partially reinstituted after 1923. Each of these workers in turn attempted to work out these core ideas in his or her own way.

They lacked, however, the more refined theoretical machinery that was developed later. Concepts of self and object representations, the distinction between ego and self, developmental and maturational concepts (object constancy or scheme), and a more sophisticated terminology for instinctual phenomena, which would have enabled these theoreticians to distinguish biological from behavioral manifestations—all these were still in an embryonic state at that time, and the fumblings for clarity and for a better handle on things are strongly felt in these writings. In spite of these difficulties, however, these thinkers did break some new paths, particularly when they endeavored to give expression to the many faces and many roles of affects. These authors helped bring an era to an end in which affects were regarded as simple accompaniments of something more important, which had to be let out or expressed through the affects. They seem to have established a whole tradition, and the technical need to consider affects and object relations as the most important element in the clinical situation continues in London, in contrast to the United States, where the structural approach dominated the scene until recently.

No systematic approach to affects, however, was developed by these thinkers. It seems that, with the exception of Brierley, they were basically interested in the affects themselves rather than in affect theory, and so they developed the important subject of the interrelationships among affects. This subject can be divided into several components:

1. The view was developed that affects are complexly layered (Jones, 1929); that they weave together different ideas through the binding power of their intensity (the 'complex' of Jones, 1920, 1929); or that they have a logic of their own (Alexander's 'emotional syllogisms,' 1935).

2. As to the modes of operation of the affects, it was noted that affects can diminish or annul their own effects (Jones, 1929); that feelings can be mastered by manipulating their objects (Brierley, 1937); and that integrated feelings comprise the perception of the body as contrasted with 'affective attacks' (Landauer, 1938).

3. Distinctions were made at this period among different types of affects, such as simple versus compound affects (Glover); tension and discharge affects (Glover; Brierley saw all affects as tension phenomena); affects, passions, moods, and 'affective attacks' (Landauer), and so on.

4. Affects were linked to the ego in various ways. Affects were considered ego expe-

riences (Brierley, 1937) or products of conflicting response tendencies within the ego (Landauer, 1938); or feelings were linked with the ego and with objects (Brierley, 1937; Landauer, 1938). On the whole, the idea was rejected that affects are mainly instinct derivatives or superego phenomena (Glover, 1939; Landauer, 1938).

The concepts of ideas and affects became reunited into complexes (after they had been separated by Freud) and were attached to objects and to the ego. On a theoretical level, there was a return to the view that affects serve to charge different ideas with different tensions and action tendencies, in contrast to the theory of affects as deriving from the drives (as assumed in the first topographical theory and its outgrowths) or as receiving their structure from the superego (as claimed in the second topographical theory and its later developments).

3
Ego Psychology and the Affects

Freud's structural theory was taken up by the proponents of what came to be called ego psychology, who attempted to develop psychoanalysis from a psychology of neurotic phenomena and dreams into a general psychology, in line with some of Freud's latest concerns. According to Kanzer, one of the spokesmen of ego psychology twenty years ago:

The predominant lines of development in psychoanalysis during the post-Freudian period (since 1939) have continued the historical progression toward an analytic psychology that views the abnormal in relation to the normal, regards states of consciousness as aspects of, rather than divisions and goals of, psychic functioning, and approaches the diverse determinants of human behavior . . . through their manifestations in mental events (1971, p. 13).

Discussions of affects within this framework include primarily efforts to account for their development and structuring and the process of their 'binding' by the ego. Affect development and maturation were discussed mostly in terms of the ability to delay, to tolerate tension, or to bind energy. The blocking of affects was assumed to change their nature, sometimes by increasing their pressure and peremptoriness, at other times by helping them to differentiate and eventually to become thresholds, linked with secondary processes (Rapaport, 1953), or to become desomatized (Schur, 1966). Moreover, in parallel to the neutralization of the drives, affects were assumed to form new structures (Hartmann, Kris, & Loewenstein, 1946).

Affects were conceived in the framework of early ego psychology as energies that become increasingly structuralized, even tamed (Fenichel, 1945). This interest in the relationship between the ego and the affects reflects one of the main theoretical concerns of ego psychology in those days, that of the relation between structure and energy and, on a more general level, between the structural and economical points of view in psychoanalytic theory. Gradually, a theoretical framework evolved in which different 'degrees' and states (e.g., signal versus discharge affects) were studied from the perspective of their different relations to the ego. Some workers (e.g., Fenichel, 1941, 1945; Rangell, 1955, 1967, 1968; Schur 1953, 1960, 1964, 1966) set themselves the task of spelling out and explaining the relations and transitions among strongly experienced (discharge) affects and informational (signal) affects and the manner in which the two were related to traumatic states, which, at the inception of ego psychology, were still defined in energy terms. All this was studied and argued mainly with respect to the affect of anxiety.

Gradually, a change became discernible in the stipulated relationship between the ego and the affects. From driven powers opposing the ego in blind animosity, which needed to be 'tamed' and domesticated, affects came to be seen either as experiences to be defended against or as cognitive and motivational tools of the ego, having the role of indicators that provide the ego with the most sought-for and valuable knowledge about psychic states.

The 'annexation' of the affects into the domain of the ego, which was begun by Freud in 1926, made the affects dependent and contingent on the degree of maturation of the ego and superego (Jacobson, 1953; Krystal, 1975; Sandler, 1972; Spitz, 1972). Affects were regarded now partly as ego functions (both adaptive and defensive) and partly as stimuli controlled by the ego. They were considered to be developing, becoming structured and hierarchical, and used by the ego purposefully; affects were regarded as being anticipated by the ego, scanned and evaluated, or given free rein to influence the various spheres of action.

Thus, the concept of the ego became in many ways vital for understanding affects. The period under discussion, the years following 1933 (the year in which Freud had expanded the concept of the ego for the last time, endowing it with relative secondary autonomy), was a period full of intellectual ferment and growth. In 1936, Anna Freud published *The Ego and the Mechanisms of Defense*. Waelder, who in 1930 had proposed his important 'principle of multiple functioning,' wrote in 1936 about reality testing. In that year, the famous symposium on the "Theory of Therapeutic Results in Psychoanalysis" was held, in which the point of view of ego psychology reigned supreme. In that year, Bibring wrote about the relationship between drive psychology and ego psychology, and Hendrick elaborated a theory of ego development in terms of character development.

In the following year, 1937, major changes occurred and innovations were made. Increasing recognition was given to the role of external reality as a source of variability in ego development, which was now seen as not only dependent on the drives. Thus, French wrote about adaptation to reality in terms of the repetition compulsion (1937), and Fenichel discussed early stages of ego development (1939) while Balint discussed early stages of development of the ego (1939).

Let us return from this panoramic view of ego psychology in the 1930s to individual workers in the domain of affects. We may well begin with the three principal figures in the field: Heinz Hartmann, Anna Freud, and David Rapaport.

THE AFFECTS SEEN THROUGH THE EGO

Heinz Hartmann

In 1937, Hartmann presented his monograph *Ego Psychology and the Problem of Adaptation* (1939a) to the Vienna Psychoanalytic Society. Some thirty years later, Anna Freud was to write on how Hartmann and she had entered the Vienna Psychoanalytic Society in the same year. She tells us that whereas she came into the field of ego psychology "from the side of the ego's defensive activity against the drives" (1966–1970, p. 144), Hartmann, "in a more revolutionary manner, [came] from the new angle of ego autonomy" (1970–1980, p. 128). When her book, *The Ego and the Mechanisms of Defense* (1936), was discussed in Vienna, Hartmann made the point that the ego-at-war-with-the-id was not the whole story and that there were additional issues that needed clarification, such as ego growth and ego functioning as a whole, beyond conflict and defense. Hartmann argued that although the ego grows on conflict, this cannot be its only root; there are conflict-free spheres in the ego as well. In the area of conflict, Hartmann was interested not only in the clashes between the mental agencies, the so-called intersystemic conflicts, but also in the conflict within each system, particularly the ego.

Hartmann believed that, during its growth, the ego is sometimes torn within itself; therefore different lines of development exist, and the whole picture has a complexity that must be reckoned with. Hartmann dealt with this complexity by using concepts such as hierarchies, synchronization, autonomous functioning, and other terms pertaining to psychic economy. His work, which may be seen as a kind of psychoanalytic field theory that treats psychic phenomena from several different viewpoints at once, contributed considerably to the abandonment of simplistic, 'either-or' types of thinking in psychoanalysis. The ego, in Hartmann's theory, is not a monolithic construct, but the bearer of different functions, all directed toward adaptation on different levels. In fact, Hartmann established a theory of psychic functions, their energy supplies, their relationship to the outer world, their stability and autonomy, and their development, regressions, and transformations. Later workers, who saw affects as mainly ego functions, relied on Hartmann's general theory of ego functions in their discussions of affects.

Hartmann's work helped attenuate harsh dichotomies between conscious and unconscious, as a result of which the idea of gradations in consciousness could be developed further (see G. Klein, 1976). The idea of gradations of consciousness proved helpful in reaching a finer conceptualization of affects (Eagle, 1987; Krystal, 1988; Lewin, 1965; Sandler, 1972, 1984; Schafer, 1964).

The father of ego psychology, however, in his classic *The Ego and the Problem of Adaptation* (1939a), hardly ever mentions terms such as affects, feelings, or emotions. The same is true of his much later work, *Essays on Ego Psychology* (1964), in which little consideration is given to affects, except when explaining them in terms of inhibitions of ego functions. This can be understood in the context of Hartmann's theoretical commitment to mechanistic causality as the basic explanation of all phenomena to be treated scientifically. Such a methodological choice positions Hartmann in an external, 'objective' explanatory stance, a stance from which psychic reality and its experiential dimension cannot be accounted for. Although Hartmann undoubtedly realized the profound importance of feelings in the clinic (and has certainly used them in his own clinical work), his personal conception of what a theory ought to look like (very much in line with theories in philosophy of science of that time) compelled him to exclude the subjective aspect from theory. On this point, Schafer wrote that "the biological language of functions cannot be concerned with meaning, and rightly so, in terms of . . . [Hartmann's] vantage point" (1976, p. 89). This theoretical stance created and reinforced a profound split between theory and practice, and perhaps between theoretical and clinical methods of investigation as well.

What is this stance, which reigned for such a long time as the central perspective of psychoanalytic theory? In Hartmann's view, every systematic, scientific approach, including one dealing with the mind, must clearly recognize the discrepancy between experiencing and knowing, or between understanding (in the sense of 'Verstehen,' or empathy) and explaining. "Understanding in the sense of comprehending experientially," he writes (in his polemics with Dilthey's philosophy of Verstehen), is "unreliable and potentially deceptive because of the affective elements involved, and, in addition, is informative only as regards conscious factors." Experiencing is, for Hartmann, "the very nucleus of the personality which is *inaccessible to explanation*. It has to do with satisfaction of the drives, attainment and preservation of pleasure, and with a complex of drives and emotions which is the center of mental structure" (1927, p. 375, emphasis added).

Whereas experiencing cannot be explained, in Hartmann's view, mental constructs cannot be experienced; they must be inferred. He accordingly defines the goal of psychoanalysis not as the understanding of the mental but as the explanation of its causal relationships (1927, p. 377). He further asserts that "experiencing itself cannot contain within itself the criterion for the real givenness of mental connections" (p. 378), by which he means that experience cannot be the arbiter of the nonexperiential mechanisms responsible for or generative of the experiential contents.

There is one place where, juxtaposing instincts and emotions, Hartmann suggests a classification of the various categories of pleasurable experiences. He distinguishes feelings with strong somatic reverberations from the pleasurable qualities of aim-inhibited, sublimated activities, and, within the latter category, he further differentiates among (1) sensory or experiential feelings, (2) somatic and vital feelings, (3) pure psychic feelings, and (4) mental ('personality') feelings.[1]

Two general points can be made concerning affects in Hartmann's theory. Simplified, they are the following: (a) affects or feelings are inaccessible to explanation, and they cannot be causally, i.e., according to Hartmann, scientifically, explained and (b) affects are unreliable as guides to explanation in that they do not comprise any criteria for explaining anything in an objectively valid, systematic way.

Hartmann's main concern was to construct a theory of psychoanalysis as a general psychology, and since he did not believe that affects as experiences had a place in theory, he was not theoretically interested in them. He took an interest, however, in the 'neighboring concepts' of affects (e.g., energies and cathexes), which he deemed better tools for his theory-making. Hartmann believed that affects could be discussed meaningfully by using such concepts as cathexes, particularly in the sense of a positive load attributed to an object or an idea, that is, the value with which objects and ideas are invested in the subject's personal world.

Hartmann has had a tremendous impact on psychoanalytic thought, which reached far beyond ego psychology proper. His attitudes, inextricably involved with a certain theoretical allegiance, played a formative role in the way succeeding conceptions of affects were formulated.

Anna Freud

While Hartmann focused on the conflict-free ego in his theorizing, Anna Freud developed at the same time a conception of what may be called a 'defending ego.' Her belief that whatever an analyst sees is seen in terms of the ego, was very innovative at that time. In those years, in which the concept of the ego was introduced and elaborated in psychoanalytic discussions, the assumed importance attached to the concept was suspect to those analysts who worried lest the ego concept oust the concept of the id, the importance of which, they felt, made psychoanalysis what it is, uniquely different from any other realm of knowledge.

It was in this atmosphere that Anna Freud put forward her views and defended the concept of the ego against criticisms, particularly as to the relations of the ego with the drives. The articulation of her insights about the ego made it necessary for her to sharpen the dichotomy between the ego and the drives. This may have been one of the reasons for her conception of the ego as an alien (and even hostile) territory to the drives. According to her, the ego basically defends against the drives and against the affects. With all the differences between affects and drives, the ego employs the same defenses against the affects as against the drives, so that the two kinds of defense may be regarded as equivalent. Thus she assumed that the reason that an expected affect does not occur is that the ego operates against it, i.e., defends against it.

In the 1930s, Anna Freud conceived of affects mostly in terms of something the ego has to defend against, and she believed that the study of affects was important because affects were a kind of contrasting background against which the operation of the ego could be better perceived and understood. Analyzing the defenses, in her view, always teaches us something about the ego by teaching us about the various techniques employed by the ego. She believed that analysis "offers us rich opportunities for learning about affective life, which in the child is less complicated and more easily observable: in observing the child's affective processes, we are largely independent of his voluntary co-operation; his affects betray themselves against his will" (1954, p. 42).

Later, in 1952, she modified her views, acknowledging Hartmann's influence on her, and added: "The ego's role as an ally to the id precedes that of an agent designed to slow up and obstruct satisfaction" (p. 236). Yet she did not pursue the implications of this change of view concerning the rapprochement of ego and id on the concept of affect, although the gain won by her conception of defenses against affects was, and continued to be, a strong influence on later thinking on the subject. In this context, she wrote that when the ego defends against instinctual claims, it must as a rule first defend against the affects associated with them (1954, p. 34).

Many years later, in 1977, she added to her statement that any unpleasant affect can give rise to defense by asserting that "all defense activity, whether benign or pathological, is set in motion by token anxiety" (p. 90); with this assertion, the ego was now endowed with token affects of its own.

An illuminating account of her last views is given in the discussions she held with Joseph Sandler shortly before her death in 1981. In these discussions she admitted that defenses against affects are not necessarily derivatives of defenses against the drives, and she agreed with Sandler that conflicting feeling states within the ego should be regarded as motives in their own right. This realization marked an important step in the more recent theory of affect developed by Sandler (see chapter 5).

Anna Freud's most important contribution to affect theory is her conception of defenses against affects. The meaning of this is that consideration of pleasantness and unpleasantness, that is, experiential attributes, were now regarded as motives. It is not only excess stimulation or moral condemnation that is feared and avoided, but also feelings themselves. Also, by spelling out the existence of defenses against affects, she made their structural status clearer and moved a further step in the understanding of unconscious affects. She would not, however, grant affects an independent status; she always saw them as essentially drive derivatives, or drive equivalents.

David Rapaport

Whereas it was Anna Freud who first wrote on defenses against affects and on the relationship between the ego and the affects, it was David Rapaport who for a long time was considered the spokesman of ego psychology on affects. In 1953 appeared his monumental paper "On the Psychoanalytic Theory of Affects," preceded by his 1950 book, *Emotions and Memory*. As his comparative survey of the literature on affects up to his time has itself been surveyed by several writers (Arlow, 1952; Jacobson, 1953; Sandler, 1972; and others), I shall not repeat it here. Instead, I have chosen for discussion from his work some points of special concern or difficulty.

Like many thinkers before (and after) him, Rapaport stresses the notorious difficulty of delimiting and unifying the domain of the affects, a domain that encompasses an enormous variety of states and manifestations. Another related difficulty in theorizing about affects stems from the necessity, in Rapaport's view, of rendering compatible different writings of Freud, each of which is intelligible only within one of Freud's changing theoretical frames of reference, in which affect is variously linked to theories of catharsis (of a charge of libido), theories of conflict (between a drive and its expression), and theories of signals (about meanings and situations).

Rapaport exposes and orders the implicit theory of affect in each phase of Freud's writings in a penetrating and scholarly manner. He pays great attention to the transition from one phase to another, while demonstrating how each phase also contains assumptions and notions from the phase preceding it. The last phase of the psychoanalytic theory of affect, beginning roughly with *The Ego and the Id* (S. Freud, 1923) and its conception of affect as an ego signal, is for Rapaport the overture to a structural-adaptive point of view.

Within this point of view, Rapaport attempts to explain how ego development brings about the delay of action and of drive discharge by invoking the concept of thresholds as the structuralizing factor in affect development. In his view, structures develop out of innate, discharge-regulating thresholds, which are fostered by delays of discharge (themselves enforced by reality conditions) and proceed by internalization of this delay, in this way establishing an 'ability to delay.' Rapaport believes that this ability is achieved through the defenses.

The establishment of defenses acts as an obstacle to the flow of energy. The analogy Rapaport uses is that of an obstacle that is put in the way of a stream and forces the water to take various detours and to form different paths, so that various drive derivatives, i.e., new affects with their specific discharge thresholds, are formed. When prevented from discharge, these derivatives have the power to modify the thresholds. This process, constantly repeated during the course of development, builds up a complex hierarchy of motivations, drives, and affects, spanning the most different shading of feelings, from massive affect attacks to mere signals and even signals of signals. This development of the motivational and affective hierarchy is, in Rapaport's view, one aspect of the development of the ego structure.

Rapaport posits three basic components that a psychoanalytic theory of affects should integrate: (1) inborn affect discharge thresholds and channels, (2) affect 'charges' (formed through threshold modifications and undischarged drive derivatives) and (3) affect signals, released by the ego, with which the ego progressively 'tames' the affects. Of these three parts, the first, the concept of thresholds, seems to be of the greatest interest for a working out of a theory of affect, in that it allows for more complex relationships and states than either discharge or tension, opposition or quietude, and has some explanatory power concerning the problem of unconscious affects.[2] Rapaport shows how affect formation incorporates aspects of the various metapsychological models of psychoanalysis. Thus, at each level of the hierarchy, the dynamic aspect of affect formation consists of the conflict between the discharge cathexes and innate thresholds, or between the discharge cathexes and reality (i.e., the absent object), or between discharge cathexes and countercathexes. The economic aspect of affect formation is apparent in the (partial) discharge of motivational cathexes of ever increasing neutralization. The structural aspect of affect formation is discernible in the integration of the ascending motivational systems into id, ego, and superego, and the creation of mutually controlling systems of organization. Rapaport understands continuous affective states to occur as integrations of complex balances and conflicts of components from the three structural divisions of the psyche.

This 1953 paper, whose impact on psychoanalytic thought was very important for a long time, reveals both the long way traversed since Freud and the extremely difficult conceptual problems still waiting to be elucidated, perhaps never to be completely settled within this framework. The impressively thorough and detailed overview Rapaport offers us of the history of affect theory, together with his addition of the genetic and adaptive points of view of what may be called 'affect metapsychology,' has made the paper an obligatory reference for every worker on the subject.

Rapaport's paper represents a giant effort to analyze the concept of affect from a formal, objective position, to depict the varied structural vicissitudes and genetic stages of the affective phenomenon, and to encompass all of Freud's statements and perspectives on affect. The interiorized, experiential aspects of affect, however, are not addressed theoretically. In so doing, Rapaport, like Hartmann before him, has chosen an epistemological position that succeeds in reconciling many dimensions of the vexing mind-body problem of the affects, but at the cost of excluding the realm of subjective experience and reflective meanings from analytic theory. This prevented Rapaport from using the 'felt' aspect of affects for explaining motivation in terms of feelings. Rapaport's model is consequently mechanistic rather than teleological. What motivates a person, in his theory, are energic disequilibria, not feeling states.

THE EGO EVALUATES, EXPERIENCES, REACTS

Otto Fenichel

A common thread running through the work of Rapaport (1950, 1953) and of Fenichel (1939, 1941, 1945) is the theme of the 'taming' of the affects; there are, however, considerable differences between the two thinkers in their approach to affects. In his writings, Fenichel seems to wrestle with defining affects, which, as late as 1941, he still conceived of as being drive-derived forces confronting the ego, which has the task of taming them. Fenichel disagreed with the conception of affect found in the psychoanalytic literature of his day, which he thought was borrowed from psychology and descriptive, and thus emptied of the dynamic and economic dimensions entailed in the psychoanalytic view of affect. He believed that the common and most specific characteristic of affects is their being basically 'spells,' occurring without the consent of the conscious will; during their occurrence the normal function of the ego is eliminated. Emotions in Fenichel's eyes are either in the nature of overwhelming spells, or, alternately, are akin to neurotic symptoms, the difference being that whereas in the neuroses symptoms are subjectively determined (by the history of the individual), in the case of affects the substitute is "objectively determined" (the symptom is roughly the same for all individuals). Both emotional spells and neurotic symptoms are, in Fenichel's view, archaic substitutes for healthy ego motility.

Fenichel sees development in terms of the following stages. Initially, the ego is weak, and affects are an alien and dominant force. At a second developmental stage, the ego becomes stronger and has also learned to use affects for its purposes. A third stage, however, is also possible, in which an elemental affect may once more overwhelm the ego. Fenichel demonstrates this 'triple stratification' through the affect of anxiety.

Fenichel regards the ego's attitude to affects as similar and equivalent to its attitude toward alien forces, which can traumatically overwhelm the ego or, if the ego is strong enough, be met with its countercathexes, or which may be absorbed and used within the structure of the countercathexes. Fenichel understands these three reactions (shock, distortion, or learning) to be the ego's ways of handling all events. When the ego tames the affects, writes Fenichel, it anticipates and actively apportions the automatic id reactions; the ego then actively uses the affects for its own purposes, either by using negative affects, which Fenichel calls 'automatic protective affects,' such as disgust and shame, as defenses against sexual impulses, or by using affect signals, including signals of shame, disgust, and pain, as a means for reality testing. In line with his model of neurotic symptoms that he applies to the affects, Fenichel writes about the 'secondary gains' from affects, their use as rationalizations, and their various functions in conflicts between ego and superego.

Fenichel, like most writers in this framework, is particularly interested in the affect of anxiety. The central concept in his theory of anxiety (1939), as well as in his theory of affects (1941) and in his theory of neurosis (1945), is that of the 'dammed-up state,' which occurs when there is a relative "insufficiency of the discharge apparatus," so that quantities of dammed-up excitation accumulate. Such states are associated with subjective feelings of tension, and anxiety is a mode of experiencing tension "arising from urgent needs" (1939, p. 49). All anxiety is, at base, fear of experiencing a traumatic state (1945, p. 133). For Fenichel, traumatic and infantile anxieties are experienced passively by the ego, while signal anxiety is seen by him as resulting from the ego function of judging danger, that is, judging the liability of a traumatic excess of excitation. This is achieved by the ego's setting up conditions in the id similar to a traumatic situation. According to Fenichel, the ego simulates a mini-traumatic situation so as to be able to handle it with its own means (see also Rangell, 1967; this explanation, however, begs the question of how an ego function can cause excessive excitation).

Fenichel is strongly influenced in his thinking by models of psychopathology, which consider affects as analogous to symptoms. This explains the neglect, in his affect theory, of the pleasurable affects and of the richness and subtlety of affects as a whole. The result is the most mechanistic, dated model of the affects since Freud. Fenichel's model of the affects stands in marked contrast to his deep and sensitive approach to other mental phenomena of treatment (1941) and of psychopathology (1945). While historically such an approach was perhaps inevitable, it imposed serious limitations on psychoanalytic thinking on affects. Fenichel's stress on what may be called 'psychopathological psychodynamics' leaves no room for the autonomous status of the affects and for their constant, though sometimes silent, influence on thought and behavior. Fenichel's work on affects is a reflection of a conservative tendency, which came as a reaction to the fear that in changing older notions of psychoanalytic theory, important psychoanalytic insights achieved in the past might be lost.

Max Schur

A considerably broader perspective on affects, their development, and their relations to the ego was offered by Max Schur (1953, 1958, 1964, 1966). Drawing on many disparate sources, such as developmental psychology, ethology, and models of ego and id functioning, Schur succeeded in dispelling some of the confusions in this area, and, on a long and somewhat tortuous path, he worked out a more refined and tenable concept of anxiety, modifying his views as his thought evolved over the years. In presenting Schur's work, I shall follow the chronological unfolding of his ideas and the emendations he introduced in them.

Schur's early clinical encounters with his medical patients convinced him that an intense study of the anxiety reaction was indispensable for a better understanding of his clinical observations. Schur began where Freud had left off with his famous *non liquet* [Latin for 'it cannot be clarified or decided'], through which Freud had expressed his resignation at failing to establish a unitary theory of anxiety. Scrutinizing Freud's 1926 *Inhibitions, Symptoms and Anxiety*, Schur discovered that throughout the ten chapters of this essay, Freud had written only about actual, real danger, to which the anticipated reaction was defined as anxiety. Only in Addendum B of this essay did Freud introduce the concept of a traumatic situation, defined as a situation in which the organism experiences utter help-lessness. From this point on, Freud regarded danger as an event in which a traumatic situation is anticipated. This formulation broadened the scope of anxiety. Also, by considering both kinds of anxiety to be caused by sexual frustration, Freud came very close to a unitary theory of anxiety, writes Schur. But Freud had felt that this formulation led to confusion, because anxiety was now the name Freud himself had given to both the reaction to danger and the reaction to the traumatic situation itself, whereas the term anxiety, which denotes an economical occurrence (overwhelming libido, or energy), cannot be given at the same time to a signal, that is, to virtual, rather than actual, danger.

If one keeps in mind the categorical distinction between a traumatic and a signal reaction, then the nonunitary nature of Freud's concept of anxiety becomes clear. Having realized this, writes Schur, Freud withdrew from the problem and drew his *non liquet*; the concept of anxiety was left divided into separate id and ego components. This situation led, according to Schur, to the deepening of the dichotomy between somatic and mental phenomena in psychoanalysis and psychiatry. To bridge this unacceptable gap, Schur set himself the goal of con-structing a unitary theory of anxiety. To this end, he experimented in 1950 with eliminating from his definition of anxiety the component of 'thoughtlike aware-ness of danger' (corresponding to signal anxiety) by reasoning that this thought-like awareness lacked any affectlike characteristic and therefore could be ignored when conceptualizing affects. Schur thus defined affects within an exclusively somatic conception.

But in 1953, in "The Ego in Anxiety", Schur acknowledged the error entailed by the step of excluding signal anxiety from affect theory and redefined anxiety as the response of the ego to a traumatic situation, that is, to danger. Signal anxiety, considered an ego response to danger, had now to be encompassed within a theory of anxiety. In order to include signal anxiety within his theory of anxiety, Schur introduced the distinction between present and anticipated danger. To this end, he included the factor of time in the definition of affects and used the genetic point of view (see Rapaport & Gill, 1960) and the concept of 'complementary series' (Freud, 1916–1917, p. 347), the reasoning of which is too complex to be detailed here. According to Schur's conception, there are two sets of basic factors, innate and environmental, which act and react to each other in a complementary and dialectical way.

Another important extension of the theory of anxiety was Schur's interposition of the ego system—particularly the ego functions of experiencing and evaluat-ing—between the situation of danger and the reaction of anxiety. Schur also added the concept of potential danger to the situation of present danger and of trauma (past danger). This model now enlarged the scope of anxiety situations as well as the domain of ego functioning and allowed for more variability and freedom of perception and reaction. Now Schur's theory could account both for hierarchies of situations and for variations in reactions.

In the next phase of his theory, Schur deepened his study of anxiety, danger, and trauma by relating them to ego development. He suggested that at the beginning of life all danger is perceived as coming from the inside; it is sensed in terms of a disturbance in the inner equilibrium of the organism. With maturation, the conception of danger undergoes a series of changes. The realization that an external object can initiate and/or end a traumatic situation displaces the danger from, as Schur calls it, an 'economic situation' (a physical situation, such as hunger) to the conditions that determine the situation (the psychological situation, such as mother's absence). Thus, inner danger has changed to outer, potential danger, which has now become 'danger of danger' and to which the ego reacts as it would to real danger. Schur believed that the traumatic impact of a situation depends on two factors: the quantity of excitation and the quality of regression of the ego, which determines how the ego experiences the situation.

Implied in these new formulations is the view that there can be no anxiety without the ego, and traumatic situations can no longer be explained by Freud's hypothesis of automatic anxiety, which is said to be produced exclusively by the id. Schur believed that only if there is regression of the ego is there trauma. It is the ego's regressing, and not the id's overflowing, that makes a trauma. But trauma is 'produced' neither by the id nor by the ego. We cannot say, writes Schur, that the ego 'produces' an affect (a formulation prevalent in the writings of early ego psychologists, which echoed Freud's early conception of affects as secretory phenomena) any more than we can say that it 'produces' a percept or a memory. Instead, Schur uses Hartmann's conception of the ego as an organization and argues that the ego perceives and evaluates the danger and experiences various shades of anxiety and that both evaluation and experience act as signals to induce defenses. Here Schur takes a step away from the view of anxiety as a quantity and attributes to the ego the functions of perception and evaluation of danger and even the experiencing of anxiety.

By taking this step, Schur radically reformulated and broadened the concept of signal. His new conception implies that even in the actual presence of danger, and even with a regressive ego reaction (e.g., resomatization), an experience may still serve as a signal for the rest of the ego to take the necessary measures! According to this view, all shades and grades of anxiety, except for outright panic, that is, totally uncontrolled anxiety, represent an attempt of the ego to regain control and to avoid danger (the implications for a theory of therapy are momentous; see Krystal, 1988).

But to gain control and avoid danger, Schur found it necessary to postulate an instinct to avoid danger. He reinforced this thesis in his 1966, "The Id and the Regulatory Principles of Mental Functioning," in which he assumed two different bases for the regulatory principles of pleasure and unpleasure, namely, response and withdrawal, respectively. He now maintained that the instinct to avoid danger functions according to the unpleasure principle; it develops out of the need to withdraw from danger. The trouble with this solution is that it put Schur back in the old and no longer tenable position of postulating a separate instinct for each kind of behavior.[3]

In setting himself the task of continuing in Freud's footsteps, while at the same time trying to clarify the difficulties resulting from Freud's conceptualizations of affects in predominantly somatic and energic terms, Schur wished to reject notions incompatible with newer clinical findings and theoretical formulations.

Schur also made considerable efforts to link the somatic and the psychological aspects of the affects. From the beginnings of his work, he linked both aspects through a common, extended ego-id matrix. On this ego-id continuum, Schur worked out the notion of affect as consisting of two basic, innate, simultaneous elements, a cognitive (signaling) process and the reaction to this process. This conception made it possible for Schur to draw the analogy between affects and thought processes.

Schur believed that he could embrace within a single consistent framework the entire spectrum of affective 'variants.' Whereas older formulations could only suggest the transformation of the instincts into ego judgments of negation and affirmation, Schur felt he could now trace in detail the successive stages from affect-dominated to ego-dominated responses to personality needs.

In Schur's theory affects are seen as partitioned between the ego and the id in a kind of balanced flow between these two agencies of the mind, in a series of innate and learned behavior patterns. The ego here both serves as mediator and modulator of excitations and tensions arising from the instincts and determines the reaction to them within each particular situational context. What has been said above describes the cross-sectional part of Schur's theory. The longitudinal aspect is also given prominence in his thinking. Schur saw maturation as leading to the differentiation between traumatic and bearable anxiety.

Thus, Schur's main moves were away from a somatic view, via an exclusively ideational (thoughtlike) view, eventually to a psychosomatic, compromise-formed view of affects, in line with the trend in ego psychology of considering psychic activities as attempts to reconcile the strivings of the different functions and agencies of the body and of the mind.

AFFECTS MEDIATE BETWEEN THE EGO AND THE DRIVES

Charles Brenner

Charles Brenner (1953, 1974, 1982) is another thinker who broached the conceptual difficulty inherent in the dual (mental and somatic) nature of affects by positing a unitary model aimed at encompassing them both.

At the beginning of his work, Brenner focused on anxiety and sought to eliminate from affect theory the energic and somatic side of the affects (in contrast to Schur, who, at the beginning of his work, chose to exclude 'thoughtlike awareness' from affect theory).

To this purpose, Brenner culled recent findings and conceptions from ethology that he believed could replace energic and discharge conceptions of the working of the mind in general and of affects in particular. Brenner used many extra-analytic data to make the point that the test case of anxiety coming from an energic source, the 'Aktualneurose,' does not exist. In addition, he claimed that neurotic anxiety arises not from energic vicissitudes but from the interplay of external events and unconscious conflicts (1982, p. 21). He contended that the only situations in which there is something like 'economic' anxiety are found in early infancy; however, this kind of anxiety should more correctly be called unpleasure. This initial state of unpleasure is understood by Brenner to be later differentiated into more specific emotions.

If it is accepted that unpleasure precedes anxiety, it follows that unpleasure, rather than anxiety, should be regarded as responsible for defense and for conflict. Thus, in Brenner's view what causes conflict in the first place is unpleasure. Unpleasure, in his view, later becomes differentiated into anxiety and into depressive affect.[4] Brenner proposed to revise Freud's theory of anxiety by abolishing Freud's distinction between qualitatively overwhelming traumatic anxiety as a product of the drives, and signal anxiety as a product of the ego's activity.

With the abolishing of this distinction, the contrast between ego and drives was greatly attenuated. To understand this point better, let us look at Brenner's concepts of the drives and drive derivatives, of the ego and its relationship with the drives, and, consequently, of psychic conflict.

Brenner argues that the conception of the drives as a borderline phenomenon has become untenable, particularly since 1920, when the dual drive theory was better elaborated. His point is that the drives have no specific extra-cerebral, somatic sources and, in addition, that the designation of the drives as 'somato-psychic' is a tautology, because everything psychic is somatic as well, in his view, since all mental phenomena are rooted in the body, i.e., in the brain.

Brenner considers the drives to be a highly abstracted theoretical construct that explains the general nature of people's basic motivations. Brenner sharply distinguishes the concept of the drives from the concept of the drive derivatives. The concept of the drive derivative refers to the wish as a particular instance of drive activity; the wish is ''personally and situationally determined and object-related'' (1982, p. 89); it is specific and personal, in contrast to the drive. Drive derivatives being essentially wishes for gratification, they function according to the pleasure principle (there is no repetition compulsion in Brenner's theory). Consequently, the old issue of the transformation of pleasure into unpleasure occupies a central place in Brenner's thought.[5] Instead of asking, as Freud had, how it happens that pleasure turns into unpleasure, Brenner sees the ego, which he considers as the executant of the drives, as the agency that gratifies the derivatives on the one hand, while on the other hand it sometimes opposes the drives (1982, p. 40). Ego functions serve both to gratify drive derivatives and to oppose them. If a wish arouses too much unpleasure, the ego functions appear as defenses; if not, they appear as mediators of satisfaction. The ego is seen here as being definitely in the service of the drives and their derivatives and hence inseparable from the drives, except in situations of conflict.

Conflict, in Brenner's theory, ensues when a drive derivative arouses unpleasure and hence defense. Brenner's theory considers every psychopathological manifestation to be the result of conflict. Psychic conflict, writes Brenner, can never exist between different drives or their derivatives, because they all function according to the pleasure principle. Conflict can arise only if one drive derivative is used to ward off another, to alleviate unpleasure, for purposes of defense, and at this point the ego comes in.

What links drive derivatives and ego functions is the affect of unpleasure. Brenner sees affects as related both to the gratification and frustration of drive derivatives and to the development of ego and superego. In other words, affects are the common denominator of the ego, superego, and the drives. Conflict and psychic disturbances are rooted in affects, and what causes psychopathology is anxiety and depressive affect, which derive from wishes and trigger defenses, rather than the 'intensity of the drives' as pure quantity.

Let us turn from the role of affects in Brenner's theory to the nature of affect itself. To Brenner, an affect is a complex mental phenomenon that includes constitutionally given, unchanging sensations of pleasure and unpleasure, and ideas, such as memories, fantasies, representations, and the like. Brenner believes that this definition of affects enables him to classify them according to the intensity of sensations and according to the content and origin of the ideas that constitute each affect, and to explain individual differences in the affects and in their expression. In his book, Brenner repeatedly uses this definition of affect, which he believes to constitute the basis for a unitary theory of affect in psychoanalysis (he sees himself as the first theoretician to put forward such a unitary theory). He considers his theory to be unique in its hypothesis that the ideational content is part and parcel of the affects themselves.[6]

Brenner is a recognized authority in ego psychology, and his formulations and assumptions are representative of prevailing views in ego psychology today. The controversy about whether affects belong to the ego or to the id has been reformulated in such a way as to considerably alter, in fact abolish, the distinctness (or, in Anna Freud's words, the 'animosity') between the ego and the drives, except in situations of conflict. According to Brenner, the ego is in conflict with the drive derivatives and opposes them via unpleasurable affects, which in turn are produced by the activity of the drive derivatives. At the same time, the drive derivatives function as signals for the ego to stand up to and oppose the drives. The drive derivatives then may produce unpleasurable affects. In Brenner's eyes, affects serve to link soma (sensations) and mind (ideas). This view leads to the situation in which the concept of affect supersedes that of the drives; the drives no longer possess their status of a frontier concept. Instead, it is the concept of affects that is now at the forefront of the theory.

Brenner introduced some major modifications in the psychoanalytic theory of affects that are germane to the very character of the ego-psychological outlook. In the following, some of the most pertinent points in this context are listed.

1. In Brenner's theory, as in other contemporary work in ego psychology, emphasis shifts from the sources of the drives (which, according to Brenner, are extra-cerebral) to their aims. Consequently, explanations in terms of energy are superseded by functional considerations. No recourse to neurophysiology or to energy is therefore needed. Ego psychology has become more confident of its own methods and its conceptual frame, and Brenner considered it legitimate to rely on so-called analytic data, i.e., observations obtained exclusively from the analytic situation. With this approach, functional and teleological considerations now become acceptable, and the circularity in explanation against which Hartmann had admonished his followers is not feared anymore.

2. The paradigmatic affect for theorizing, in Brenner's view, is no longer anxiety, but an earlier, more inclusive, and psychologically less specific affect, in fact, a sensation—unpleasure. The original meaning of anxiety as based on memory traces of fear or pain (Freud, 1895) is thereby restored. Anxiety loses its status as the primary affect (see Ramzey & Wallerstein, 1958).

3. The pleasure principle is here elevated to the primary regulatory mechanism. According to this view, everything functions in accordance with the yield of pleasure (or unpleasure) or a specific wish at a given time. Conflict is wholly based on considerations of pleasure and unpleasure, rather than on dissension between mental agencies, as had been assumed until then.

4. Brenner maintains that there is no fundamental opposition between the ego and the id (1982, p. 34), and in 1987 he writes, "Rather than the ego overwhelmed by drives, it is disorganization of ego functioning resulting from wishes that causes unpleasure" (p. 39). Ego functions are regarded by him as executants of the drives (1973, p. 41) and their derivatives, and as inseparable from them except where the drives arouse unpleasure and give rise to defenses.

5. Brenner's central tenet is his definition of affects as complex psychic phenomena that include (a) sensations of pleasure, unpleasure, or both and (b) ideas. Ideas and pleasure-unpleasure sensations together constitute an affect (1982, p. 53). He further adds that whereas pleasure and unpleasure have no developmental history, ideas develop, and the development of affects is therefore entirely dependent on the development of ideas.

Some of Brenner's hypotheses accurately reflect recent ideas in ego psychology, but there are some basic points that are extremely problematic, such as his claim that pleasure and unpleasure sensations do not develop with time or the statement that affects are simply made up of sensations and ideas. It is not clear what exactly is meant in this context by 'ideas' and what the difference would be between primitive and mature, global and differentiated affects, beyond the addition of ideas to the latter category of affects. The attractiveness of Brenner's theory of affect may lie in its neat packaging of many diverse phenomena into few elements and simple statements about the relations among them; its simplistic cast, however, seems not to take account of the complexity of the phenomena it addresses.

AFFECTS AS TENSION AND DISCHARGE PHENOMENA DETERMINED BY PSYCHIC STRUCTURES AND BY SELF AND OBJECT REPRESENTATIONS

Edith Jacobson

Edith Jacobson began her study of affects out of her clinical work. Treating patients with affective illnesses made it clear to her that these disturbances lent themselves to the study of ego and superego pathology, in which she was deeply interested. As early as 1937, she studied superego formation in women, which then stimulated her to explore the links between depressive syndromes and ego and superego formation, and the relations between normal and pathological affects.

Her comparative study of affects and effective configurations culminated in her 1971 book, *Depression*, which had been preceded by considerable work, done mostly in the 1950s and 1960s, some of which had been published in two monographs, *The Self and the Object World* (1964) and *Psychotic Conflict and Reality* (1967).

Jacobson's thinking draws upon various sources, such as Freud's 1917 paper, in which he linked melancholia with internalized object relations, his structural theory (1923), and his anxiety theory (1926); Abraham's ideas on depression (1924); Hartmann, Kris & Loewenstein's papers, particularly on structure formation (1946); and Mahler's work on infantile psychoses and moods (1961, 1966, 1974). Marked by its integrative thrust, Jacobson's thinking has nevertheless a distinctly personal quality, and her complex ideas, although not very often referred to directly, impregnated the entire psychoanalytic literature in the 1970s and continue to do so even today.

Having entered the domain of affects, Jacobson soon became aware of the tremendous conceptualizing and clarifying work waiting to be done, and she chose to advance along several theoretical lines of investigation simultaneously. Her interests lay in economic issues, in the developmental vicissitudes of the ego and the superego, in self and object representations and their ways of crystallizing into a mature identity, and in general regulatory principles of mental functioning, embedded in all of which, and influenced by each of which, lay the affects. Her major efforts, throughout her work, were directed into bringing all this under one cohesive roof. In presenting her ideas, I have chosen only that part of her extensive work that bears directly on the subject of affects.

Jacobson chose as her point of departure two issues that had been preoccupying affect theoreticians in those days. The first concerned the question whether affects should be regarded as essentially discharge processes or as tension phenomena;

the second had to do with the equation Freud had made between discharge and pleasure, on the one hand, and tension and unpleasure, on the other.[7]

On the basis of extensive clinical and theoretical work, Jacobson came up with some answers to these questions. She rejected any attempt to answer the first question, whether discharge equals pleasure and tension equals unpleasure, in an either-or manner; instead, she offered a more comprehensive framework, which assigns affects both roles of discharge and of tension in varying proportions that change with development. As to the question concerning the equation of discharge with pleasure and tension with unpleasure, Jacobson's answer is a definite no. In her view, both discharge and tension can be either pleasurable or unpleasurable. Empirical (clinical) and theoretical considerations convinced her that affects must be considered central subjective states that include, but are not identical with, discharge processes. Neither, to her mind, do affects eventually become mere signals; affects in their full experiential quality are vital for mental life. She thinks, however, that under a metapsychological description affects should be regarded as dispositions,[8] which may originate from each of the psychic systems or between them.

In Jacobson's view, affects are basically discharge processes, differing in quality according to the site of the "underlying energic tension by which they have been induced" (1953, p. 59). This site may be one, two, or all of the three psychic systems, and affects may arise from intersystemic or intrasystemic tension. The site in which an affect arises determines the identity of the affect; hence metapsychologically speaking, it is the structural constraint that shapes the differences among the affects. Jacobson proposed these distinctions as guidelines for a basic classificatory scheme of the affects. In this classification, affects that arise from intrasystemic tensions may be the instinctual drives proper, arising from the id, or fear of reality, pain, or enduring ego attitudes, arising from the ego. In contrast, affects arising from intersystemic tensions between the ego and the id express themselves as fear of the id, disgust, shame, pity, etc., while affects arising from tensions between the ego and the superego assume the form of guilt or depression.[9]

Jacobson realized that such a structural classification of the affects was inadequate; it can define the type of an affect, but it cannot convey the experiential meaning of even one simple affect. She considered affective expression in the mature, highly differentiated psychic organization to develop from a series of intersystemic and intrasystemic psychic tensions that are interrelated, condition each other, and arise simultaneously or sequentially at various sites in the psychic apparatus. She believed that such highly complex affects can be understood only by studying the experiential and ideational processes associated with them as well.

With this realization, Jacobson took another route; now she attempted to refine the use of the terms 'discharge' and 'tension' in the context of affect theory and tried to give these terms more precise definitions. In her view, discharge refers to "the energic processes themselves," i.e., the emotional processes that energize the biological strata, whereas tension is expressed by feelings. Feelings are described metapsychologically by Jacobson as the rises and falls of tension in the course of one or more discharge processes. These rises and falls occur in the psychic apparatus, which she visualizes as a vast field where numerous different energic tensions and potentials grow and decline in different loci at the same time. While mobile energy is being dispersed and tied down at one point, it is being gathered, released, and discharged at another point (she gives the example of a bathtub, where the water is simultaneously flowing in and being drained out; as long as the influx is stronger than the outflow, the water level will rise). This is analogous to psychic release processes that develop from the depth to the surface of the psychic apparatus, where the strength of the stimulus increases the tension even while the discharge has already begun, until the point is reached where the energy, having come to the surface, can be fully dispersed and the level of tension falls (1971, p. 21).

Implied in this description is the existence of tension within the discharge process itself, even in orgasm, the paradigm of pleasurable discharge. On the other hand, the wish to move from forepleasure to the sexual act itself cannot be said to be a wish to move from an unpleasurable to a pleasurable state (see Freud's 1900 definition of wish), but the wish to move from one pleasurable state to another pleasurable state. Jacobson proposes in this context to understand the wish in a broader sense than the original Freudian one; wishes, in her view, should be regarded as wishing for more pleasure or for a different pleasure quality.[10] According to Jacobson, we are constantly alternating between excitement and relief, while striving all the time for more cycles of pleasure. These perennial cycles represent the deep course of instinctual life; even if tension is pleasurable, we may nevertheless not wish to maintain a specific pleasure indefinitely. Thus, Jacobson has reconceptualized the regulatory principles and the theory of affect that she aligned with them.

In this view, the pleasure principle (and later in her thought the reality principle), rather than aiming at effecting relief from tension, directs the course of biological swings around a central axis of tension. The swings of the tension pendulum to either side feel pleasurable under certain conditions, "depending on certain still unknown proportions between the amount of excitation and the speed and rhythm of discharge" (1971, p. 28).[11]

While the pleasure principle directs the course of swings around a central axis of tension, the tension axis itself is regulated and stabilized by a general homeostatic law, the constancy principle, which Jacobson sees as the most general law governing mental life. The constancy principle dominates the pleasure principle and sometimes replaces it. The pleasure principle, however, can reassert itself in proportion to the strengthening of the ego, as more tension can become tolerable and even pleasurable for the ego. The constancy principle is thus invoked by Jacobson to explain the integrating of unpleasurable tension affects with signal affects, which, experientially, means increasing tolerance for tension affects. The hallmark of affective development is, in Jacobson's view, the growing tolerance for tension affects, and their integration and fusion with pleasurable affects.

Affective development proceeds along two interrelated dimensions: (a) increasing tolerance of tension, which leads to what she calls 'adult tension tolerance and tension pleasure' and (b) establishing, through ego maturation, increasingly variegated discharge channels. Jacobson sees affects as progressively changing from crude, almost exclusively biological discharge phenomena into tension affects. Tension prolongs the duration, refines the shadings, and increases the awareness of an experience. Tension that is tolerated becomes amalgamated into various pleasurable experiences, creating new, richer interweavings of diverse feeling qualities into one felt emotion.

Jacobson draws the extremely important distinctions between tension tolerance and taming of affects. She agrees with Fenichel's description of the progressive taming of the affects with development, but she suggests that although some affects become safety valves for discharge when adequate motor action is excluded, affective responses in general should not be too strictly opposed to adequate drive action or to reasonable ego functioning; on the contrary, the more developed the psychic apparatus, the less do affects function as safety valves. This function, so central in early life, decreases in importance and leaves the stage for the differentiated and full experiencing of various kinds of tension.[12] In her 1964 book, *The Self and the Object World*, Jacobson describes the stages of transition from a low-tension, discharge-dominated to a tension-oriented affective life. She posits several stages in affective development.

The first affective phenomena constitute what she calls "affective organ language" (1964, p. 11). Discharge at this stage is directed inward into the body and is equivalent to the cathectic investment of the self. What is discharged to the inside is undifferentiated psychophysiological energy. From this stage, the child advances to "the colorful affect qualities of the oedipal period," when "self-expressive affectomotor activity alternates with the most touching expressions of object-related feelings" (p. 23). With the establishment of stable self and object representations, true object relations, and ego activities, the child becomes able to experience affectionate feeling qualities and rich feeling shades. In latency, the superego establishes a lasting and dominant control over self representations, and superego fear becomes the leading affect signal. In the process of modifying and repatterning the affects under the influence of the superego, enduring large-scale feelings and feeling states develop as an expression of the ego's states and its relations with objects.

The Self and the Object World may be said to be an extension of Jacobson's theory of affects, in that it links affects with the development of the psychic structures and of self and object representations. Here Jacobson indirectly provides us with a complex developmental and structural model of the affects.

Another area to which Jacobson contributed is that of moods. She believed that the superego had a crucial role in controlling moods and affects. Its main function is to control, modulate, and regulate emotional expression. The normal superego, in her view, functions to delimit guilt feelings so that they remain localized and refer to specific forbidden strivings only. In this way, guilt feelings can serve as an effective warning and directing signal, mobilizing the defensive activity of the ego. She contrasts this process with the defensive or regressive superego, which has lost its signal function and is replaced by a tendency to diffuse moods.

In 1971, influenced by Weinshel's 1970 paper on moods, Jacobson revised her ideas on the subject. Weinshel had spoken of the ambiguous, shadowy, or even 'slippery' quality of moods, emphasizing their complex, highly refined nature. His work stimulated Jacobson to place moods in a broader perspective than before; she now no longer saw moods as predominantly primitive, even archaic structures, and she no longer associated them primarily with the superego. Recognizing more clearly their richness and complexity, she stressed their inherent usefulness as psychic structures that allow prolonged discharge in small, modulated quantities, which helps maintain the emotional equilibrium of the psyche. In her view, an experience causes a change of mood only if it can lead to qualitative changes in the representations of the self and the object world. The very existence and complexity of moods, however, and the ease in which the sweeping worldview that they induce can be corrected or delimited, are indicators of ego development. An immature or an altered ego creates anomalous vacillations of moods and leads to the restriction and reduction of finer emotional shadings in favor of crude or strange affects and moods; it also cannot prevent the ascendancy of cold affect qualities over rich, warm, and affectionate ones.

Jacobson's study of moods is closely associated with her famous work on depression. She explains depressive and masochistic phenomena in terms of the renunciation and sacrifice of the pleasure principle in an effort to restitute psychic equilibrium; in extreme cases, the self-preservative function fails altogether, and self-destruction results. In such cases, the victory of the constancy principle is mentally or physically fatal. Reading Jacobson on depression, one appreciates the complexity and subtlety of her handling of the many structural and representational factors involved in these syndromes. Throughout her writings, on whatever subject, Jacobson stresses the great extent to which the quality, intensity, and differentiatedness of affects are determined by the psychic structures in which (or among which) they originate and by the maturity of these structures, and, inversely, the tremendous extent to which affective development determines the differentiatedness of self and object representations and the functioning level of intrapsychic structures.

Jacobson is the theoretician who has made the boldest large-scale attempt at updating affect theory with a structural framework before the 1970s and 1980s. She built a classificatory system for the affects that was based on the tripartite model. She may be considered the last writer who seriously attempted to classify all affects in accordance with a unitary, overarching scheme. These attempts, begun in the late 1930s by such writers as Glover and Landauer, eventually proved unrewarding and incommensurate with living emotional reality.

Later, Jacobson replaced the structural taxonomy with an account of affects in terms of the development of self and object representations. This new framework proved to be more dynamic and fruitful and to contain finer and more discerning categories for the affects.

This shift occurred parallel with Jacobson's later study of moods, and both mark the later phase of her theory, in which she renounced structural elegance in favor of a more refined understanding of experiential qualities. In this vein, Jacobson studied the developmental aspects of affects. She believed that affect development is characterized by growing tolerance for tension, on the one hand, and by a growing variety of means of discharge, on the other. She regarded affects as an immensely complex interweaving of discharge and tension, which recurs incessantly and ubiquitously in the psychic apparatus.

Jacobson did much to bring varieties of affective manifestations into the normal range of psychic phenomena. This work helped bring about the discarding of the narrow, fallacious conflict theory of the affects, which regarded all affects as potentially pathological drive derivatives. Jacobson repeatedly stressed that tension is not synonymous with conflict and that affects are essentially the structured products of the three psychic systems and cannot be understood apart from these structures. One may say that Jacobson 'normalized' and 'structuralized' the affects in psychoanalytic theory in alignment with the structural theory.

AFFECTS AS PROGRAMS OF THE SELF

Pinchas Noy

Noy opens his 1982 paper, "A Revision of the Psychoanalytic Theory of Affects," with the observation that different and sometimes incompatible theories have been developed around various aspects of the phenomenon of affect in the past. This situation stimulated Noy to try to reconcile these theories by adopting a view of affect as a general, organizational phenomenon. In his view, affect should be understood as a kind of program, whose function is to organize and coordinate "in a goal-directed manner the various psychological and physiological systems and processes taking part in behavior, perception and communication" (p. 140). Noy asserts that affect should be regarded as a global phenomenon that rules over a wide range of physiological systems activated according to a fixed, repeatable pattern, where each particular affect is recognizable by its typical pattern of psychophysiological changes. Noy conceives of an affect as an essentially automatic response to an inner or outer stimulus, which, once it has been activated, runs its full course, even in cases in which its outward expression is inhibited.

As mentioned, Noy hoped to reconcile various extant affect theories with the conception of affect as an overall organizing plan. There were also, however, other problems that awakened Noy's interest in affect theory. One of them was the so-called organizational discrepancy Noy believed to exist between primitive drives and highly organized behavioral manifestations, a discrepancy that he felt needed bridging. Another issue was that of psychosomatic phenomena, which he thought needed better explanations than those provided so far. All these subjects and issues comprise the background of Noy's work.

Noy's basic biologically rooted and evolutionary stance entails viewing affects as phenomena that have survival value for the organism by virtue of their preset, immediate availability in preparing for action. In cases in which an immediate response to an acute situation is required, prompt arousal is necessary. In addition, the pattern of changes that occurs in an affect has to be sustained, occasionally over a considerable period of time. Noy argues that this double requirement, for immediacy and for sustained effort, is met by the double transmission of affect, as he calls it. Affect is transmitted through (a) the neural channels, where instructions for activation travel in fractions of a second, a fact that makes possible the prompt arousal of the whole pattern of required changes, and (b) the secretory channels, which ensure that the pattern of changes induced will be sustained until the raised hormone level returns to its baseline. The reverse side of this immediacy and sustained arousal level, however, is the fact that affects lack adaptiveness to new situations demanding deliberation or novelty. Affects are not resilient enough to meet complex changes in a given situation, for which thinking is needed.

Essentially, affect is believed by Noy to activate the systems necessary for turning a motive or a drive into behavior. Affect is thus placed in Noy's theory in an intermediary position between the motive and the action. In Noy's view, an affect is not a motive; rather, an affect is aroused by a motive, while the motive in its turn has the power to lead the organism to a specific action only to the extent that it succeeds in activating all the physiological and psychological components that participate in this action. In Noy's view, a motive (i.e., any need, instinctual drive, wish, or stimulus that leads the organism to action) arouses an affect, and the affect helps the motive to push toward perceptual or behavioral action. Thus, Noy clearly separates affects from motives; motives arouse affects, but to do so, they must be represented by the imagination, which evokes and represents the motive on the so-called inner screen.

Thus, imagination and affect are interlaced in Noy's theory. Motives ride on the affect's back, so to speak, thus leading to action. But, owing to Noy's definition of the motive as a stimulus, as some force that exists in an unactivated state and has to be aroused, another entity is needed to serve as the element that 'pushes' the motive forward and starts it going. This role is filled by the imagination. Imagination, according to Noy, is what 'ignites' a motive, thus leading, through affect, to action. Imagination is both the igniting spark (one could perhaps call it the 'motive') of the motive, *and* its product.

Noy regards the concept of imagination as the intentional and nondeterministic component in his affect theory. Imagination serves, so to speak, as the 'representational provider' to the (blind) motive. In positioning imagination within affect theory, Noy's theory purports to encompass representational contents as an integral part of the typical automatic (contentless) activation pattern of each affect. In Noy's view, it is only through the activity of the imagination that tension can be released and relieved: it is imagination of contents that causes or permits discharge (Noy equates discharge with feelings of relief of tension). This inclusion of the component of imagination in his affect theory is regarded by Noy as his original contribution to a theory of affect in psychoanalysis. Viewed from another perspective, introducing the component of imagination into the conception of affect seems to compensate for the ousting of the concept of motive from the realm of affect, i.e., the separation of affect from motive. Noy asserts that in every mental act, affect is not the motive. Even in cases where affect ostensibly acts as a motive, it should not be mistaken for a motive, and he goes on to say that "close examination will show . . . that in these cases it is not the affect as a pattern of activation that arises or serves as a motive, but only imagination" and that "imagination can create an inner situation in which various motives are aroused out of the blue" (1982, p. 151).

Noy's definition of affects as automatically activated action patterns (which induce prepatterned changes in various physiological systems) leads him to the conclusion that affects cannot be directly controlled by the ego. The ego is therefore unable to intervene in affective processes and can control the affects only indirectly. It can block their access to behavior or defend against subjective awareness of them. There is, in Noy's view, a gap between the ego and the affects, which is bridged by the imagination, that is, a conscious and unconscious fantasy of some action by which the ego has the power to change the intensity of an affect after it has spread.

Noy believes that a theory of affects should begin with simple, elemental affects, and he therefore regards the affects of anxiety and depression as unsuitable concepts to use in theorizing about affects, because he sees them as pathological by definition and as compounded of other, more elemental affects. In his view, only at a later stage should a theory of affect advance to explain the combined and pathological affects. In divesting negative affects of their central status in theory, Noy joins the emphasis given in ego psychology to adaptational and conflict-free functioning. In Noy's words, affects are positive "steering mechanisms." Stressing the negative affects would amount, in his view, to a conceptual bias toward conflict, avoidance, or disorganization.

When potentially disruptive affects are activated, writes Noy, a problem is created for the ego, for which it has to find a solution. The optimal solution is one that does not entail the distortion of reality and/or the development of symptoms. Such a solution brings about the 'sealing' of the potentially disruptive affect, together with its induced bodily changes, or at least the neutralization of the most dangerous bodily changes through an opposite affect. In the case of a 'suboptimal solution,' however, the neutralization of changes is achieved only at the price of creating pathological symptoms. Noy divides the suboptimal solutions into three kinds: the psychosomatic, the anxiety, and the depressive solutions, in which the price paid for the existence of conflicting affects is, respectively, psychophysiological disturbance, unsettling anxiety, or a retardation or reduction of activity. In cases where the ego is strong enough to confront the affects of anxiety and depression, writes Noy, it may use these affects as signals that something has gone awry and needs appropriate action to rectify it.

Noy believes that a great many normal human affects, and presumably all pathological affects, are in fact combinations of two or more interlocking programs. Very often, two or more conflicting motives arise at the same time and compete for the activation of the neurophysiological systems, which prepare for a specific action; at such moments, in Noy's view, disturbances arise. Since each motive carries its own specific program of instructions about how to activate the systems, the result is a situation of multiple affects, either mutually reinforcing each other or conflicting and calling for contradictory action.

These ideas led Noy to consider psychosomatic diseases as grounded in conflicts between two opposing affects that have become interlocked and act simultaneously on several organs or on bodily systems, inducing pathological changes in them. Thus, Noy regards conflict as coterminous with the interlocking of the psychophysiological programs of different affects. Psychosomatic illnesses derive from a conflict between two or more specific, opposing affects. Noy believes that further research will reveal the specific pair of opposing motives that are active in each of the known psychosomatic illnesses.

Noy regards affects as belonging to the primary process. Affects, in his view, do not take objective reality into consideration but operate in terms of 'autistic thinking' (Bleuler), mirroring wishes and strivings as fulfilled, and doing away with obstacles in the imagination. On this level, the motive is 'translated' into an actual action with the aid of a preset program, and at the moment in which the motive (drive) is aroused, everything proceeds automatically along preprogrammed lines, in contrast to actions on the level of the secondary process, where an ad hoc executive program has to be constructed for each specific action. Noy believes that we need the affects because secondary processes have no access to the autonomous and extrapyramidal physiological systems necessary for the execution of the most immediate and vital functions.

In evaluating Noy's theory of affect, I will first take up the subject that stimulated Noy's interest in affect theory in the first place, namely psychosomatic theory (personal communication, 1985). I shall then discuss Noy's conception of negative and complex affects, which is a direct consequence of his ego-theoretic allegiance and of his interest in psychosomatics. This discussion will lead us to consider Noy's perspective on the relationship between the ego and the affects. I shall also evaluate his basic definition of affects-as-programs, which is borrowed from the automatically functioning structures of the autonomic nervous system and whose description is couched in computer language. My main effort, however, will be directed at discussing the metatheory grounding Noy's affect theory, which can be shown to lead, by its nature, to some problematic views on affects.

Let us begin with the psychosomatic issue. Basically, Noy's view of psychosomatic phenomena draws on theories such as that of Alexander and French (1946), who consider psychosomatic illnesses as caused by the transmission of psychic events to the autonomic nervous system. These theories speak about the 'organ specificity' of an affected organ or system in a psychosomatic illness. This prototype of explanation dominates psychosomatic medicine to this day, although psychoanalysts have found that clinical observation fails to bear it out (see, e.g., Blanck & Blanck, 1974, p. 96). In psychoanalysis, this theory of psychosomatics has been superseded by theories that, rather than talking of unproved 'organ specificity,' talk of psychosomatic affection as essentially a regressive process, whereby the person reverts to the infantile use of the body in a general way and only secondarily uses a bodily organ or system as a vehicle for the discharge of affect. According to this view (e.g., Schur, 1966, and chapter 3 in this study), verbalization is the means for the neutralization of libidinal and aggressive energies, which can then be contained and later discharged through this verbalization, thereby reversing the regressive process. These new theories regard psychosomatic phenomena as much less specific than either Alexander and French or Noy do, and they no longer assume that further research would enable us to discover "the specific pair of opposing motives, involved in any of the known psychosomatic diseases . . . and by this to explain the specificity of the disease" (p. 155). Psychosomatic theory today considers psychosomatic phenomena as inherently complex and based on complex affective structures that sometimes fail to function, as in the phenomenon of alexithymia (Krystal, 1982) or in the 'operational thinking' of the persons studied by Marty and de M'Uzan (1963). Recent collections of psychosomatic theories and research speak about 'disregulation theory' (Cheren, 1987) or stress the importance of object relationships and the psychology of the self in psychosomatics (Taylor, 1987). In these works, very little, if anything, is discussed in terms of organ specificity.

The view of psychosomatic phenomena as the interlocking of two elemental affects is associated with Noy's claim that complex affects cannot serve as a basis for building an affect theory. Noy eschews anxiety and depression as starting points for theorizing about affects, on the ground that these affects are, themselves, composed of more elemental or simple affects and, moreover, that they are a priori pathological. Both grounds given for this strategy seem questionable. It is doubtful whether the right way to build an affect theory is by starting with 'simple,' 'elementary' affects as building blocks for further conceptualizations. In general, it may be said that 'simple' elements do not necessarily yield a more fruitful understanding of mental life than do complex structures. On the contrary, all metapsychological perspectives, particularly the dynamic point of view, deal with conflictual, complex, multilayered, and defended-against mental products, born of complex processes; 'simple,' univalent affects—if there are such things—are schematic and static, and say very little about the complexity of mental life.

On the whole, the general trend today in modern theories (one might see it as the zeitgeist) is opposed to atomistic theories (see, e.g., Calhoun & Solomon, 1984).

Noy assumes that anxiety and depression are not only complex but pathological affects as well and are therefore unsuitable to serve as demonstration cases for an affect theory. But as both clinical practice and the theoretical study of affects have shown, the assumption of the a priori pathogenicity of specific affects seems unwarranted. The picture is rather more complex; if depression and anxiety are avoided at all costs, this in itself is a sign of pathology. The assumption that anxiety and depression are pathological per se contradicts clinical knowledge, which shows that anxiety and depression are often welcome signs of awareness of conflict, of the avoidance of more primitive or costly defenses, and experiencing them (up to a certain degree) helps attain emotional depth and growth.[13] On the other hand, anxiety, depression, and in principle every other 'negative' affect may be eroticized, or mixed with different sorts and degrees of other feelings, and, in short, made to yield pleasure in innumerable ways.

It seems to be more in line with clinical evidence to assume that, allowing that there are more or less pleasant affects a priori, affects are, to begin with, neither 'good' nor 'bad' per se but that each affect is suffused with individual meanings and past learnings and is built into variegated personal inner schemes, whence each affect derives its particular quality and 'feel,' including its felt desirability or undesirability for the individual. Taking a further step in this direction, one may argue that the pathogenicity or 'health' of affects is tied with the fit, or mutual adaptedness, of inner states and outer situations. But such a formulation contradicts a view of some affects as a priori pathological or healthy, that is, 'negative' or 'positive.'

Noy makes a sharp distinction between ego and affects, which he considers as two opposing entities. The issue is analogous to the problem of the relation between the ego and the drives. In the earlier stages of psychoanalytic theory, when the drives were regarded as energy or as blind forces, the concept of the ego as a means of controlling the flow of energy was indeed necessary and appropriate. But as theory developed, the drives were increasingly conceived as specific (libidinal and aggressive), complex structures capable of development, variation, and change. This view in turn led to the problem of how to relate the old conception of the ego as the governor of discharge of forces to the new conception of the drives as no longer shapeless, blind, reality-alien forces but as relatively cohesive, persistent, aim-directed, and reality-oriented structures. Now it was clear that the distinction between the ego and the drives is much fuzzier and more problematic than was thought before (on this issue, see Schafer, 1976), and some thinkers, e.g., Bibring (1941) and Apfelbaum (1966), went so far as to consider the drive to be essentially a function of the ego. For a time, the problem could be ignored by keeping the scope of the ego concept narrow; the ego was viewed as implementing the defenses and as regulating discharge. But further developments made it clear that there are non-drive motives (e.g., Holt, 1976; Sandler & Joffe, 1969; White, 1963), that the drives are more structured and complex than had been thought in the past, and, lastly, that many ego functions are themselves molded on the pattern of instinctual drive manifestations (e.g., the modes of giving and taking, projection and introjection, and so on). These developments led to the conclusion, succinctly put by Krystal, that "structural theory, which . . . is but a means of classifying mental contents according to their relation to drives and conflicts, creates some clumsiness in our consideration of affect: affects are described . . . as both drive derivatives and as possessing characteristics [of the ego]" (1975, p. 181). As we shall see in the following chapters, it has become increasingly clear that structural theory is not enough to explain mental phenomena and, among them, the affects.

But, in contrast to these developments, Noy's theory still opposes ego and affects in sharp dichotomy. In many ways, Noy's approach is a revision and continuation of Rapaport's and Fenichel's affect theories and of some theories of emotion in academic psychology (Noy, personal communication, 1985). Thus, he writes that "the attempts of the ego to control affect represent . . . its never ending struggle to ensure its functional autonomy and independence. The main instrument the ego uses . . . vis-à-vis the affects is the secondary process-dominated rational thought" (1982, p. 159); the resemblance of this passage to Rapaport's or Fenichel's approach is unmistakable.

A theory of the type suggested by Noy is in the tradition of ego psychology, which stresses two basic dichotomies, that between the ego and the drives (or, for that matter, between the ego and the affects) and that between the ego (and sometimes the self) and the environment. The lines in these divisions are sharply drawn. Such views are aided by the dichotomization of mental functioning into primary and secondary processes; the former operate, as Noy put it, "according to obligatory demands of the self," while the latter represent "autonomous, disengaged functioning." Noy brings together the two divisions, of the primary and secondary processes and of self and outer reality, by attaching primary process thinking to the self and secondary process thinking to the ego when dealing with external reality. Affects are conceived by Noy as inherently linked to primary processes, to psychic reality, and to the self in opposition to reality. Noy contends that affects make use of what Bleuler called 'autistic thinking' (Noy, 1982, p. 167; Rapaport has shown Bleuler's concept of autistic thinking to be identical with Freud's concept of primary process thinking), and Noy agrees with Bleuler in regarding this type of thinking as "distorting reality . . . by mechanisms familiar to us as influence of affect" (Bleuler, 1913, p. 404, cited by Noy).

This simple, neat division, although useful in some ways, fails to transcend an old and very problematic dualism between the drives and outer reality. It is presented by Noy in a new guise as a dualism between the self (and its interests) and reality. This dualism is reflected again in another area as being between the affects and the ego. If, as Noy suggests, affects are automatic programs for action on behalf of the self that the ego can influence only indirectly, then the ego must be limited to the role of dealing only with outer reality, while affects become, by definition, autistic and deranged types of thinking. But this idea flies in the face of what we know about affects.

Another separation of parts that seem inherently to belong together follows from the role of imagination in Noy's theory. Noy's theory separates elements that belong together creating a static conception of motivation. Hence, Noy is compelled to introduce 'imagination' in a manner of deus ex machina so as to account for freedom of choice and for the expansion of the human motivational scope beyond that of mechanistic, 'deterministic' motives or drives. Noy claims that bringing in the conception of imagination saves his theory from a causal, deterministic fate (he seems to be erroneously equating 'causal' and 'deterministic') and endows it with intentionality, so that affect can be explained teleologically. It is not necessarily the case, however, that so-called causal theories are a priori incompatible with intentional theories (see discussions on this point by Eagle [1980] and Rubinstein [1980] in psychoanalysis and by Hampshire [1983b] and Davidson [1963, 1982] in philosophy). Furthermore, 'causal' is not synonymous with 'deterministic.' In the end, it all depends on the vantage point and the purpose of our endeavor; in investigating a phenomenon, be it theoretical or empirical, we always have to look, very pragmatically, for the level that will provide us with the best explanation for a given purpose. In this way, there is no a priori danger that a theory will be deterministic because it is also in some sense causal, or that we shall have to assume in theory some external agency or power to 'push' some other part of the theory 'from behind,' as it were. But Noy seems to fear these very dangers, and therefore he needs the concept of imagination to stimulate the motive and trigger it into action. An additional goal reached by introducing the concept of imagination into Noy's affect theory is that of saving the concept of affect from becoming vacuous, as it was liable to become if it was neither in the role of a motive nor linked with experiential contents beyond bodily sensations. By being subserved by the imagination, affect is invested with thinkable content.

On the whole, affect serves in Noy's theory as the bridge between the drive and action. Noy conceives of the drive as a partial, simple manifestation, whereas behavior is regarded as a compound, highly organized phenomenon. Hence, Noy believes, there is a gap, a difference in levels of organization, which needs filling. This filler and organizer is the affect, which in his theory has organizational properties. Noy sees Hebb's theory in psychology as a fitting model for such a viewpoint. Hebb's theory is basically physiological, however, whereas Noy's theory takes affect to include psychological systems as well as physiological ones.

Noy regards the basic idiom of his theory as borrowed from the realm of computers, and this choice is manifest in some formulations of his theory. Thus, for example, the language used to describe the relationship between the ego and affects is like a flowchart. Most of the reasoning underlying Noy's model about how affects work is put in terms of "if then." Thus, for example, he writes that the ego decides if the affect is threatening, nonthreatening, or only partially so and then proceeds accordingly. Noy invokes general terms from computer language to explain neurophysiological processes and actions, which he regards as forming the rock bottom of affects. But this commits him to a data language that can only be indirectly applied to clinical theory, for such a language is, as a rule, extra-phenomenological and impersonal, not to say mechanistic. This commitment penetrates into his theory and is expressed in his assumption that the ego can have no direct control over the affects. In this sense, Noy's orientation has a strong affinity with the earlier ideas of Pribram (1970), who considers emotions as 'plans' or 'neural programs' that are activated when the organism is disequilibrated. In Pribram's theory, when the execution of any plan of action upon the environment is hampered, mechanisms of internal adaptation and control are activated. These mechanisms are represented by emotional states. A lively example illustrating this conception is adduced by Noy at the beginning of his paper on affects.

To summarize, Noy's theory of affect is a large-scale attempt at a revision and unification of diverse theoretical views on affects by according affects a central, organizing, unifying function in our mental economy. Noy's message, to the effect that affects are compound events that recruit many bodily and mental systems to help us deal with ourselves and our environment in ways that are both complex and immediate, is an important contribution. The more specific formulations as to how this is done, however, meet with considerable conceptual difficulties.

4
Affects and Positions:
Melanie Klein, Wilfred Bion

MELANIE KLEIN

This section presents a proposed new reading of some aspects of Melanie Klein's writings. Briefly, it is suggested here that a reading of Kleinian theory from the point of view of affects makes for a better understanding both of this theory and of the affects. I shall start with a historical part, which is a reading of Klein's theoretical writings from the angle of affects. I will then show that some of the most central concepts in Klein's theory can be profitably read as a discourse on affects and their laws of functioning.

I will begin with a few words about the theoretical soil on which Klein's ideas grew. In 1923, Freud elaborated the concept of the ego. From being regarded as an entity that repudiates the drives, which were conceived as external to it, the ego came to be regarded as a complex structure possessing libidinal and aggressive energies of its own. Another development was made concerning the concept of anxiety. Anxiety was no longer regarded only as a product of tension or frustration, but predominantly as a motive, a cause for defense, located in the ego (1926). With these reconceptualizations, Freud modified his theory of anxiety and the instincts. After the instincts had been divided into the life and the death instincts (1920), anxiety became an ego signal and a motive. In 1924 Abraham's paper, "A Short Study of the Development of the Libido in the Light of Mental Disorders," appeared. In this paper, a study of sadism in the young child, Abraham did not mention Freud's hypothesis of the life and death instincts (1920), but he explored the roots of destructive impulses and then applied the understanding gained from this exploration to the etiology of mental disturbances with more detail and specificity than had ever been done before.

These seminal works of Freud and of Abraham gave a central role to aggression and to unpleasurable feelings in mental life and development. The foregrounding of the concept of aggression in 1920 marked a milestone in psychoanalytic thinking. This concept was now moved from its place as a secondary by-product of defended, excessive, or perverted libido to be the prime source of guilt, the motive leading to renunciation of pleasure and to reactive identification with prohibitory parts and with the superego. The basic psychic conflict postulated by psychoanalytic theory was no longer seen to be exclusively focused on sexuality. It was no longer the conflict between sexual, pleasure-seeking instincts and reality-oriented, self-preservative instincts, but the opposition between pleasure and self-preservation, on the one hand, and the need for unpleasure and the urge to repeat painful, destructive, and self-defeating experiences, on the other. The essential strife of a person was no longer with pleasure-prohibiting external reality; it was realized that even when reality and pleasure were in agreement and on one's side, strife continued in the inner world, between different parts of the person.

Klein took up this basic view of conflict from the beginning of her work, in 1919, and interpreted it, with increasing emphasis, as the conflict between the life and death instincts, and, in 1927, as the conflict between love and hate. She was concerned with this conflict throughout her work, and made it into a cornerstone of her theory.

In my approach to Klein's thinking I shall try to elucidate those aspects of her theory that seem most pertinent to the clarification of her views on affects. This selective emphasis will inevitably give her theory a particular slant and will not do justice to some areas of her thinking, but it will hopefully prove to be of interest in the endeavor to reach a clearer conception of what may be called the implicit Kleinian theory of feelings. As a first step, some of the major assumptions in Klein's thinking and how they evolved with time will be spelled out. The main issues and problems germane to the concept and theory of affect in her writings will then be summarized and discussed. A hypothesis will then be offered according to which Kleinian theory can be profitably regarded as a kind of affect theory, provided one interprets some Kleinian concepts from the perspective of her views on affects. In addition to the above, the problems and shortcomings of this theory will be discussed.

As said, Klein took off from Freud's latest instinct theory, which she saw as a theory of two basic impulses in conflict. On elaborating this conflict, she came to see it as manifesting itself in the interplay of feelings (of love and hate) in relation to objects (1952, pp. 93, 271). It can be seen that Klein shifted the focus from Freud's predominantly cathectic explanations to the concepts of objects and the feelings attached to them. Essentially, Klein believed that when the ego repudiates the drives, it is not so much because they clash with reality or because they have accumulated in excessive quantities, but because they arouse intolerable feelings in the person. Persons in Kleinian theory are seen as being torn all their lives between love and hate both toward themselves and toward their internal and external objects, and they are particularly and painfully helpless against them during infancy. Individuals attempt to deal with the emotional conflicts by unconsciously manipulating (i.e., splitting and projecting, introjecting, or idealizing) parts of themselves and of their internal objects in ways corresponding to one of two basic emotional positions, the paranoid-schizoid and the depressive. To get a picture of how this process occurs, let us take a closer look at Klein's ideas as they developed over some forty years. This overview was guided by Hanna Segal's work (1964), to which I added some relevant emphasis. I have divided Klein's work into two main periods, from the 1920s to the mid-1930s and from the mid-1930s to the end of her writings, at the dawn of the 1960s.

The Mid-1920s to the Mid-1930s

At this period, Klein followed Freud's and Abraham's models of the psychosexual stages, but with an eye constantly on the concept of the object. Gradually, however, she shifted her emphasis from phases of libidinal development to the study of anxiety, down and back to its earliest roots. On the basis of her assumption that the death instinct operates from the beginning of life, she thought that there is no preambivalent stage (Abraham, 1924). One may say that Klein believed that there is never love without hate (there is no 'primary love,' as Balint was to suggest in 1952). Since, in her view, the destructive impulses and hate operate from the beginning of life, life begins with ambivalence, although at this earliest stage aggression is split off so as to protect the weak young ego from the unbearable impact that the extreme anxiety born of such aggression may have on it. Anxiety at this stage is basically fear of retaliation by the bad persecutory object, itself a product of the infant's projection of his own aggressive and destructive impulses. This basic idea with its many implications was spelled out in several of Klein's papers in the 1920s.

The change from libidinal and economic considerations to formulations in terms of internal object relations becomes increasingly pronounced in the course of development of Klein's thinking. Klein holds that good internal objects build and comprise the core of the ego and the superego, whereas bad objects, which consist of the externalized products of the child's anxieties, become persecutors and necessitate the activation of defenses. Her perspective of the dual instinct conflict and the inner object world constitutes a shift from Freud's account of psychosexual development to a very different account in which the explanatory terms are those of impulses and instincts (1930, p. 232). Already in her 1927 paper, however, Klein analyzes feelings (fear and particularly hate) in the child. The etiological significance of feelings in Klein's theory is striking. Klein's is not a trauma theory, in which feelings arise or accumulate secondarily to the trauma, as is assumed in Freud's theory. Rather, it is a theory in which feelings per se call forth defensive constellations that comprise the various psychopathologies.

Thus, at the beginning of her thinking Klein was writing about issues similar
to those discussed in Freud's *Inhibitions, Symptoms, and Anxiety*. Like Freud,
Klein focused on anxiety, but she addressed herself to other unconscious affects
as well. At this early stage of her thinking, she writes about anxiety that can be
repressed, that is, inhibited, turned into pain, or taken up by the libidinal cathexis
of ego instincts. A little later, she was to change her mind about the role of
anxiety. While formerly she had regarded anxiety chiefly as an inhibitor of
capacities (in the tradition of the beginning of Freud's 1926 paper), she now
additionally saw it as the precondition of mental development, an idea that was
to become the center of her later theories. In the same paper in which she adopts
a new view on anxiety (1930), she also comes to think differently about the
ego's first mode of defense; she believes it is not repression, as Freud thought,
but rather expulsion. Infants are now seen as expelling their impulses to protect
themselves, as well as to destroy the object. Nevertheless, she writes, there
always remains some residual anxiety in the ego, "so that it is faced at the very
beginnings of its development with the task of mobilizing libido against its death
instinct" (p. 193). Here and later, in 1933, Klein formulates her own view on
anxiety. Whereas Freud's first anxiety theory considers libido as leading to
anxiety, and his second anxiety theory regards danger as leading to the anxiety
signal, Klein posits sadism as a cause for anxiety. Sadism can be represented
in the mind of the child as "*fear* of suffering unimaginable cruel attacks" (1933,
p. 251, emphasis added). Anxiety in turn also increases the sadistic impulses
by pushing the child to destroy the hostile objects so as to escape their onslaughts,
and a vicious cycle sets in.

With the increasingly important and normative role Klein gave to aggression,
she began to consider early sadistic fantasies as part of normal development and
to stress the normal child's numerous oral, anal, and oedipal sadistic fantasies,
which, no less than traumatic experiences, create distorted and frightening conceptions of objects and relations to them. Still, there is no theoretical discussion
of affect at this period. The distinction between fear and guilt is still only of
descriptive significance, and this lasted until 1935.

The Mid-1930s to the Mid-1940s

In 1935, Klein formulated her concept of the depressive position. Now she
no longer accepted the classical, psychosexual account of development that she
had used until this time alongside a different set of terms to describe the ego's
relations with objects. Now, for the first time, Klein bases her work solely on
the interaction of the life and death instincts, expressed in love and hate. In this
paper, she describes how the infant begins to perceive his mother as a whole
person, loves her, and identifies with her, as he was not able to do before. It is
to this whole and loved mother that the infant turns to relieve his persecutory
fears; he strives to introject her so that she may protect him against inner and

outer persecution. But at the same time, the loved mother is herself felt to be exposed to the same attack the child fears and needs protection against. Furthermore, the mother herself is not only loved but hated as well, so that she is experienced by the infant to be in danger of being destroyed by his own hatred and sadism. The ego has now arrived at a new situation in which it experiences the psychic reality of the danger to its internal objects as being due to its own impulses and fantasies. The fantasied loss of this loved and identified-with mother is experienced by the infant through a whole gamut of feelings—sorrow, pain, pining, and guilt. According to Klein, when the child feels that he has destroyed his inner good object, he tries to rebuild it by his love (1940). Mourning for the lost object is not only a process of reality testing, as Freud conceived it, but, according to Klein, a regular developmental task of coming to terms with feelings, including feelings concerning the oedipal situation (1945).

Bad conscience, says Klein, is the feeling of being prey to contradictory and impossible claims from within. It is a mixture of feelings: the fear lest the good object be lost or turn bad, the child's hatred of the id, his gnawing uncertainty as to the 'goodness' of his object, and so on. The deeper source for the motive for reparation is not guilt alone, but an innate aversion of the ego toward the id (this formulation expresses the Kleinian conception that every part of the inner world can be endowed with feeling) and conflictedness about the possession and durability of the good object and, concomitantly, of one's love for it.

In Klein's writings the development from the most primitive part object relations toward relations to a whole, separate, and realistic object follows the vicissitudes of love and hate (1935, p. 264). Love and need drive the child to want to devour the mother and introject her, particularly if the child's inside is felt to be a safe place for harboring the love object. But there is anxiety lest the inside might not be safe enough to protect the good object against the internalized persecuting objects and the id or lest the good object be expelled together with the bad. "A little child which believes, when its mother disappears, that it has eaten her up and destroyed her (whether from motives of love or of hate) is tormented by anxiety both for her and for the good mother which it has absorbed into itself" (1935, p. 266). It is as if the little child would say to himself, "Oh, what have my feelings done!" To counteract these feelings, says Klein, a defense comes into being—that of making reparation to the object.

We can see here that the theory of the depressive position implies that in normal development there is no hate without love, and that the mitigation of hate and suspicious fear by love has enriching and creative aspects (1940). In this period Klein elaborates the concept of love, notes its ubiquity, and shows how, by decreasing anxiety, love can grow, how vital the import of good emotional experiences is for the child's mental life, and how crucial it is that these pleasurable feelings and a sense of trust should be experienced. She also shows the lasting part that the internalized mother plays in life. But there is never love alone; Klein says that the very young infant's emotions are "particularly powerful and are dominated by extremes'' (1935, p. 304), and for that reason early feelings of love are seriously inhibited and disturbed by the impulses of hatred and the unconscious sense of guilt that are aroused by the very feelings of love.

In 1935, there appears for the first time Klein's 'feeling talk' (to paraphrase Mackay, who contrasts Freud's 'structure talk' with Klein's 'object talk,' 1981). In the 1930s, Klein's conceptual language becomes increasingly that of feelings, and even her titles bear witness to this change. In 1936, Klein and Joan Riviere, her co-worker and follower, gave a series of public lectures that became the basis for a small volume called *Love, Hate and Reparation*. They divided their subject matter so that Riviere spoke about *Hate, Greed and Aggression*, and Klein spoke about *Love, Guilt and Reparation*. The two parts of the monograph deal with the two powerful impulses of love and hate, which are in constant conflict and interaction, both being attached to the infant's first object of love and hate, his mother. These mixed feelings and the struggle between them are then carried over to the father and siblings. At the very beginning, the baby loves his mother (the destructive, hating death instinct is still totally split off) and feels secure with her, but when he is hungry and his desires are not gratified, or when he is feeling bodily pain or discomfort, the whole situation suddenly changes. Hatred and aggressive feelings well up in him and impel him in fantasy to destroy the very person who is the object of all his desires and who in his mind is linked with everything he experiences. Thus, "[the] first love is already disturbed at its roots by destructive impulses; love and hate are struggling together in the baby's mind and this struggle . . . persists throughout life and is liable to become a source of danger in human relationships'' (1937, p. 309; see also 1935, p. 287).

The Mid-1940s

In her "Notes on Some Schizoid Mechanisms'' of 1946, Klein elaborated her concept of the paranoid schizoid position, which she had introduced four years earlier. She sees the schizoid mechanisms (e.g., splitting) as necessary for the overcoming of paranoid or, as she later called them, persecutory anxieties. Persecutory anxieties comprise the infant's dread of annihilation by his own unbearable destructive impulses, which arise from his death instinct and which, projected, have become persecutory objects (see Riviere's [1936] vivid description of the infant in the throes of his own raging and frenzied body parts and bodily sensations). All occurrences at this stage are seen as extremely violent and excessive. An example is a fantasy underlying the schizoid mechanism, which is that of omnipotently annihilating the persecutors. Another example is the assumption that, at this primitive stage, the absence of the good object is equivalent to a positive attack by a bad object, an invasion of the body and psyche by persecutors who threaten it with annihilation; frustration is felt as persecution. There are many more examples in which emotional processes are described that produce different states of self and object (e.g., projective identification leads to idealization and dependence, or flight from the reintrojected object attaches one to another internal object). The schizoid mechanisms have a momentum of their own; starting with the relation to the breast, they continue to operate in relation to the mother's whole body, which is attacked through projective identification and fantasied as full of and identified with the child's projected parts. With all its violence and 'craziness,' the paranoid-schizoid position is considered a developmental step in that it implies the capacity to differentiate (between good and bad, internal and external); projective identification, one of the principal mechanisms of this position, is, according to Klein, the first step in relating to the external world.

The Mid-1950s

In 1957, Klein wrote her famous book *Envy and Gratitude,* in which envy is singled out as a primary constitutional feeling, the oral sadistic and anal sadistic expression of destructive impulses (p. 176). By introducing the concept of envy and distinguishing it from jealousy and from greed, Klein launched an important development in psychoanalysis, that of psychodynamically thematizing a particular emotion.[1] Klein had proceeded in a similar manner when she had earlier traced the different (persecutory and depressive) qualities of mental anxiety, but anxiety had already received the most intensive treatment by Freud, whereas the treatment of envy is something particular to Klein. Klein's *Envy and Gratitude* is a prime example of a treatise on the constellation of one single emotion, where various combinations of feelings emerge, which would not be thinkable without this delving, as Klein did, into the world of one emotion. Examples are the idea that envy, the feeling that the source of goodness lies outside oneself, is aroused not only by gratification but by frustration and deprivation as well; that envy arouses hopelessness (as good experiences become bad, hope is lost); and that envy results in the early, precocious onset of guilt, because of the persecutory flavor of envy at this early stage of a weak ego.

Envy is a relentless, self-vitiating process for which, according to Klein, there is no relief, only defenses. This harmful, almost lethal emotion can diminish and become tolerable, in Klein's view, when it is mitigated by love (1946, p. 232), which may then arouse gratitude. Gratitude is closely linked with trust in good figures, which implies the ability to accept and assimilate the loved primal object without greed and envy interfering too much (p. 188). Gratitude brings about generosity, the feeling of inner wealth, and the wish to share.

The dialectic between envy and gratitude may be seen as another variation on the theme of the strife between love and hate, which is the core conflict in Klein's theory. In the following section, the place of the conflict between love and hate will be traced as it occurs in the two basic positions, the paranoid-schizoid and the depressive.

The Love-Hate Conflict

Klein writes that the central conflict between love and hate is the thread running throughout all development (1927, pp. 172–73; 1935, pp. 271, 285, 286, 287; 1936, p. 293; 1937, pp. 308, 309–11, 316n, 321; 1940, pp. 349n, 353). Many, perhaps most, of Klein's formulations are based on her observations of infants and children, which showed her that emotional and intellectual growth is thrust forward by this core conflict (e.g., 1960, p. 271) directed at the mother's body and person. Love and hate, fantasies, anxieties, and their defenses are regarded as being all-operative from the beginning of life and as being ab initio indivisibly linked with objects. "This insight," she wrote, "showed me many phenomena in a new light" (1952, p. 52). Objects, according to Klein, possess psychological features in the infant's eyes from the beginning and stir up many feelings in him. The object is not only an instinctually gratifying or frustrating object but a loving and loved, a hating and hated, or an envious and envied object. The ego's task in all this is—simply put—to deal with the struggle between the life and death instincts by doing all kinds of things with itself and with the objects (1957, p. 191).

It can be said that the developmental process, according to Klein, is the account of the vicissitudes of love and hate and their multifarious outcomes (1952, pp. 59, 93), and even the Kleinian concepts of regression and fixation derive from this view. Thus, Klein says that, following the early developmental splitting, the earliest defense against the death instinct, the struggle between the instincts, is manifested in the war between the loving, good part of the ego, identified and identifying with a single, whole, ideal object, on the one hand, and the persecutors, which are the projected fragments of destructive impulses, themselves fragments of a 'bad' ego, on the other. To prevent the anxiety that the persecutors will destroy the ego and its ideal object, schizoid mechanisms are activated, increasing the split between good and bad, in an attempt to protect the good ego and the good object from the bad object. The good object, not separable from the good feeling it gives, is craved by the infant, writes Klein. When she writes about the urge, rooted in anxiety and existing from the earliest days of life, to get constant evidence of the mother's love, she writes in a way that has not been seen before in psychoanalysis (except perhaps in Ferenczi's writings) about the urge to get love to allay inner destructiveness.

Klein believes that at any point in development when aggression and anxiety become excessive, libido is called upon to overcome the anxiety and becomes fixated there. Klein's concept of fixation is another instance in which she puts feelings at center stage and does not distinguish between impulses and feelings. Klein says that when anxiety, stirred up by aggressive impulses, cannot be mastered, a fixation is formed by the mobilization of large amounts of libido to counteract the anxiety; however, this mobility of libido depletes and weakens the ego and lessens its capacity to withstand frustration. The ego then becomes prone to regression, and a vicious cycle sets in. Regression itself is seen by

Klein as a return to crude feelings and primitive defenses (rather than to the predominance of earlier erotogenic zones and modes of behavior, as is the case in Freud's formulations). In regression, according to Klein, feelings change and activate specific, primitive mechanisms; feelings 'regress' too. In Kleinian thought, 'regressed' feelings differ in quality, as well as in intensity, from more mature feelings.

These two groups of feelings, the 'regressed' and the 'mature,' are grouped by Klein in two basic positions, the paranoid-schizoid and the depressive. Once Klein crystallized the concept of the two positions, she used them as an explanatory scaffolding and discarded the concepts of fixation and regression. The concept of position is not comparable to a developmental concept such as that of a libidinal phase (although Klein claims ontological priority for the paranoid-schizoid over the depressive position). The paranoid-schizoid and the depressive positions are structural rather than chronological concepts, and they coexist autonomously. The concept of 'position' may be said to refer to a grouping together of characteristically conjoint phenomena, such as the state of the ego, the nature of the internal object relations, the quality and intensity of anxiety, and the characteristic defenses.

But essentially, the two positions differ in being built around different core feelings and nuclear affective structures, which imply differences in states of ego integration. The concept of 'position' is used by Klein to draw a large-scale, dual model of anxiety and guilt and to explain their vicissitudes. In the context of affects, the two positions may be regarded as two basic psychological configurations, which differ fundamentally according to the individual's capacity to tolerate unpleasant or conflictual feelings (1937, p. 348). We may say that it is the person's way of handling feelings that determines and defines his position. In what follows, the different qualities of the core feelings in the two positions, particularly those of anxiety and guilt, and how they are handled will be delineated.

"The first set of feelings and phantasies are the persecutory ones," writes Klein in 1937 (p. 348). In her view, the characteristic way of handling persecutory feelings in the paranoid-schizoid position, where feelings are extreme and polarized, 'all-good' and 'all-bad' and unbearable most of the time, is by splitting and partial denial. As these feelings are projected, the object is infused with exclusively good or exclusively bad feelings. Another way of dealing with such feelings is by projective identification, i.e., by shifting ego and object boundaries so as to realign the parts of self and object that contain the good and the bad feelings.

The second set of feelings and fantasies is around depressive anxiety and pining. In the depressive position, the person deals with his feelings by bearing (with) them, by acquiring the capacity to tolerate their essentially ambivalent and fluid nature. The way of handling them is by mourning, that is, by acknowledging the bad feelings and their consequences, by avoiding manic controls of omnipotence and denial, and by mitigating the depressive feelings with good feelings such as love, tenderness, and concern and with fantasies of making reparation. When good feelings and experiences predominate, there is less need to project bad impulses and parts of the ego outward, projection is thereby diminished, and persecutory anxieties lessen. A benevolent cycle sets in; lessening the persecutory anxieties diminishes the aggression and decreases the anxiety and with it the need to project; the person becomes more whole.

As said, the two positions can be seen, from a certain perspective, as two portraits of anxiety and guilt. The typical anxiety is different in the two positions, and so is guilt. In the paranoid-schizoid position, the anxiety is fear for the survival of the ego (or the self); it is the fear that the persecutors will destroy the ego and its ideal object. In the depressive position, anxiety is of the loss of the object or the injury done to it. Here the object is not turned bad or attacking (by projection of aggression and bad feelings); it remains good, but it is experienced as vulnerable to harm or destruction inflicted on it by oneself.

In the paranoid-schizoid position, the guilt is fear of revenge from the object, a fear that results from projected aggression and destructiveness, which becomes persecutory anxiety. In the depressive position, the guilt consists in the sense of one's own responsibility for badness or harmfulness and is ineluctably accompanied by reparative urges to re-create the lost or harmed object. Anxiety is about the ego (which in Kleinian theory is not distinguished from the self) in the paranoid-schizoid position and is about the object in the depressive position; guilt is, inversely, fear of an object in the paranoid-schizoid position and fear of oneself in the depressive position. Anxiety and guilt, which Klein distinguished from 1927 as two separate forces emanating from the superego, are, in her view (e.g., 1948, p. 42), the inevitable outcome of the co-existence of love and hate, which in turn are close in meaning to libido and aggression (1952, p. 82) in mental life. Because of his anxiety and guilt, the child is compelled to form an Oedipus complex. Anxiety and guilt increase the need to externalize (project) bad figures and to internalize (introject) good ones, to attach desires, love, feelings of guilt, and reparative tendencies to some objects and hate and anxiety to others. Klein, in contrast to Freud, regards the Oedipus complex as being the outcome rather than the cause of anxiety and guilt.

Discussion

A look at Kleinian theory from the angle of affects reveals the central place given in this theory to aggression and its vicissitudes in mental life. It may be said that in Kleinian theory there is the assumption of a 'psychoaggressive,' no less than psychosexual, development. In elaborating on the vicissitudes of aggression, Klein added to the picture Freud had drawn of psychic development.

In Klein's view, aggression and libido manifest themselves in an ever-present conflict between the feelings of hate and love, expressed in various forms of ambivalence. Conflict in Kleinian theory is not ascribed to a specific mental agency and, over the years of her writings, is ascribed less to impulses. It is not seen so much as a conflict between impulses and external reality, but is assumed to obtain between the feelings themselves. This ever-present strife between feelings, this very basic ambivalence, is the essence of psychic reality.

This core conflict is handled differently according to the 'position' the individual is in. I have argued that the concept of 'position' denotes an affective constellation, i.e., a group of characteristic affects and ways of handling them, mainly through relationships with objects. Klein postulated two such basic constellations: the paranoid-schizoid, which centers around fear and suspicion (of being attacked by bad objects), and the depressive, which crystallizes around guilt (of losing the good object) and concern (for its survival). The two constellations imply different typical object relations: egocentric and omnipotent in the first, ambivalent and mutually dependent in the other.

Kleinian theory assumes that from the beginning of life, expulsion of feelings is a ubiquitous process. Expulsion rather than repression of feelings is the primal defense. Defended feelings are not in the nature of something pushed 'downward,' 'inside' (such a conception entails discharge as the ameliorative or therapeutic operation). On the contrary, feelings experienced as extremely painful or dangerous tend to be expelled, split off, and projected to objects. These objects are assumed to exist from the dawn of life and are regarded as imbued with the feelings projected onto them to such a degree as to become figments of the child's mind and turn into persecutory villains, idealized entities, or helpless, emptied-out, and destroyed ghosts.

Because objects exist in the infant's mind from the beginning, and because they carry his strongest feelings, it is essential that there be possibilities for psychically manipulating objects through getting rid of some feelings, so as to maintain and protect psychic structure. Such a manipulation entails 'making' the internal object feel them or, alternately, fleeing from or destroying these emotionally laden objects, which are a menace to mental integrity. Freud's theory of the death instinct, an instinct that he assumed has to be deflected outside of the organism, becomes in Klein's system a theory of destructive feelings that must be projected outside of oneself onto another object. The theory is thus enlarged to include new conceptions of object relations and of affects to account for the handling and influencing of the object's feelings (projective identification), thereby assuming a much tighter and reciprocal enmeshment with the object than Freud's theory would allow. The explanation of these processes in Kleinian theory remains experience-near. The metaphor for feelings is not of alien, toxic substances that have to be removed; it remains experiential and object-related. Affect is not eliminated after its discharge but goes on 'living' in a dissociated or split-off object relation.

What has been said so far implies that in Kleinian theory there is, in a sense, an equivalence between object and feeling, with a clear tendency to assume that objects are created by feelings in mental life. This equivalence between objects and feelings can be spelled out as follows. 'Bad' (unpleasant) feelings necessitate defense mechanisms, which 'create' bad objects; mechanisms such as projective identification, splitting, denial, and manic triumph differentiate and seclude 'all-bad' objects. On the other hand, 'good' feelings (such as concern, gratitude, love) establish or restore good objects, which, once introjected, create a good self-as-object, i.e., a good core in the ego. Restoring good objects can be achieved when 'bad' feelings can be tolerated and contained, urging the individual toward reparation, creativity, and fostering of inner strength, which in turn build good internal objects, or, alternatively, projecting one's good feelings, which is tantamount to idealizing an experience and creating an ideal object (see Segal, 1979, p. 104).

One of the main arguments of the present interpretation of Kleinian theory is that the nature of early, 'regressed' feelings is qualitatively different from that of later, more mature feelings. 'Early' feelings are assumed to be harder to bear and more difficult to verbalize (see, e.g., 1957, p. 180). The quality of primitive feelings such as idealization, terror, persecutory anxiety, or triumph is characterized by being extreme and crude, unmitigated and unqualified.

Mitigation and qualifying of emotions, what Klein calls ambivalence, are found, in her view, in the depressive position. Experiencing ambivalence is a developmental achievement. "It enables the ego to assert itself against its internal persecutors and against a slavish and perilous dependence upon its loved objects" (1940, p. 349). Ambivalence highlights the existence of equivocality and multiplicity of feelings in mental life. In Kleinian theory, there is never a stage in which there exist pure feelings of one sort or another, unless some feelings are completely split off.

From all that has been said above it would be correct to say that in Kleinian theory, feelings are primary motives. Often they are seen as the spurs for, or the hindrances of, development. Here are but two of a wealth of examples in Klein's writings of the view that it is feelings that promote or obstruct development. Klein assumes that guilt arouses the desire to restore and perform constructive activities of very different sorts, whereas anxiety may give rise to the desire to attack, which may be actualized as knowledge or curiosity, which are motives for development. Another facet of the motivational power of feelings is their capacity to influence impulses; thus, "fears have brought about an increase in the destructive impulses, therefore, when fears are diminished, destructive impulses also are lessened" (1957, p. 336).

This discussion brings us to an important point concerning the meaning and role of drives in Klein's theory and their relationship with affects. As Greenberg & Mitchell contend (1983, p. 136), Klein in her theory gave the concept of drive a different meaning from the one it had in Freud's theory, but this shift has not been sufficiently noticed because of Klein's efforts to remain loyal to Freud and to employ his language. Thus, although Klein's entire motivational system rests on drives and her writing is replete with references to them, in her view drives are inherently and inseparably directed toward objects. Through their inherent object-relatedness the drives in Klein's theory possess many of the features that in Freud's theory were the province of the ego and the secondary process. Thus, "the drives themselves are fundamentally directional psychological phenomena, constituting complex emotions" (p. 138). "Libido and aggression for Klein are not groups of component instincts but personal, directional *emotions*" (p. 139, emphasis added). "In Klein's usage the motive is supplied by the feeling, the passion, which selects available body parts and functions for its expression . . . meaning is generated not in bodily parts and mechanisms but in emotional experiences she terms 'drives.' " They say that "in many places, particularly in the later papers (e.g., 1959, p. 248), Klein makes it clear that her concept of drive concerns not merely the reduction of bodily tensions, but rather a fuller, passionate relatedness to another person" (p. 141). Greenberg & Mitchell hold that "Drives for [Melanie Klein] are not discrete quantities of energy arising from specific body tensions but passionate feelings of love and hate directed toward others and utilizing the body as a vehicle of expression" (p. 146). I have quoted these passages at length because they are germane to my reading of Klein's writings as presented in this chapter—writings that, it seems, have not received enough attention in the literature.

As said, the core conflict with which Klein increasingly dealt in her writings is that between feelings of love and feelings of hate. The points at which she refers to the conflict between love and hate as the basic ingredient of emotional development and life are countless (e.g., 1937, p. 316). This conflict is not ascribed to some mental agency and is ascribed only partially and to a decreasing degree to the impulses, but is assumed to hold directly between the feelings themselves.[2] The conflict expands over a whole network of feelings other than love and hate and is grounded in their own rules of generation and combination.

This discussion brings us to a highly interesting point concerning what I have called 'emotional cycles' in Kleinian theory. These are characterized as chains of emotions described by Klein, whose consequences breed further emotional processes, and which run their own course without needing further contents, i.e., fantasies to keep them running, forming either a magic or a vicious cycle. An example of such a cycle would be that of persecutory fears, which cause aggression, which causes anxiety, which in turn increases the need to project aggression and 'bad feelings,' which in their turn, increase persecutory fears, and so on. Another example is that of guilt, which reinforces gratitude, which in turn diminishes envy. Following these 'chain reactions' of feelings introduces us to unexpected, complex, and pregnant emotional forms. Sometimes one can find in Klein's writings whole chains of emotions intertwined with fantasies (which then serve as connectives between the emotions), which build up into what may be regarded as 'emotional phrases' containing real story lines. For a touching example, see the analysis of a mother's [herself?] mourning reactions to her son's death. Her reactions included the preunderstandings or, rather, the misunderstandings woven by the primitive layers of the psyche around a momentous and terrible emotional event. In her account, Klein assumes the necessity of continuing the free circulation of these 'emotional cycles' so as to enable the mourner to overcome her loss (1940, pp. 356–59).

The common thread running through all mental development, according to Klein, may be said to be regulation of feelings. The primary principle of development in Kleinian theory is infantile omnipotence (rather than infantile sexuality), which is a form of control of feelings (e.g., defensively experiencing grandiosity instead of helplessness); development is accordingly the necessity of phase-appropriately renouncing absolute control of feelings. The developmental stages, in Klein's view, are not defined or constituted by the different erotogenic zones—all the bodily zones are regarded as active, experienced, and fantasized about from the beginning of life—but rather by the emotional qualities and the different ways of handling the impulses and feelings that mark the developmental stages and the differences between them. In particular, increasing integration brings about changes in the nature of anxiety (1952, p. 50).

If we accept the thesis that Klein conceives of development in terms of progressive changes in handling feelings, we can better understand the reason for the precedence given in her theory to feelings over objects. This may be the main reason for what is sometimes called the esoteric or strange flavor of Kleinian theory. This flavor, of something blindly yet actively preoccupied with connecting and destroying, is a vivid depiction of the psyche's constant endeavor to create objects out of its feelings and to relate to them. Klein assumes that in psychic reality, feelings create objects (see, e.g., 1957, p. 88). In 1936, Joan Riviere writes:

I have tried to show that internal conditions (feelings, sensations) are the earliest forerunners of object relations. The objects are identified with the internal conditions and so are 'internalized.' . . . A good feeling towards an object signifies (and in phantasy, creates) a good object; a bad, hostile feeling creates a bad object . . . These archaic feelings are a permanent element in the organization of the superego, even though they are certainly not at first (and perhaps never) acknowledged or accepted by the ego (p. 94).

The content of feelings is expressed by fantasy (mostly unconscious). Susan Isaacs, who further developed the central Kleinian concept of fantasy, believed that fantasy springs from feelings and sensations. She writes:

Fantasy expresses the specific content of the urge (or the feeling, e.g., anxiety, fear, love and sorrow) which is dominating the child's mind at the moment . . . Fantasies are in their turn the simplest contents of implicit meaning, meaning latent in the impulse, affect and sensation . . . The earliest rudimentary fantasy is bound up with sensory experiences; it is *an affective interpretation of bodily sensations*, an expression of libidinal and aggressive impulses, operating under the pleasure-pain principle (discussion, Jan. 7, Feb. 17, May 19, 1943, quoted by Glover, 1945, p. 95, emphasis added).

Riviere writes in 1936 that the child feels as if it were actually carrying out the desired action, and this feeling is accompanied by physical excitations in certain organs and by a kind of primitive personification of the experiences of need, urge, and feeling. Fantasies, according to Isaacs and Riviere, tell the story of a feeling or of a sensation.

Feelings themselves are said to lead to other feelings. Thus, Klein says that ambivalence, rather than the libidinal or the death instinct per se, causes guilt. Conflict is between feelings, rather than between structures, impulses, or psychic reality. To get a clearer picture of the Kleinian view of feelings as determining their own 'feeling descendants,' so to speak, as contrasted with a non-Kleinian view on this subject, let us compare Klein's view with Glasser's conception (1986), in which he contrasts aggression with sadism in discussing perversions. In Glasser's view, the same condition that arouses anxiety arouses aggression, namely threat, and it is through this common factor that anxiety and aggression are linked. Klein's theory, in contrast, seeks no common underlying root with which to explain anxiety and aggression; here aggression is said to lead directly and automatically to anxiety, whatever its cause or situational antecedent. Although the Kleinian view harbors some deep intuitions about feelings and the way they are experienced, something is lost in the process of tracing the vicissitudes of feelings. Thus, while Glasser can comfortably make the distinction between aggression and sadism on the basis of their different functions (survival value versus a need to inflict pain on the object as a compromise between controlling it and not destroying it), in Kleinian theory the two collapse.

This is in line with the view that sees Kleinian theory as a so-called phenomenal theory, which is of the type defined by Mackay as a

theory that accounts for a person's activities and characteristics by referring to *his own* perceptions, wishes, and feelings. Meaning is given in such a theory to events or interactions according to how an individual perceives, wishes or feels them (not necessarily consciously), and their validity derives from the fact of the person relating to them as though they are real (1981, p. 194).

Feelings in Klein's theory, unlike instincts in Freud's theory, are not quantitatively conceived and are not defined by their somatic sources. Klein has no theory of a mental apparatus, and feelings are not placed in any such frame.

This bears directly on the many criticisms leveled against Kleinian theory, which are well known and need no repeating here. The pertinent issue for the subject matter of this study will, however, be referred to, and that is the Kleinian ascription to the infant of highly complex, elaborate, and potentially verbalizable fantasies.

Such a theoretical stance is doubtlessly very problematical, and Klein's developmental assumptions have perhaps been conclusively refuted by contradictory empirical evidence (see, e.g., Emde, 1980; Lichtenberg, 1987; Stern, 1985). There nevertheless remain two considerations that make the central claims contained in this stance highly relevant to the realm of affects (even if not to that of infant development). The first is the realization that with all the conceptual confusion and the uncertain theoretical status of Klein's assertions, her theory has deepened our understanding of emotional processes and enriched our empathic, descriptive, and perhaps explicative repertoire of communication, particularly, but not exclusively, with children and with very disturbed patients. Klein has created a language that sometimes, perhaps at certain beneficial moments, can be grasped by the child, and by the child within the adult, because of its force and its appeal to primitive fantasies and feelings. Preverbal experiences and early psychic reality can be better articulated since the appearance of Klein's theories. The confused, chaotic, "buzzing and blooming" (James, 1950 [1890]) reality of early life has now been named and has become more comprehensible in terms of differentiated occurrences and has also become infused with specific, although crude and intense, feelings. As S. Brody remarked: "Melanie Klein contributed to psychoanalytic thought when she described the intensities [and, one could add, the immediacy and object relatedness] that affects can reach during infancy" (1982, p. 542). Today it is taken as a matter of course that the affective dimension is the most relevant in the moment-to-moment interactions between patient and analyst in the psychoanalytic situation. One may therefore easily forget the fact that before Klein there was scant mention in the literature of these "pre-verbal emotions . . . revived in the transference situation . . . appear[ing] . . . as 'memories in feelings' . . . which are reconstructed and put into words with the help of the analyst" (Klein 1937, p. 316).

The second consideration is that Klein seemed to have grasped the essence of primitive thinking beyond Freud's primary process heuristics, which seem to point mainly to the illogicalities and condensed modes of representation of ideas and, at most, impulses and wishes. In psychic reality as Klein envisioned it there is not only an overthrowing of logical rules and realistic constraints; there is not only symbolization and compromise formation, as in Freud's primary process mode; there are also active ejections and seizings, pushes and pulls of feelings, which are experienced and felt in psychic reality, in unconscious fantasy, as substances, liquids, body parts, and particles.

Perhaps the very same method (the Kleinian) that from one angle is a conceptual reification is at the same time a deeply intuitive grasp of some mental conscious and unconscious manifestations as experiences. Perhaps this phenomenon has to do with the fact that it is in the inherent nature of primitive experiences and feelings to reify and to concretize—in other words, to create objects.

A PROCESS THEORY OF EMOTIONAL EXPERIENCES: WILFRED R. BION

Wilfred Bion's work appeared in the 1950s and continued until recently. In a sense, it extended Melanie Klein's theory in some important directions. Bion's

The first part of this chapter originally appeared in 1990 as "A New Look at the Theory of Melanie Klein," by R. Stein, *International Journal of Psychoanalysis*, Vol. 71, Part 3, pp. 499–511. Copyright © Institute of Psycho-Analysis. Reprinted by permission.

thinking is difficult and intricate, and his system of ideas is very complex. For the purpose of this study, only some aspects of his work will be highlighted— those having to do with emotions or emotional experiences and their vicissitudes. Accordingly, many areas of Bion's theory will not be addressed—areas that, albeit evocative and challenging, do not directly touch on our topic.[3]

This topic will be divided into some summarizing points. They will serve as way stations as we shall proceed along a certain line of thought, which becomes increasingly clear and demarcated on close reading of Bion's various writings. This line portrays Bion's conception of thinking as a kind of processing of emotions, which eventuates in two possible outcomes. When it succeeds, thinking results in "taking responsibility for one's feelings," yields self-knowledge, and approaches truth. When this process is aborted, no transformation of raw data into psychic material is effected, and the inner world remains alien and bizarre to its owner, who does not own it psychically; it is unavailable for psychic experiencing and mental life. Instead, 'lies' propagate, and 'catastrophe,' or psychic death (psychosis) seals this process. But let us start from the beginning, that is, with Bion's views on thinking.

Basically, Bion's project has been, as he himself writes, to enhance clinical and theoretical understanding by constructing an abstract psychoanalytic theory of knowledge and thinking, whose aim is to deal with the understanding itself. Bion attempted to conceptualize this undertaking—and this is the main thrust of this chapter—by presuming that thinking and other mental activities are based on, and even 'made of,' emotions, or, as he calls them, emotional experiences.

Thorner (1981) described the difference between Freud's and Bion's theories of knowledge in the following way. Whereas Freud proposed a biological theory of the origin of thought based on sense impressions of the outer world, which he saw as primarily providing instinctual gratification, Bion was concerned with inner awareness, with awareness of emotional experiences. Psychoanalysis, according to Bion, deals with experience that is not sensuous, whereas sensuous phenomena, such as memory, recordings, and various kinds of communications consist of sensory data that are seen by Bion as 'psychoanalytically irrelevant,' actually detracting from understanding of psychoanalytic 'facts' (1962).

This distinction between Freud and Bion is very pertinent in that it helps to understand the essential function Bion assigns to thinking, which is not so much that of providing restraint from motor discharge (Freud, 1900) as providing fulfillment of the requirement on the mental apparatus imposed by the demands of reality when thinking became intimately associated with self-knowledge. In order to reach this self-knowledge, the mental apparatus has to make successive transformations on the sense impressions and the raw emotional experience impinging on it.

The basic psychic units for thinking, according to Bion, are the transformed products of raw emotional experiences. These are the so-called alpha elements (a neutral term that Bion has deliberately chosen so as to avoid any prior connotations). Alpha elements in his eyes designate those psychic elements that serve as catalysts for turning raw information into materials for awareness, that is, for thinking and for consciousness. The transformation of emotional experiences into alpha elements is mediated by the alpha function, which operates on the sense impressions and the emotions of which the patient is aware (1962, p. 6). What is this alpha function? Bion conceives of it as a kind of mental processing, akin to the dream work, that produces the dream thoughts. Bion sees a kind of dream work going on in waking life too. Both in dreams and in waking life, perceptions of emotional experiences have to be worked on by the alpha function before they can be used for thoughts. The alpha function transforms raw data and basic elements into elaborated, 'dream-worked' alpha elements. With this formulation, Bion draws an analogy between waking life and the dream, while at the same time radically differentiating between the dream and sleep, where there is no psychic processing going on. Bion's model of the dream and the dreamwork describes the selection and processing of certain stimuli and the screening out of others. In Bion's view, a person is said to 'be asleep' to stimuli when he is screening them out to protect himself against being overwhelmed by their quantity.

According to Bion, every person is in a constant struggle between the tendency to have consciousness and the wish not to have it, between his capacity to tolerate it and his inclination to avoid it because of the pain it may bring him. In a parallel manner, there are always two basic ways, two modes of mental functioning, according to whether the person tolerates the frustration and painful feelings or whether he avoids experiencing them. When consciousness is avoided, the alpha function does not operate.

The factor that is responsible for the inoperation of the alpha function is the violence or destructiveness of the emotions. This violence initiates another process, in which emotional transformation into knowledge is evaded and even attacked. This happens when a person, or a part of him (called by Bion 'the psychotic part of the personality'), cannot tolerate frustration, pain, or absence because of their intensity. Under these circumstances, violent hatred of internal and external reality, hatred that extends to the sense organs and to the parts of the personality that are used to establish contact with reality, i.e., consciousness, transforms love and appropriates it into itself; or excessive envy deflects the need (which could not be satisfied) for love, for understanding, and for mental growth into the search for material comforts; this need becomes hatred and greed, devoid of love or gratitude. Bion describes poignantly the predicament of the baby who, at the same time that he needs material food and care for his physical survival, is full of violent emotions; the baby becomes split between feeling the threat of starvation and horror of death, on the one hand, and fear of his violent, destructive emotions, on the other. The baby then greedily appropriates from the environment the material supplies he needs, while denying his own dependence on the giving object so as to avoid suffering. This process leads, according to Bion, to relentless greed without gratitude, a state that is found in adults as well.

Thus, Bion assumes that violent emotions that cannot be tolerated attack the person's links with external reality. Excessive greed and envy cause the splitting of ego parts into minute fragments, which are violently projected onto the object or onto the world; reality itself is destroyed; and a false, concrete reality springs up that is populated by so-called bizarre objects. Bion explains the formation of the bizarre objects in two different ways. Sometimes he sees them as the fragments of the split-off and propelled-out particles of the personality, and sometimes he regards them as the raw, untransformed emotional experiences misperceived and misexperienced as concrete, naturalistic objects. These two formulations seem incompatible unless one keeps in mind Bion's essentially equating (particularly when explaining psychotic states) parts of the personality, material particles, and feelings (experiences).

These bizarre objects, which become increasingly painful, persecutory, and damaging to perception and judgment, are treated by the 'psychotic part of the personality' as if they were elements for thinking. But they are not elements for thinking: They are not psychic alpha elements, and neither are they the original raw experiences; they are rather at an intermediary stage between alpha elements and sense perceptions or between thoughts and real things. Like alpha elements, they can be stored, not as thoughts, but rather as so-called undigested facts. Under these circumstances, primitive thoughts are taken for real objects of thinking; concrete, not (yet) abstracted elements are mistakenly treated according to the laws of mental functioning, i.e., as if they were thoughts, and not as objects that obey natural laws of sense perception. When this happens, the person becomes thoroughly confused and unable to give meaning to his emotions or to turn them into usable knowledge. Instead, the emotions are now unconsciously experienced as objects that have to be evacuated or used for very concrete manipulations, such as projective identification and acting out, for they are felt to be things-in-themselves, as Bion calls them, without any symbolic dimension or psychic elaboration. The person in such a state is unable to endow his emotions with meaning; Bion adduces many clinical examples of such confused, concretized emotions in the patient and their evoked emotional counterparts in the analyst.

One way out of this predicament, writes Bion, is to use another person (e.g., the analyst) as a repository of a part of one's own personality. This is done by projective identification, which is what the infant does with his mother. In this context, Meltzer's formulation is appropriate: "For Bion," he writes, "all needed objects are bad objects" (1978, p. 64). Indeed, Bion writes that when the infant is aware of a very bad breast inside it, which is a breast that is not there, and that "by not being there gives it painful feeling," the infant will 'evacuate' the breast by route of the respiratory system, or, alternatively, it will 'swallow' a satisfactory breast (1962, p. 57). By using the term 'alternatively,' Bion loses some of the power to convey the taste of such a primitive experience, an experience that is *at once* a blend of feelings of evacuation of discomfort and of being persecuted, and also of relief, experienced on having 'swallowed' a good thing-feeling-object. The good breast that is 'swallowed' is indistinguishable in fantasy from a thought, from an idea in the mind. When the baby has a good breast inside it (either by his successful projective identification or, later, by his tolerance of frustration and absence), the 'no-breast' (the absent mother) can become a thought, and the 'apparatus for thinking thoughts' develops; various thoughts are formed on different conceptual levels.

It is difficult to decide on the appropriate level of discourse (e.g., metaphorical or realistic) from which to describe Bion's assumption that thoughts exist prior to a mental apparatus to think them; in this conception, thoughts 'search' for a thinker to contain them or to 'think them out.' As this difficult issue does not bear directly on my subject, I shall leave it at that (see 1967, p. 165).

Obviously, the 'good breast' or the 'bad breast' is not the breast itself; it is not a phenomenon that can be objectively assessed; rather, it designates, as Bion writes, the individual experience of sweetness, sourness, or bitterness, which is abstracted from the (subjectively experienced) sweet, sour, or bitter breast. For Bion, the felt need itself *is* a bad breast ("to employ concrete terms," as he says) or a beta element ("to employ an abstraction," in his words). The need 'means' the feeling; it means that the infant feels that the breast in actuality is a bad object, which does not fulfill it, is empty, and has to be evacuated from oneself.

Thus, need, feeling, and object (breast) are equated in Bion's system. In the baby's mind, they are one. In a passage discussing the baby's experiences at the breast, Bion writes: "We must assume that the good breast and the bad breast are emotional experiences." And he goes on: "In the imaginary situation when the baby shows signs of needing food, the need for the breast is a feeling, and that feeling itself is a bad breast; the infant does not feel it wants a good breast, but it does feel it wants to evacuate a bad one" (1962, p. 35). This last phrase conveys Bion's idea that absence, frustration, and deprivation become bad feelings and wishes of riddance, and that consequently there is never absence of feelings in the psyche; emotional experiences always occur when there is a so-called psychic space.

This psychic space is a framework that encompasses various kinds of emotional processes, functions of the personality, fantasized interactions, and their inner conceptualizations. Bion contrasts this conception of psychic space with Freud's concept of the mental apparatus, which, to Bion's mind, is a closed system that can account only for neurotic, but not for psychotic, phenomena. Psychotic processes, which are the result of intolerance to pain and impatience (Bion's term) to let thoughts and concepts form, should be seen, in Bion's view, as occurring in a destroyed mental space. This is a space of infinite dimensions, which has nothing to restrict it and which therefore cannot act as a container. 'In' it, explosive projections, not only of psychic content but of parts of the mental apparatus itself, multiple splittings, and psychotic catastrophes incessantly burst apart its boundaries. The mental space generated by these processes is so great that the person feels "his emotions to get lost in an infinite vacuum . . . words, images and ideas . . . are remnants, debris or fragments floating in space without limits'' (1967, p. 89). Violent emotions are regarded as destructive forces that burst psychic space and strip the incipient formation of concepts of space and time of their meaning; violent emotions (which, in a sense, are equivalent to 'the psychotic part of the personality') attack and destroy concepts and thinking. These attacks are the consequence of "hatred of the emotions, which is, by short extension (hatred) of life itself'' (1967, p. 100).

I have quoted Bion at length to show his peculiar language, which leaves unsettled the question of whether he speaks metaphorically or, as he tells us, literally but abstractly, following the model of mathematical theories (e.g., of catastrophic change), so as to grasp the immutable essence of psychic events, behind and beyond their multifarious and deceptive appearances to the senses.

While in Bion's system violent emotions are conceived as massive destructive forces, it is only on emotional experiences that the mind can thrive and develop; emotional experiences are its oxygen and its food. By thinking about the emotional experiences and by understanding them, writes Bion, the mind apprehends meanings, and this very activity makes it live and grow.

Bion makes an even stronger assumption, however—namely, that elaboration of emotional experiences is more than nourishing to the mind: Understanding one's emotions has the function of protecting one's passions from being 'poisoned' and 'eroded' by "lies" that are generated by the destructive parts of the personality. He assumes positive powers of growth inherent in the emotions, against which active tendencies militate. These tendencies purposefully seek to destroy integrative emotional relationships called by Bion 'links.' Thus, projective identifications "increase in a cancerous manner," causing an endless splitting of the parts that are already split and "grown together again." In their proliferation, these malignant processes destroy the capacity to perceive and to think; this is psychosis.

This description is at least partially comprehensible if we realize the equivalence, even the identity, in Bion's theory, of emotion and knowledge. There is an equation in Bion's model between the bad breast, bad feelings, concrete (unelaborated) facts, and the (sometimes unconscious) experience of foreign bodies and false knowledge ("lies"). In an analogous manner, thoughts and ideas, food and nourishment, the good breast, and conditions for true learning and knowledge are, in psychic reality, one and the same thing. Deep down, at the lowest level of abstraction, they are the same. And this is the most essential knowledge the baby acquires about himself and about his inner world. Obviously, such a view is very different from seeing feelings as essentially body sensations in early life, as ego psychologists believe them to be. Bion differs also from Melanie Klein, who regards feelings and objects as intrapsychically identical, at least at the beginning of life. Bion is less concerned with objects than with the functions of the personality, of persons, or of relationships, all of which subserve to metabolize raw and alien materials or experiences into feelings and thoughts of an increasing order of abstraction (see 1962, p. 1).

The attitude called 'knowing' is the activity through which the subject becomes discerningly aware of his emotional experience and can abstract from it a formulation that will adequately represent this experience. The process of abstraction is essential to the emotional experience of knowledge, for then the abstracted elements can be used for learning and for understanding.

This conception of knowledge leads to one of the central themes in Bion's thought, namely, his assumption that knowledge is one of the three basic feelings of the psyche, the other two being love and hate, as they are in Melanie Klein's theory. With this assumption, Bion supplemented Klein's implicit 'theory of feelings,' as we have called it. Bion called knowledge (K) an emotion, on par with love (L) and hate (H), all of which are called 'links', a term in which the emotional, the relational, and the cognitive dimensions converge. Loving, hating, and knowing an object are links with that object (or a function or an experience). This was an intriguing step on Bion's part; with this juxtaposition, the boundary and the difference between feeling and knowing were obliterated with a sweeping stroke.[4] The implications of this move for theory and practice are momentous. In Bion's thinking, knowing and feeling are at bottom not essentially different, and both use thoughts as their material. These ideas grew on the ground of Bion's theory of knowledge, where all knowledge was assumed to have its origin in primitive 'emotional experience' (an often recurring term in Bion's writings). In psychic reality, according to Bion, there are not only love and hate, but knowledge as well; whereas L and H pertain to the present (even if frustrating) object, knowledge or the K-link pertains to the absent object, which potentially (if frustration can be tolerated) leads to thought, which can bridge the gap between the felt lack and the steps necessary for gratification.

Discussion

In singling out the main ideas in Bion's writings that are pertinent to theories of affect in psychoanalysis, I have found that they can be organized around two axes. One of them may be called Bion's basic equation of emotion and cognition, while the other is his core metaphor of affects. The basic identity in Bion's theory between feelings and cognition may be epitomized in the following two statements: (a) feelings have to be contained and processed in order for the mind to grow, and (b) feelings, or emotional experiences, 'become' true knowledge (through conceptions, concepts, K, or O, all terms developed by Bion).

Put together, these two propositions would amount to the idea that feelings have to be contained and processed in a certain manner in order to become truthful knowledge and, inversely, that there can be no knowledge that is not emotional (and personal) at root.

Repeatedly throughout his writings, Bion uses two basic, interrelated images or metaphors, which we can call the metabolic and the spatial. With the aid of these two metaphors, Bion has provided a framework (or a container, in his words) for feelings, for their modes of processing (e.g., transformations, reverie), and, in addition, a notational system for describing and communicating their vicissitudes.

The metabolic metaphor deals with the psychic transformations of emotions; within it, emotions are regarded as being processed in an analogous manner to food when it is digested and metabolized. The alimentary system and, occasionally, the respiratory system serve for Bion as models with which to explain or depict what happens to raw emotional data. The language here is that of 'metabolized elements,' 'swallowing,' 'evacuating,' 'transformation,' and so on.

Not only, however, do emotions have to be processed; they also have to be contained as a precondition for their processing. A kind of psychological space has to exist to encompass them, so that they can be linked to each other and to the different parts of the personality. The spatial metaphor in Bion's writings draws profusely on terms such as 'psychic space,' 'container,' 'contained,' 'binocular vision,' 'vertices,' and so on. When the infant is small and helpless, he is helped if, when he projects a feeling, say, that he is dying, to the mother, he can reintroject it after the sojourn of the feeling in the breast has made it tolerable to the infant's psyche, and the feeling has thereby changed its meaning (1967, p. 116).

From these two issues, the assumption of the necessity of containment and of metabolizing (processing) emotions and the assumption of the basic identity of emotion and knowledge and truth, or meaning, we arrive at a new insight. The essential dimension, the crucial axis (or 'vertex,' to use a term of Bion's) in Bion's theory of emotions is the dimension of abstractness. It seems that degree of abstractness is the crucial factor in self-awareness and inner knowledge, and vice versa. In this respect, Bion strongly differentiates and even contrasts the sensual and the emotional. Only the latter is the true source of knowledge and truth, even if absolute truth, 'O,' can never be reached.

It is difficult to discuss Bion's theory of emotions in terms of the concept of affect, as can be done with the models of other thinkers on emotion. Compared to other recent thinkers on affect theory who have arrived at not very dissimilar ideas about the primacy of feelings or about knowledge being ineluctably emotional, Bion's theory remains divorced, and purposefully so, from 'daily,' moment-to-moment sensory experience. Feelings in his theory do not tell the person whether things are functioning well and in harmony (Sandler, 1972); also, feelings in Bion's theory lack the energizing quality, the motivational fiber inherent in them in reality (see G. S. Klein, 1976; M. Klein, 1935, 1946; Sandler, 1960a, 1985; Tomkins, 1979). Neither are feelings signals or semantic symbols pointing beyond themselves (see the ego psychologists, e.g., Green, 1973). In Bion's thinking, one has to let oneself be steeped in and brood over and reflect upon one's emotions in order to 'know' oneself. One has to possess curiosity (but not stupid, arrogant, or excessive curiosity, which then becomes destructively intrusive) to arrive at authenticity and truthful knowledge.

Bion's conception may be seen as a theory of emotional wisdom or an epistemology of emotions. Perhaps what saves his theory from becoming a philosophical system that has lost touch with clinical or daily reality is his continual reliance on emotional experiences as the clinically most essential ingredients of psychic processes.

5
Affects as Feeling States and as Value Functions: Joseph Sandler

Joseph Sandler is a central contemporary theoretician on affect. His writings show many developments and shifts of emphasis in an effort to adapt psychoanalytic theory to clinical practice, while at the same time attempting to capture the clinical experience itself. In all his work, the subject of affects and feelings is predominant; it is constantly present and returns to occupy him in most of his writings. Sandler argues for a conceptual divorce of the affects from the drives, for linking affects with the concept of object relationships (and even making the former the precursors of the latter in development), and for positing affects as the regulators of the whole mental apparatus. Before discussing Sandler's theory of affect, a few words will be said about the background against which these ideas have been elaborated.

Sandler's work revolves around two axes. One is the striving to conceptually and theoretically account for the experiential (in the sense of the German 'Erlebnis') aspect of the mental, as well as for clinical experience (in the sense of the German 'Erfahrung') and its cumulative yield of knowledge. The other axis is the concern with the dialectical development of psychoanalytic theory. According to Sandler, psychoanalytic theory develops out of the problematics of existing theories. The continuing use of formally accepted theory gradually eventuates in loss of precision, conceptual strain, and theoretical disharmonies that become increasingly obstructive of fresh developments. At such a stage, "ideas arise, aimed at dealing with very real areas of weakness or unclarity in the theory. These ideas give rise to counterformulations, and this in turn results in a process of development which makes psychoanalysis alive and growing in a truly organic fashion" (1983, p. 3).

Such a historical process occurred, in his view, with the theory of affects, and he traces this process with a keen sense of the crucial importance of affects in the clinical situation and in theory construction. The sources that nourished his work in this area can roughly be divided into three categories. One is Anna Freud's work, particularly her defense theory, her simultaneous use of the topographical and the structural models, and her emphasis on ego functioning. The second source is Sandler's undertaking, with the assistance of other workers and empirical data from the Hampstead clinic, of a conceptual analysis of psychoanalytic theory and its central concepts. In this project, Sandler attempted to examine and reformulate various psychoanalytic concepts in a more precise and historically differentiated way than had been done before. The third source for his work on affects is empirical studies in the psychology of perception, which point to the existence of a constant, constructive, balance-maintaining adaptational activity across different states of consciousness. Formulations in this vein have always been germane to Sandler's thinking.

Let me begin with Sandler's dialogue with Anna Freud, which has been going on for many years and whose last chapters have been recently documented in a book (1985a). One of the topics that occupied Sandler in his early thinking concerned the implications of Anna Freud's view (1936) that affects are not only drive derivatives but also motives for defense. The conception of affects as motives for defense, which Anna Freud introduced into the theory from clinical practice, was at that time a relatively novel perspective in psychoanalysis. Sandler realized that any motive must be indissolubly linked to the affect that accompanies it and that it is ultimately the affect, and not the drive, that is defended against. Thus, he conjectured, the ultimate and necessary factor motivating each attempt at defense must be the affect. Sandler maintained that the view (to which Anna Freud herself subscribed occasionally) that affects were only drive derivatives, or even merely "adjuncts, things accompanying the drives," lacking an autonomous status, hindered analysts from effectively dealing with the psychoanalytic theory of affect. He argued, basing himself on various observations, that a person defends not against the 'causes' of his feelings, but against the feelings themselves, which may be regarded as causes; feelings cause wishes, although they are also reactions to wishes. In general, Sandler prefers to speak of wishes rather than of drives, and of the relations between feelings and wishes, rather than between feelings and drives. In his view, drives are hypothetical constructs, whereas wishes entail feelings, as well as self and object representations. Feelings are expressions of wishes, and sometimes they have to be defended against. This last statement seems to be the most pertinent point for affect theory emerging from Sandler's work with Anna Freud.

Another area where Sandler's conception of affect has evolved is the study of the different phases of psychoanalytic theory and the changing frames of reference of its concepts. Sandler pointed to the muddled situation in which, first, energies and affects were confused and, in addition, the bodily aspects of affects were not differentiated from their experiential aspects. The lack of distinction between affects and energies created a wide gap between theoretical explanations (based on the hypothetical drives) and clinical work (done via understanding of affects and ideas). The failure to differentiate between the somatic and the experiential dimensions of affect led to the erroneous equation of instinctual threats from within with dangerous stimuli from without.

Sandler raised these issues and circumscribed them, choosing Freud's 1926 signal concept. The concept of signal is used by Sandler in a two-stage reasoning process. First, he shows that Freud's thesis that anxiety could also arise as a consequence of the perception of danger, and not only following impulse threat, constituted a forward thrust in divorcing affects from the drives by implying that affects can arise from perceptions too, not only from the drives.[1] Affects, in Sandler's view, are in fact linked to perception even more completely than to the drives. As a consequence, affects could now be more closely studied and their role clarified. Sandler considered the signal as mobilizing both adaptive and defensive behaviors, i.e., as a motive, and as being absolutely necessary for the functioning of the ego. He concludes from his study of psychoanalytic theory (1969–1972) that, in their role of signals, affects are indispensable components of ego functioning. This idea was to be elaborated by him later (particularly in his paper on motivation, 1985b).

This links with the third provenance for Sandler's theory of affect, the domain of perception. Here Sandler was inspired by Freud's 1900 notion of 'identity of perception' and by work done in experimental psychology. Sandler extended Freud's notion to the whole of mental functioning, including object relations, by aligning it with studies on perception (e.g., Gardner et al., 1959; Koehler, 1964; Werner & Wapner, 1955; all cited in Sandler, 1967). According to Sandler, the foremost integrative activity of the ego is that of perception. Every act of perception is essentially an act of integration, and it is accompanied by a feeling of mastery. It is an active ego process meant to protect consciousness from being overwhelmed by unorganized sense data. Perception endows incoming stimuli with meaning, in terms of some internal frame of reference (which was articulated, two years later, as the 'representational world'). Sandler maintained that identity of perception is sought after and its achievement is inherently satisfactory not only in the dream work (Freud, 1900) but also in the work of perception. It brings with it a feeling of safety, a derivative of the earliest experience of the suckling's positive body state of satiation. This feeling is assumed by Sandler to direct all behavior. The idea of a background feeling of safety proved to be seminal in Sandler's thinking in the years to come.

These three strands in Sandler's thinking branch out and come together again in his various writings. We may epitomize them in the following way: the influence of and work with Anna Freud inspired Sandler's conception of affects as motives; Sandler's study of Freud's theoretical phases gave rise to the further elaboration of the conception of affects as signals; and the perceptual studies Sandler brought to bear on psychoanalytic theory sharpened his conception of affects as background feelings of mental functioning. Sandler's thought developed in a to-and-fro movement between general psychoanalytic theory and affect

theory. I shall now follow, in chronological order, some of Sandler's writings
that are most pertinent to the theory of affect.

In 1960, Sandler discussed the problem of the superego. Drawing on notions
of the inner world found in Piaget. Hartmann, and Jacobson, Sandler extended
the concept of schemata to internal sense data as well. He contends here that
feelings of well-being arise in the child and adult from the experience of being
loved by the superego, which reaches back to experiences of feeling one with
highly esteemed, idealized parental figures. These good feelings are constantly
sought after by the individual, who not only fears the superego but also deeply
wishes to be loved by it. This affective state, experienced early in life as a bodily
good feeling, is later localized in the self; it becomes attached to what Sandler
called 'the ideal shape of the self.'

In 1962, Sandler, together with B. Rosenblatt, introduced the notion of the
representational world, which proved very fruitful and a point of reference for
much future work. This notion served as a central concept in the discussion of
the child's subjective world and denoted the authors' belief that internal representations within the ego must precede perception of objects in the external
world. The representational construction of an internal world is an ego function,
which provides for the perception of external objects and their internalization.
The representational world is likened by the authors to a radar or television
screen, which provides meaningful information as a base for action. It consists
of self, object, and affect representations, used by the ego in an effort to maintain
its equilibrium, while its prime motivators are conscious and unconscious feeling
states. Good feeling states indicate that there is congruity between the actual
and the ideal representations, whereas pain and unpleasant feelings accompany
discrepancies between representations. The overall aim of all ego functions is
to reduce representational discrepancy and to attain a feeling of well-being, that
is, to reach a feeling homeostasis.

In 1967 appeared Sandler's paper "Trauma, Strain and Development," in
which he suggested that discrepancy between mental representations causes pain.
Sandler believes that, subjectively, pain is seen as part of all unpleasurable
feeling states; it roughly equals the experience we call suffering. On a theoretical
level, pain denotes the discrepancy between an ideal and an actual state of the
self (the ideal state being well-being). He assumes that discrepancy can be
perceived only through experiential input, which is the only kind of information
with which the mental apparatus can work and make judgments. Pain is regarded
as a motivating factor because it is an affective state that has to be defended
against. The ideas expressed here lead to a psychoanalytic motivational explanation on a different basis than the drives; motivation is explicated as a function
of perceptions and wishes, ideas and feelings. In the same year, Sandler also
discussed, with Joffe, the concept of narcissism in terms of feeling states rather
than in terms of libidinal cathexis of the ego or of the self.

Sandler's 1968 paper with Joffe on the psychoanalytic psychology of adaptation contains two important points for the subject of affect. The first is a move

of the authors from using the term 'shape of self representation' to talking in terms of self and object relationships. The other point is the renewed discussion of representational discrepancy in terms of its association with feelings of pain. In terms of the functioning of the ego, Sandler is now in a position to say that the prime motivators are conscious and unconscious feeling states, associated with various forms of representational congruity or discrepancy. The aim of all ego functions is said to be the reduction of discrepancy so as to attain or maintain a basic feeling state of well-being.

In 1972, Sandler delineated the role of the concept of affect in the different phases of psychoanalytic theory. That year marked the termination of his study of the evolution of psychoanalytic theory in terms of the different frames of reference within which it is to be understood. Out of this study, only those points will be singled out that are most pertinent to the subject of affect.

Sandler pointed out the fact that in the first phase of psychoanalytic theory (after 1897 and particularly in 1915) the unconscious became differentiated into the dynamic, repressed unconscious and the descriptive, unrepressed unconscious, or preconscious, in contrast to the period when the concept of the unconscious comprised only one kind, that of hysterics and of the hypnotized. This distinction had repercussions on affect theory, particularly on the framing of unconscious affects.

Sandler felt that what was needed at this point was the adoption of a basic, unifying assumption of a mental apparatus, with an overall aim of psychic adaptation, which bears an inherent relationship to affects, particularly to feeling states, in the sense that feeling states are its exclusive fuel and its avenue of knowledge and action. The mental apparatus, as Sandler conceives it, develops out of the interactions between subjective experience and mental representations of action. These interactions take place on the basis of a dialectic relationship; the mental apparatus handles experiential contents, and its functioning is assessed in turn on the basis of feeling states, particularly those of safety and well-being.

In his 1974 paper on psychic conflict, Sandler criticized the structural model as being incapable of accounting for the core concept of conflict in light of clinical experience. Sandler argued that when the sharp distinction between ego and id had been shown not to hold, it was no longer tenable to conceptualize psychic conflict as obtaining among the three psychic agencies of the mind. Instead, he proposed to conceive of conflict as obtaining between the unconscious, peremptory urges and the so-called delaying tendencies of the mental apparatus. Rather than consider conflict as an intersystemic phenomenon, as does the structural theory, conflict should be seen, according to Sandler, as existing between the different functioning aspects of the total mental apparatus. With this move, Sandler discarded the highly problematical distinction between ego and id in favor of notions of degrees and hierarchies of structuralization (see Gedo & Goldberg, 1973; Gill, 1963; G. Klein, 1976).

To this picture of the mental apparatus, Sandler adds the temporal dimension and posits a sequential process along which mental events change their meaning;

in this way, psychic conflict is seen to occur in historical layers in different temporal modes of mental functioning. According to this model, conflict takes place between graded tendencies and defenses and between developmentally determined censorship (1983), rather than among the three mental structures. The temporal dimension in mental functioning accounts for the phenomenon that what were once solutions to conflicts may later become conflictual themselves, once they are found to clash with the ego's present needs to maintain self-esteem and safety.

All these ideas are worked out within an adaptational and object-related framework, which assumes that the mental apparatus functions to maintain a 'steady state' of feelings. According to this view, incessant activity continuously goes on in the mental apparatus, where external stimulation is scanned by the ego for its experiential content and significance, unconscious fantasy serves as a stabilizer, a kind of gyroscope (with A.-M. Sandler, 1986), and feeling states act as indicators of the momentary state of the mental apparatus. These moment-to-moment changes of feeling states in the mental apparatus are profoundly influenced by object relationships.

In a 1978 joint paper with Anne-Marie Sandler, called "On the Development of Object Relationships and Affects," the Sandlers presented what they called a theory of object relationships, which they attempted to integrate into what they called 'intrapsychic psychoanalytic psychology.' The gist of their argument is that object relationships should be conceived as inherently and unexceptionally mutual in a dynamic sense, rather than in terms of a unidirectional energic investment of an object. They suggested that a relationship to an object consists of an actual or fantasized interaction between the representation of the self and of the object (one fantasizes about oneself in some relationship or interaction with an object; one does not fantasize about the object in vacuo).

Object relationships, in their view, serve essentially to fulfill, or to represent the fulfillment of, needs that appear as wishes. To Sandler, wishes are not necessarily instinctual but are seen as motivated from various sources such as disequilibrating external stimuli or unpleasurable affects or the need to gain or restore feelings of well-being, safety, and control. A wish is a complex structure, involving a self representation, an object representation, and a representation of the interaction between the two. A representation of a gratifying interaction (or, in many cases, of an interaction per se, even a painful one) is what provides good feelings of safety. The desired aim is directed at the object not for gratification of a drive or need, but for a wished-for interaction between self and object representations, in reality or in fantasy. Thus, object relationships and wish fulfillments are at bottom the same.

The Sandlers hold that, from the beginning of life, the subjective experiences that register on the infant's sensorium are predominantly feeling states, mixed with other sensations, and, stretching the concept of object "a little further than usual," as they propose, they suggest that the first objects of the child are the experiences of pleasure and satisfaction, on the one hand, and those of unpleasure and pain, on the other (p. 292). Experiences of pleasure and unpleasure are seen by the authors as the two 'primary objects' of the child, who has two kinds of reactions to these two classes of feeling: joy and excitement, on the one hand, and rejection, avoidance, and withdrawal via anger and fear, on the other. The first division of the child's world, according to this perspective, is that of pleasure and unpleasure as 'nice' and 'nasty' objects, respectively. These primary affective objects are regarded by the authors as chaotic masses of subjective experience in which 'self' and 'nonself' have not yet been differentiated and which are divided into two clusters of pleasurable and unpleasurable feelings and sensations (see Furman's 1985 paper, which expands and applies Sandler's notion of well-being in the clinic and in development).

The authors hold that after the primary affective objects have been formed, further boundaries are laid down between self and object representations, and increasingly complex representations are established of the interactions between them. These developments are said to proceed along the lines of feeling states. The result of these ideas is that psychic economy becomes an economy of feeling states in a double sense. In one sense, J. Sandler posits that reality is apprehended only through feelings; experience is organized through and around feelings. In another sense, it is assumed that at later stages of development, the person will always strive (but will never permanently succeed) to get back to the situation of absolute good feelings of his link with the good mother of his early beginnings. Thus, the authors write: "Generally speaking, the development of object relationships consists in the departure from the close primary relation to the affects of pleasure, well-being and security giving rise to vigorous attempts to recover that relationship" (p. 294). They stress, in contrast to older views in psychoanalysis, that the need to gain feelings of safety and well-being precedes and predominates over feelings associated with instinctual satisfaction.

The shift in Sandler's theory of the concept of affects in relation to the drives and to objects, where feeling states of well-being become the ultimate goal, raises the question as to what it is that makes the feelings of nonsensuous well-being or security more attractive than the direct sensual pleasure associated with sexual satisfaction. Sandler attempts to address this question with the help of the concept of an 'affective value cathexis,' which is said to determine the priorities of motivation. Affective value cathexis is defined by Sandler as the feeling state with which a particular mental representation is invested and which is a measure of its positive or negative attractiveness to the ego or of the pressure that motivates one toward it (1985b, p. 33). The affective value cathexis, i.e., the attractiveness of an object, is seen as a variable quantity, which depends on the "intrinsic potential for pleasant feelings associated with that state, goal, aim or object" and also on "an added investment provided by the need to do away with unpleasant feelings" (p. 35). The idea of cathexis of value appeared for the first time in Sandler & Joffe's 1966 paper on sublimation and was reintroduced in his paper on motivation (1985b). 'Value' is defined by Sandler as the feeling qualities (positive or negative, simple or complicated) or sign values "which give all representations their significance for the ego" (1985b, p. 22; see also Sandler, 1967, p. 65). The gist of the argument is that even if feelings of well-being and safety are less 'driving' and passionate than sexual feelings, they have their own inherent attractiveness, their own value.

The important point here is the introduction into theory of the dimension of an object's significance for the person. With this step, what was until now called 'cathexis' in the sense of investment of psychic energy, or else given the name of a particular feeling (such as love), could now come under a more satisfactory (because exact) description; 'objective' stimuli become, so to speak, 'subjectivized'; i.e., their meaning to the person is now taken into account. The link existing between feelings and meanings, which Sandler had posited earlier (in his view of feeling states as indicators of mental functioning), has now become stronger; meaning and feeling now converge in the concept of value. Thus, feelings motivate a person toward an object according to the affective value cathexis that the object carries for the person. This view sees objects not as cathected with libido but rather as loaded with feelings, i.e., having emotional significance, which is private and specific to each object in the eyes of the person who, by definition, evaluates it.

With the addition of the concept of affective value, motivation theory can now be built, according to Sandler, on formulations in terms of affects (rather than drives). Feelings and feeling states are linked with the most general issues of motivation. In a way, Sandler has come full circle to the theme that had occupied him in his early theoretical writings. At the beginning of his dialogues with Anna Freud, he had come to the conclusion that it is mostly affects that motivate defense. Subsequently, he dissociated motives from their one-to-one relationship with the drives. Now, he speaks of affects as general and primary motives, and he bases psychoanalytic motivation theory on affect. If we bear in mind that psychoanalytic theory as a whole may be regarded as essentially a theory of motivation (see, e.g., G. Klein, 1976), then we can realize the status that affects are accorded with such a strategy.

The upshot of Sandler's ideas concerning affects is his view that the equation of affects with drives is the Achilles' heel of affect theory. In his work, Sandler contributed to the final divorce of affects from the drives by showing that explanations in terms of affect (e.g., of sublimation, depression, narcissism, object relations) are superior to explanations in terms of drives. Sandler also helped uncover the misleading double use of hybrid concepts such as 'tension,' 'discharge,' or 'cathexis,' in which biological or quasi-biological states and experiential contents or processes are condensed.

On the other hand, Sandler effected a rapprochement between the concept of ego and the concept of affects, and he helped break the old picture of the ego standing in inherent opposition to the affects by maintaining that ego and affects are not in conflict (1974), but, rather, that the ego harbors the feelings within its realm. The ego defends against feelings, but it also attempts to use them for the benefit of the whole mental apparatus.

Sandler put forward explanations in terms of the perceptive, evaluative, and object-related role of feelings. Thus, he regards the first objects in life as sensations of pleasure and unpleasure and the feeling reactions that accompany them. He asserts that it is the dynamic gestalt of the experience of interactions between child and mother that gives rise to the 'nice' and 'nasty' objects.

The point for which Sandler is probably most known in affect theory is his postulation that feeling states are regulators of mental functioning. Feelings and feeling states are the only channel to assess and handle mental contents to which the mental apparatus has to adapt.

Sandler's assertion that feelings states regulate mental functioning implies that feelings are endowed with motivational status. Feelings may in themselves motivate defenses, which change experience, and feelings also cause wishes (1985b). The feeling values attached to an object determine its attractiveness and its power to motivate a person toward it or away from it. Thus, feelings have a double function in Sandler's theory, stabilization and perception. Feelings have motivational power as pointers to the road to attain or regain feelings of pleasure, well-being, and safety; they essentially function as set points in a homeostatic system. This role is their stabilizing role. On the other hand, feelings also provide information; that is, they are assessors of the significance and value of various stimuli and events. The notion of value, so central in Sandler's later theory, bears an affinity with Hartmann's seminal idea (mentioned by Sandler) of 'positive value accents' (1927).[2]

It is evident from Sandler's formulations that the informational (the perceptual) and the motivational (the stabilizing) aspects of feelings must strike a certain balance between them. Our most profound striving, in Sandler's view, is to feel safe and esteemed; this puts considerations of reality in second place to those of safety. The capacity itself to take reality into account depends on the maturity of the ego apparatuses, which function so as to widen the tolerable range of experience without unduly disrupting the basic feeling tone of safety or well-being. The apparatuses, according to Sandler, depend on the ever finer use of changes in feeling states by the scanning ego. Thus, development proceeds from gross and diffuse to ever more nuanced feelings, which instigate ever more complex adaptive activity; in this way, the perceptual and the motivational aspects of feelings converge.

By way of summarizing this discussion, we may say that Sandler's theory of affect springs from a view of mental functioning that stresses the exclusive role of the experiential (conscious or unconscious) side of affects as the gateway to apprehending inner and outer reality. This view also points to the role of changes in feeling states as signals for further adaptation. This theory is essentially a motivational one, which maintains that the striving for feelings of safety and harmony is a basic motive. Motives in this theory are squarely worded in terms of 'feelings of,' rather than in terms of higher-order, abstract goals, such as 'genital primacy,' 'cohesion of the self,' 'differentiation of self and object representations,' 'attainment of the depressive position,' and so on. This convergence of the two levels, the motivational and the experiential, rests on the basic underlying assumption, to my mind, of the necessity for a kind of experiential harmony as a precondition for mental functioning.

Sandler is known for his conceptualizations of feeling states, well-being, and safety, and for his having linked affects to object relationships. What is perhaps less recognized (because it bears more on metapsychology than on clinical theory) is that he has done much to banish energic formulations from psychoanalytic theory, in particular from the domain of affect. Sandler suggested that we should substitute a unified conception of the mental apparatus for energic explanations and for the structural theory. He also clearly distinguished between the two kinds of unconscious, the dynamic, repressed unconscious and the descriptive unconscious, which is actually the preconscious. This distinction bears many implications for the important issue of unconscious affects, which waits further exploration (a beginning of which is found in his 1987 paper on unconscious guilt). There are many issues that need further clarification, such as the unconscious status of affect, the relationship between the mental apparatus and the ego, and notions about the form general psychoanalytic theory will take when this new affect theory has taken root and further developed.

6
An "Ego Psychological Object Relations" Model of Affect:
Otto Kernberg

Kernberg calls his perspective on psychoanalytic theory an 'ego psychological object relations model' (1984). This model is an attempted integration of ideas from three dominant psychoanalytic schools: the Kleinian school, British object relations theory, and American ego psychology. Kernberg adopted Melanie Klein's perspective on some intra-psychic processes, particularly her conception of splitting and integration of 'good' and 'bad' experiences as primary psychic operations. Object relations theory, mainly as expounded by Fairbairn, influenced Kernberg's emphasis on object-relatedness as fundamental to psychic structuralization, while ego psychology, particularly Jacobson's thought, provided in his theory the account for the integration and differentiation of self- and object-representations into the tripartite structure of the personality.

Kernberg's work on affect sprang mainly out of theoretical considerations, and his ideas on affects are found mostly in his non-clinical, theoretical writings, particularly in three works. In his 1976 book, *Object Relations Theory and Clinical Psychoanalysis*, Kernberg presented his general scheme of the affects in a chapter called "Instincts, Affects and Object Relations," in which affects were regarded as representing inborn dispositions to a subjective, pleasurable, or unpleasurable experience. In 1980, in his *Internal World and External Reality*, Kernberg stressed the key function of affects as subjective experiences at the boundary between the biological and the intrapsychic realms and as organizers of internalized object relations, drives, and psychic structures. In 1982, in his paper called "Self, Ego, Affects and Drives," Kernberg proposed a modification of drive theory by considering the drives as higher-order organizations, whose building blocks consist of affects, a step that reverses the hierarchical and motivational order of drives and affects.

The starting point for Kernberg's specific study of affects in 1976 is his opposition to Freud's 1915 policy of separating the concept of drive cathexis from that of affect cathexis and of separating the concept of (psychic) drives from that of (biological) instincts. Kernberg claimed that this policy moved affects two steps away from their biological foundations. He therefore set himself the task of linking "affects back to the psychological correlates of biological instincts" (1976, p. 85), using as his framework the structural theory, which he considered the best available theory of mental phenomena. But now he found that his work was hampered by two problems inherent in the structural model. One was its neglect of the central role of object relations in the structuralization of the mental apparatus. The other problem, not independent of the first, was the lack of a theoretical account of the role of affects in mental life.

Kernberg believed that efforts to accord affects a place in ego psychology should lead to their conceptualization in such a manner as to allow them to be linked in a new way with self and object representations and with the drives. To this end, Kernberg then used findings from experimental psychologists, such as Young, Tomkins, Pribram, Schachter, Leeper, and Arnold, as well as from researchers in ethology and attachment theory, e.g., Tinbergen, Lorenz, and Bowlby, and in neurophysiology, e.g., MacLean, which showed that instincts in humans are complex, flexible structures.

Kernberg now began to use the concept of instinct as consisting of a hierarchy of inborn, physiologically based, integrated behavior patterns, which are subordinated to higher-level, purposive drive structures. He now adduced supporting evidence and examples for the claim that with evolution and development, purely physiological mechanisms are replaced or expanded by psychological behavior regulation and that these regulatory constellations are themselves integrated into more comprehensive intrapsychic structures.

In this context Kernberg formulated his general conception of affects, according to which affects represent inborn dispositions to subjective experiences on the dimension of pleasure and unpleasure. These inborn dispositions are activated simultaneously with inborn behavior patterns that elicit environmental (mothering) reactions, and with general arousal, which enhances (up to a certain level) the perception of external and internal stimuli occurring during this interaction. The products of these different sources are stored as memory traces in a so-called affective memory, which incorporates self components, object components, and the affect state itself.

Thus, Kernberg's project of linking affects back to their biological substratum proceeded systematically in two stages, reversing their separation by Freud. Kernberg dealt with Freud's differentiation between biological instincts and psychic drives by putting forward the view that instincts are extremely complex structures that rest on psychic as well as on biological foundations. The second step now concerned the reconnection of affects and drives. Here the question was the status of affects in relation to the drives. Should affects be viewed as marginal to physiological mechanisms, through which they are automatically conditioned and released (as in Freud's conception in his drive theory), or should affects be considered central and subjectively variable states?

Kernberg opted for the second view. He said that neurophysiological, ethological, and experimental findings in psychology led him to accept as valid the so-called central theory of affects. This view regards affects as central motivational processes, as perceptions or appraisals of situations, and as subjective states, whereas the physiological changes that are so impressive in emotion are ancillary to them. In this view Kernberg endorses (1976, p. 103) Arnold's view (1970a). Implied in the 'central' theory of affects is the assumption that subjective states, the experiential qualitative aspects of affects, have an autonomous motivational power to determine the formation of psychic structures. These subjective states need to be theoretically explored and studied.

This leads us to the next point, where Kernberg speaks of what happens within the realm of affects as subjective experiences. He argues that differentiation of affect occurs concomitantly with the differentiation of internalized object relations. In this view, pleasurable and painful affects are the major organizers for a series of 'good' and 'bad' internalized object relations. Kernberg repeatedly stresses that libido and aggression are not external givens in this development but represent the overall evolution and organization of drive systems out of these 'good' and 'bad' affects. He sees self and object representations as invariably falling into two main categories: 'good' experiences and 'bad' experiences. 'Good' or 'bad' affect (love or hate) is therefore the link between each pair of self and object representations, and it lends them its specific color.

At the most basic level, says Kernberg, there are the affect dispositions, which are the inborn 'Anlagen' for differential, subjective experiencing of pleasure and unpleasure. As successive experiences of gratification and frustration accumulate, affects separately organize 'all-good' and 'all-bad' experiences, each in the context of undifferentiated self and object representations. Eventually, this leads to the differentiation of self, object, and affect at a given moment. Throughout this development, the role of affect changes; affect dispositions first build up experience, which, entwined with constitutional and cognitive givens, evolves into affect states. The affect states in turn determine the integration of both internalized object relations and the overall drive systems. Later, affect states signal the activation of the drive and represent it in the context of the activation of specific internalized object relations.

Kernberg's main points in 1976 can be summarized as follows:

1. After establishing that affects are motivationally and subjectively 'central' rather than peripheral (and that physiological expression is secondary to experience), Kernberg calls for the study of subjective experiences and for according them a place in theory.

2. Kernberg assumes, on the basis of his interpretation of evidence from many fields, that drives are hierarchically higher-order organizations rather than low-level, linear, and simple responses.

3. The first two points are linked in Kernberg's conception of affects as developing,

together with the integration of internalized object relations, into signals and monitors of activated drives.

In 1980, Kernberg discusses Jacobson's ideas, including her ideas on affects, as one of the main sources of his own thinking. He adopts Jacobson's view of affects as arising in the undifferentiated psychophysiological self, as then becoming integrated in the context of 'good' and 'bad' object relations, and—and this is the point on which Kernberg differs from Jacobson—as subsequently contributing to the differentiation of the drives into libido and aggression (1980, p. 89). Kernberg sees libido and aggression as motivational systems that incorporate in their organization both affects and object relations.

Kernberg's statements in 1980 about affects are mainly concerned with their structural aspects. He puts forward the following statements:

1. Affects represent inborn dispositions to a subjective experience along the dimensions of pleasure and unpleasure.

2. Affects are fixated by means of memory traces into a primitive 'affective memory' unit, incorporating self components, object components, and the affect state itself.

3. Differentiation of affects occurs in the context of the differentiation of internalized object relations. Pleasurable and unpleasurable affects are the major organizers of the series of 'good' and 'bad' internalized object relations, and they constitute the major motivational or drive systems that organize psychic experience.

In his successive attempts at theoretical synthesis, Kernberg realized that the task of integrating the structural, the object-relational, and the drive theory viewpoints necessitated a basic alteration in the postulated relationship of affects and drives. By positing affects, rather than drives, as comprising the primary motivational system of psychic life, and by relegating the drives to later-stage structures evolving out of the affects, he solved many theoretical problems and conceptual muddles, such as accounting for the psychological component of the instincts or for the clinically proven priority of object relations in mental functioning. The conceptualization of affects as being, together with self and object representations, the building blocks of the drives signifies a reversal of the developmental priorities of affects and drives and a major revision of drive theory. Drives are no longer viewed as the sources of motivation but as higher-order organizations of experience.

By considering affects as the primary motivational systems, Kernberg says that affects are indeed the earliest motives in life. This motivational priority given to the affects is accorded neither to the drives nor to object relations. Kernberg argues that the drives themselves can never be actually seen in the clinical situation—only concrete experiences and interactions are visible, appearing as wishes directed toward objects, that is, wishes embedded within a specific, activated object relationship. Consequently, the drives should better be regarded as overall trends that can be discerned only indirectly, in a mediated way, through affects and object relationships. Neither would object relations serve as the primary motivational system, because, to quote Kernberg, "the organization of intra-psychic reality in terms of love and hate is more important for the understanding of the continuity of psychic development, unconscious conflict and object relations than the fact that these contradictory states are originally directed toward the same object" (1976; see chapter 4). According to Kernberg, the object, or rather, the relation to it, is fundamentally and satisfactorily explained by the vicissitudes of feelings of love and hate toward it that are then organized into libido and aggression.

In his attempt at a theoretical synthesis, Kernberg uses a general systems model, in which the personality is regarded as a hierarchical system, divided into dynamically organized systems and subsystems, each of which represents a subsystem for a higher system in the hierarchy, while at the same time serving as a super-ordinate system for a lower one. The superordinate system of the whole personality comprises the subsystems ego, id, and superego and the two drives (the drives are defined by Kernberg as the psychical representatives of the biological instincts). These in turn are constructed of units of internalized object relations linked by an affect, and these units of affects and internalized object relationships function as an integrating system for the lower subsystems, which consist of inborn perceptual and behavioral patterns, affect dispositions, neurovegetative discharge patterns, and arousal mechanisms (1976, p. 85). Thus, the three levels of what Kernberg calls the personality are the neurophysiological (inborn cognitive and affective patterns), the object-relational (where self-affect-object units are established), and the structural level (the tripartite system and the two drives). According to Kernberg, affects in this three-level personality system occupy the intermediary level, on a par with internalized object relations.

In 1982, Kernberg is concerned with the place of the self in structural theory. Again we see his concern with the removal of experiential concepts from theory, which Hartmann effected by placing the 'self' in opposition to the object. This step, argues Kernberg, excluded the concept of the self from metapsychology. Kernberg also thought that Hartmann's fateful separation of the concept of ego from self and of self from self representation created an artificial separation of structural, experiential, and descriptive aspects of ego functions. Hence, he proposed to eliminate the use of the concept of self as opposed to object and to define the self as an intrapsychic structure that develops from the ego and is clearly embedded in the ego. The self, according to Kernberg, is thus an ego structure that originates from self representations while they are still enmeshed with object representations in the undifferentiated symbiotic phase. Accordingly, the libidinal investment of the self is related to the libidinal investment of the representations of the significant others, and all these investments are related and reinforce each other. Affects link a series of undifferentiated self representations and object representations so that gradually a complex world of internalized object relations, some pleasurably tinged, others unpleasurably tinged, is constructed.

Let us epitomize Kernberg's points in 1982.

1. Following Mahler, Kernberg assumes that at the beginning of life there is no differentiation between self and object; there is just an undifferentiated phase, or matrix, to start with.

2. The self is seen as an ego structure, a psychic system built on the integration of libido and aggression invested in self representations; it does not stand in a polar relationship to the object but originates from the time when there was still no differentiation between self and object.

3. The self does not originate only from blissful states of merger, pleasure, etc. (as Fairbairn and Kohut assumed, each in his own way); rather, the self is also assumed to be built up of painful or even catastrophic experiences; self development occurs under both libidinal and aggressive conditions. Kernberg believes that this conception supports Freud's dual drive theory.

4. The experiences, and later the affects of love and hate, become stable intrapsychic structures, which exist in genetic continuity through various developmental stages and, by that very continuity, consolidate into libido and aggression. Affects are the building blocks or constituents of the drives; eventually they acquire a signal function for the activation of drives.

SUMMARY AND DISCUSSION

Kernberg applies general systems theory to his theory of personality and development. Within this framework, affects are placed at an intermediary level, superordinate to the neurophysiological level of inborn affective, perceptual, and cognitive patterns and subordinate to that of the three psychic structures, the ego, id, and superego, and the two drives, libido and aggression. Affects form part of the so-called S-A-O (self-affect-object) representation level. Thus, Kernberg's theory speaks of low-level neurophysiological phenomena, consisting of inborn affective dispositions and perceptual and cognitive patterns; an intermediary level, consisting of affects; and a high level of the three intrapsychic structures and the two drives.

Another three-level hierarchy in Kernberg's theory is that of affect dispositions developing into affects, which then develop and become organized into the drives.

In postulating that affects are structured into 'overall drives,' Kernberg has turned the table on drive theory. Affects are no longer regarded as the representatives of the drives but as the sources, or particular instances, of the drives. A drive, in Kernberg's theory, is said to be an action tendency, a basic attitude. He calls the drives "stable intrapsychic structures consolidating in their continuity libido and aggression." Kernberg thinks that dual drive theory cannot be dispensed with (personal communication, 1986).

Affects are defined by Kernberg as the primary, i.e., the earliest, motivational elements in development. Pleasurable and unpleasurable experiences, and later 'good' and 'bad' affects, form the basis on which object relations are integrated and on which the broader configurations of the drives are built. Kernberg regards affects as developing into a series of subjective experiences, which start out from the primary undifferentiated states of pleasure and unpleasure.

The interactions initiated when the infant's inborn affect patterns communicate his needs to the mother are continuously integrated with corresponding levels of perceptive and cognitive organization and are laid down as 'affective memory.'

Kernberg considers affects as 'organizers' of development, in Spitz's sense. He regards self and object representations as a priori falling into two main categories of experience, 'good' and 'bad.' At a later stage, these two kinds of experiences differentiate further into specific and variegated feelings of enjoyment or displeasure. These in turn determine new concepts of the self and the object, which eventually, under the sign of 'love' or 'hate,' crystallize into stable intrapsychic structures, in genetic continuity through various developmental stages, and, through that very continuity, consolidate into libido and aggression.

With this last point, Kernberg's early concern with the concept of cathexis in Freud's theory also finds a solution. The yield of his theoretical work on affects led Kernberg to conclude that 'cathexes' are, to begin with, affective. They represent, in Kernberg's eyes, the quantitative element, the economic factor, involved in the intensity of primitive affect dispositions, which are activated in the context of primitive units of internalized object relations. The primary 'affect cathexes' organize overall 'instincts' into drive systems, and they eventually become 'instinctual' or 'drive cathexes' in the very process.

One of the results of Kernberg's work on affects is the articulation of vicissitudes of the aggressive drive, which placed the latter on a par with the libidinal drive. Kernberg argues that inborn patterns may activate aggressive behavior and that, on the other hand, aggression in the form of hate builds the self and the psychic systems.

Kernberg effected a reversal of Freud's first and second affect theory in that he regarded affect as transformed into the instincts of libido and aggression, rather than the other way around, i.e., libido transformed into the affect of anxiety or affect being defined as a drive derivative. With this step, Kernberg attempted to accomplish two goals: to complement the missing first part in Jacobson's account of the development of libido and aggression and to provide a model for earliest affective development by theoretically accounting for the crucial function of affects in activating self and object representations. Kernberg's reversal of the respective roles of affects and drives may also be seen as a kind of response to Brierley's and Jacobson's call to improve instinct theory before proceeding to work on affect theory.

If what has been written here on Kernberg looks like a summary of his writings, it is because I found it very difficult to proceed differently in presenting this kind of material. Kernberg's writings on affects are very well organized, and his aim is very clear. Kernberg's interest in affects comes mainly from a theoretical perspective. His objectives in this context are to integrate major existing psychoanalytic theories, to accord the experiential dimension a place in theory, to reconnect affects with their neurophysiological matrix, thereby clarifying the relationship between the affects and the drives, and to connect affects with internalized object relations.

Did he succeed in his tasks? It seems that he did so in great part. Kernberg's affect theory accounts in some important senses for the centrality of affect in life. His concept of 'affective memory' is useful and resonates with similar ideas emerging at present from other quarters (see the Sandlers' concept of the 'past unconscious' and the 'present unconscious,' 1983, or Stern's 'episodic memory,' 1985). Also, Kernberg's conception of the drives as complex structures tallies with most recent formulations in ego psychology as well as in ethology and experimental psychology. His reversal of the roles of affects and drives, through regarding the drives as constructed out of affects, is a very interesting idea, which bears the influence of much contemporary thought concerning the increasing 'psychologization' and decreasing biological determination of the human drives.

Kernberg's version of the concept of the drives, however, is still considerably different from the accepted use of the concept. He regards drives as overall organizations of love and hate, of pleasurable or unpleasurable feelings toward self and objects. This version is very different from prevalent conceptions of the drives as biological motives or, as in more modern drive theories (e.g., Brenner, 1982; G. Klein, 1976; Loewald, 1971), as overall tendencies, purposes toward a goal, and from frameworks that limit and even minimize the importance of the drives or abolish them altogether (e.g., Holt, 1967; Schafer, 1976).

The same tendency to directly translate the biological into the psychological is discernible in Kernberg's use of the terms 'central' and 'peripheral' for different types of emotion theories. This distinction between 'peripheral' and 'central' theories of affect is tenuous and somewhat vague. What in psychology (from which he seems to have borrowed the terms) are called 'central' emotion theories are those theories that hold that there are specific, localized 'emotion centers' in the brain, as opposed to the theories claiming that there are no specific neural mechanisms for generating feeling experiences (see Leventhal (1984) for a very clear discussion of the subject), and that affects are diffusely represented in numerous regions of the brain. Kernberg uses 'central' and 'peripheral' in a different sense, that of denoting whether emotions are motivationally central or whether they are just by-products of physiological processes. As Kernberg is concerned with placing affects within his overall theoretical framework, his theory does not tell us what happens further along in development and what the role of affects is once the developmental stage of structural integration has been reached. In his theoretical model he positioned the affects at the first stage of development out of theoretical considerations, mainly of according the experiential and object-relational dimension of life a place in metapsychology, but it cannot be said that he built a full-scale affect theory. It seems that until now Kernberg has integrated data from psychology and related disciplines that had been obtained in the 1950s and 1960s; the integration with knowledge on affects in neighboring disciplines, as he had hoped to achieve in launching his affect theory (1980), is yet to be attained. Perhaps some of the most recent ideas and researches in psychology and infant research, some of which will be surveyed in this book, may contribute to a further updating and rounding off of Kernberg's psychoanalytic theory of affect.

7
The French School: André Green—
A Discourse on Affects

HISTORICAL BACKGROUND

Beginning in the 1960s, theoretical debates on the problem of affects in France arose mainly as a response to the then very influential work of Jacques Lacan, which had begun to appear a decade earlier. Lacan had attempted what he called a "return to Freud" through the reading of Freud's writings in a new way, which was informed and heavily influenced by certain philosophical and linguistic concepts rooted in French thinking. This was done as a protest against American ego psychology, which Lacan had criticized as biologistic and behavioristically tinged. Lacan claimed that only in reading Freud in an interpretive and linguistic way can one have a correct conception of the unconscious, called by him 'the Other' (1977, p. 142). For Lacan, knowledge or, rather, truth[1] was something that by definition can be written as a kind of logic having a linguistic structure. Hence, he contended, the key to understand the unconscious is to realize that it is structured like a language.

Lacan's work had a tremendous impact on French psychoanalysis at that time (although it later waned, except in some circles, mostly literary ones), and his dictum that "the unconscious is structured in the most radical way like language" (1977, p. 234) led to a widely held belief in linguistics as the only route to the unconscious and to mental functioning. In line with this idea, Lacan had maintained that it was fruitless to try to give affect, which is an expression of undifferentiated psychic functioning, conceptual status (1977, p. 799). Since the basic unit of any structure must be linguistic, in attempting to understand a person (a 'subject') it would be inconceivable to place him outside the functioning of linguistic structures.

In his emphasis on discourse and linguistics, Lacan relied on Saussure's theory, which proposed that language is a system of signs, constituted as a relationship between a signifying component called a 'signifier' (which, according to Saussure, is a physical sound or an image) and a signified (which is the concept or what is meant by it). Lacan adopted this model in his theorizing, in which what are regarded as signifiers are the linguistic elements. For Lacan, the flow of associations consists of a constant flow of signifiers. The signifier, contends Lacan, does not refer to its individual signified (a word in psychoanalysis does not, in his view, refer to a thing), but rather to another signifier, and this in turn refers to another signifier, and so on, in a chain of signifiers. The meaning (the signified) of this series of associations resides not in any association in particular, but in the whole sequence. Thus, unlike British and American psychoanalysis, in which the concept of object relations is used as a basic tool for understanding in the clinical situation, in French psychoanalysis in most cases the model of object relations is overshadowed by that of the signifying relation.

In this climate grew André Green's work, which today comprises the most important and articulate body of ideas on affects in France. Among other things, Green's work is a disclaimer of the strategy of Lacan and his followers, who had excluded affects from psychoanalytic theory and then attempted to explain this move as absolutely necessary on theoretical grounds. Green was initially attracted to some aspects of Lacan's theory, but then he realized that something essential and vital was missing (see his early paper of 1966, translated and reprinted in Smith & Kerrigan, 1983). Green therefore set out to investigate the topic of affects in Freud's writings so as to undo the Lacanian "amputation of affect from the theoretical corpus of psychoanalysis" (see Lacan, 1977, p. 799) and to proceed to build an affect theory of his own.

In addition to this particular concern with affects as a response to Lacan's theory, another direction inspiring Green's interest in the subject of affects has been the perennial discontent of psychoanalysis with existing affect theories. Green felt that after Freud's days affect theory had lagged behind other parts of psychoanalytic theory, which was constantly unfolding and developing. In contrast to significant steps made in other parts of psychoanalytic theory, the handling of the concept of affect had not moved, in Green's eyes, beyond Freud's original models of affect, molded on the neurotic phenomena observed in Freud's patients; the 'broadening scope of psychoanalysis' did not find expression in affect theory.

Green's ideas began to appear in the 1960s in a series of papers. One of them grew into a monograph called *Le Discours Vivant* (The living discourse). It begins with a survey of Freud's models of affect, continues with the taking shape of the concept of affect in the writings of several post-Freudians, goes on to examine affects, rather abstractly, in the clinical situation and in pathological structures not dealt with by Freud, and concludes with Green's own model, which, as he says, draws mainly on the ideas of three authors: Freud, Melanie Klein, and Jacques Lacan.

In presenting my reading of Green's work on affects, published mostly in French, I have summarized, reorganized, and partly simplified his views and thoughts, which are couched in an occasionally elliptic style and in terms steeped in the traditional French usage of Cartesian and German philosophy and structuralist theories. This intellectual background explains Green's basic interest in the structure of affects (rather than in their function or evolution) and also his interest in tracing the multifarious forms in which affect manifests itself as a part of mental functioning. In line with Green's structural, ahistorical approach, my presentation of his ideas will be an exposition intended at clarification of some of his ideas (the wealth of which obliged me to be highly selective in the short space available here), rather than a historical account of these ideas.

Green's main interest and the thrust of his work have been to give affects the same representational status that accrues to ideas and, concomitantly, to preserve and strengthen the notion of the unconscious in psychoanalytic theory. He therefore opposed Lacan's tendency to use a model of analytic communication whose paradigm is language, which excludes affects and body states. In agreement with several other analysts in France, notably Viderman, David, Bouvet, and Mallet, Green considered Lacan's model as incapable of accounting for the obvious fact of the central and vital role of affects in clinical experience and practice. Admittedly, the analysand makes himself known mainly by words; however, taking language as the sole frame of reference for the unconscious creates a situation in which words are meant to communicate something that by definition cannot be strictly translated into words. Green believes that it is unjustifiable to give identical meaning to the same words told once and then retold, because the state of mind in which they had been originally uttered is different from the later one (1977, p. 147). States of mind spring from the unconscious, which, however, is *not* constituted like language. Whereas language is a homogeneous body, a unified structure, consisting of phonemes, words, and sentences, the unconscious is made up of heterogeneous elements and "speaks more than one dialect" (Freud, 1913, quoted by Green, 1977).

In the unconscious, writes Green, there exist 'meaning chains,' which are concatenations made up of representations of things, words, affects, body states, and actions. All of these various elements are regarded as semantic meaning units. Within such a chain, affect has a full semantic function and is equivalent to the other elements of meaning (signifiers) in the unconscious. These elements taken together set up a flowing, ever-present chain of signification. This chain is not linear, as is language, but polygraphic and polysemic; that is, it has multiple forms and meanings, as has the unconscious itself, in which psychic material is coded in diverse keys. Green regards affect as having the same status as language, which is likewise a product of psychic work; both have the function of representation, which Green deems the fundamental and most profound psychic activity.

But the situation is even more complex. Up to this point, we have been discussing one type of affect, whereas Green belongs to the group of investigators who postulate the existence of two types of affect (e.g., Schur, 1966). According to Green, there is one type of affect that is a meaning carrier,[2] an elaborated psychic product, a signifier, like other meaning bearers of discourse, to whose chain and flow it adapts, while there is yet another type of affect that is intense and qualitatively different, which overflows the unconscious chain of meaning and breaks the 'sense-making structures,' as Green calls them. Under such circumstances, affect is no longer a signal or a symbol, but disruptive energy, chaining the self, "clasping it tight, in pleasure or in pain" (Green, 1973, p. 286); it invades and dominates the realm of consciousness, until eventually no space is left for any other psychic activity.

Green notes that Freud entertained two different views on affect, whose compatibility is problematic. I shall call them the one-dimensional and the two-dimensional definitions, respectively (recently, Green abandoned this division of affects and turned more directly to the question of representation [see 1984, p. 774]).

In the first definition, affect is a concept designating a quantity or sum of excitation, capable of quantitative and topographical change, which is distributed over the mnemic traces like an electric charge (Freud, 1894, p. 60). In this conception affect corresponds to an energic affectation, that of a mobile, variable, transformable, and dischargeable quantity. These characteristics account for the mobility and tranformability of affect, but not for its other aspect, its quality, its experientiality, nor for the different degrees of consciousness involved in affect.

The second definition of affect appears under various forms in Freud's work (e.g., 1915b, p. 152), but it always has two clearly distinguishable parts: (1) discharge, oriented toward the interior of the body, and (2) feelings (emotions, in French), which are either perceptions of internal movements of the body or those direct sensations of pleasure and unpleasure that endow each affect with its uniqueness and specificity. Unlike the former definition, this definition reckons with two dimensions of affect, a bodily, mainly visceral reaction and a psychic dimension, itself comprised of a self-observing activity of inner physiological changes and sensations of qualities of pleasure and unpleasure. Affect is regarded as both a bodily and a psychological experience, the former being the condition for the latter. This idea is taken up and elaborated by Green, mainly around the notions of bodily passivity and reflexiveness, which he sees as a kind of falling back upon oneself when in the process of feeling. Green stresses the passivity of the body in affect, at least in some of the phases of affect. The body in affect, he says, is an object and is acted upon, and Green's effort is directed at seizing the experience of those moments. In his words (1973, p. 221; my translation): "The body is not the subject of an action, but the object of a passion," and "Affect is the look at the 'moved' or 'emoted' body ("L'affect est regard sur le corps ému").

Green adopts as a central conception Freud's definition of affect which differentiates affect from idea (in contrast to Freud's former view of affect as the quantity that charges an idea with intensity) and Freud's consideration of affect as a separate entity, as another element representing instinct (1915b, p. 152).

Consistent with Green's view that affects have their own representations, which are more tightly linked to the body that those of ideas, Green dissects this passage of Freud into three parts, which, put in the first person, would read: 'I,' 'my body,' and 'its speaking' (to me). In affect, writes Green, 'my body speaks itself to me'; when I am feeling, I possess my body, but at that same moment, the body is also its own speaker, and the three terms join together and link my possession ('my'), the object of this possession ('body'), and that which denies my possession ('it speaks'—and in that it is its own master, or speaker, thereby denying my possession of itself).

At this point Green introduces the idea, taken from Lacan, of the imaginary mode, linked with the mirror stage. According to Lacan, a whole mode of mental functioning is organized around the (estranged) image of oneself as identified with one's reflection in the mirror, whose effect is to show, to present the subject to himself as another, so that one becomes the other, or another, to oneself. In being mirrored, one feels toward oneself what one would feel toward an object. What Lacan stressed in the role of the image (1977, pp. 1–7) seems to Green to be very much the case with affects. "Affect is an object of almost hypnotic fascination for the ego," writes Green, for it reflects oneself to oneself (1973, p. 224).

Such passages illustrate the fact that Green's affect theory is not object-oriented in the usual sense; rather, it seems to be a theory based on the assumption of primary narcissism (see Green, 1967), in which affects are seen as narcissistic phenomena in the sense that they serve for self-reflection and self-mirroring. At several points, Green indeed links affects with narcissistic phenomena and with identification, mostly primary identification. In identification, writes Green, there is suppression of representations of objects and perceptions of the outside. In this state, there is no awareness of an object 'out there,' but rather the knowledge of tension and of inner movement that comes from the 'body-unconscious.'

This brings us to the cardinal issue of the relationship between the unconscious and affects. Green maintained, like some ego psychologists (see the 1973 panel of the American Psychoanalytic Association), that affects are situated between two thresholds of consciousness that delimit different intensities. When affect is above the first threshold, it attains consciousness and enlivens and enlarges the field of perception. When it surpasses the second threshold, however, affect disturbs consciousness; it has now become a blind and blinding force that does not leave much space for any other psychical activity. According to this description, the awareness of affect is thus limited by two thresholds; it is delimited by two kinds of unconsciousness: the body (the so-called physiological unconscious) and the ego grown blind. In the clinical situation, writes Green, whenever an affect appears suddenly and unexpectedly, it may be assumed to spring from the unconscious. In his words,

Something has been activated, in the interior or exterior, which cuts across and shakes the patient's organization, breaking the repression barrier. These are moments of surprise when the Unconscious reveals itself through the affect. The non-possession of the body by consciousness, the powerlessness of the ego, are starkly exposed at such moments in which the experience that occurs may be put thus: "I am affected, therefore I do not belong to myself" (1973, p. 223).

In these states, the subject appears to himself as an other; he is not recognizable to himself, being placed outside himself and experiencing the power of the unconscious erupting. The 'otherness' is immediate, and understanding and explanation follow later ('après coup' in French, 'nachtraeglich' in German, see Freud, 1918 [1914], pp. 37–38).

Green contends, however, that the concept of the unconscious cannot explain the essence of the affective event, its experienced quality, and the continuous transformations between pleasure and unpleasure that it undergoes. The particular quality of pleasure and unpleasure characterizes each separate affect and endows it with a unique quality among the other affects. The unconscious cannot explain the essence of affect because it is comprised of a whole gamut of pleasure states, but not unpleasure. The contrary of pleasure, like the contrary of anything else, cannot exist in the unconscious; the unconscious, which is the repository of contents, can bear no contradictions and hence no opposites. Green feels strongly that we need a conceptual construct for dealing with unconscious rules (not only unconscious contents), which will enable us to deal more fully with unconscious structures. A concept is needed that will include markers of contradiction and difference between states of feeling and that will account for the registration of the ebb and flow and the fine gradations and nuances of feelings.

This concept is that of the system id. Pleasure states are located in the unconscious, but the formation of these states can be understood, in Green's view, only by going deeper than the unconscious—to the id. In the unconscious, writes Green, there are only the wish and repression and the pleasure principle. The unconscious, as Freud discovered in 1900 and later, is the locus of repressed representations and the seat of symbolic processes, but it has no gradations among qualities of affects. Freud felt that his topographical theory with its concept of the unconscious failed to elucidate the nature of unconscious processes and to describe a refined, affective subsystem, such as is evident in the clinical situation, and he consequently turned from the topographical (or what the French call the first topographical) theory to the structural (or second topographical) theory.

By taking this step of giving the concept of the id center stage, Green follows the general trend in French psychoanalysis, inspired by structuralism, of which Green is a representative. Thus, Green explicitly states that the aim of psychoanalysis is gaining access to the most fundamental system that regulates the basic functions of the psychic apparatus, which to him is the id.

Green regards the unconscious as experience-near and as governed by primary process thinking and by the pleasure principle, whereas he maintains that the id is characterized by impersonality and spatial nondelimitation. The manifestations of the id are condensation, displacement, and the use of special symbols. Green reiterates Freud's statement to the effect that the id is contentless, that is, neutral as to what it contains. While in the unconscious there are both affects and representations, in the id there reign the diverse motions and movements of the contradictory drives themselves. The id, in Green's view, is fundamentally structured around the tension between the life and death instincts, and these contradictory impulses constantly seek discharge.

According to Green, the borders between the id and the ego in the structural theory are more fluid than those between the Ucs and the Pcs in the topographical theory. Fragments of the id can be taken up by the ego; these fragments from the id are made of material that makes it impossible to separate affect from representation. There is permeability and movement between the ego and the id; the id continually and tracelessly traverses the ego, leaving some of its elements there, while the other elements fall back to its domain, 'hoping,' as Green puts it, to become affectively and ideationally represented at some other time, in this never-ending search for form and representation.

The policy of sharply distinguishing between the unconscious as the seat of pleasure and the id as the seat of the drives that represent a demand for psychic work helps Green with the problem of the double edge of affects. It accommodates, on the one hand, the unruly, pleasure-seeking character of affects and, on the other hand, the fact of their obedience to structures and rules. This dual nature of affects makes them amenable to being experienced in contradictory ways. Another problem about which Green is concerned, however, still remains unsolved, and that is the problem of the representation of affect.

Freud's structural theory indeed accorded affects a more prominent role than they had in topographical theory, and the concept of 'Affektrepraesentanz,' which was coined within the structural framework, attests to this change. But this concept always seemed to Freud basically a conceptual contradiction, a paradox in terms, because the id as it is defined has no notion of representation embodied in it. Green, from a perspective that regards Freud's affect theory as an increasing refinement in conceptualizing the representation of affects (even at the cost of other mental elements, such as ideas ['Vorstellungen']), asks how the central problem of affect representation is to be solved with the concept of the id.

The answer, to his mind, lies in the concept of the drives. The concept of the id in Freud's theory is supported by that of the drives, and Green chooses as his starting point in this task one of Freud's definitions of the drives, namely, that of the demand made by the body on the mind for work. Green then stipulates a sequence of transformations from the more organic to the more psychic functions. The beginning of this process of 'psychization' is the drive, and the end point of the sequence is a product that contains both the word representation and the affect. In Green's view, the essence of psychic work is constructing and elaborating representations (by representation here is meant what we today call representation, as contrasted with the English translation ['idea'] of the German 'Vorstellung'). Representation is therefore of the most profound importance in Green's model of the mind.

Concerning representations, there is an important distinction of Freud's that Green feels to be pertinent to the issues he deals with. Freud distinguished between the psychic 'representant' of the drive and the drive representation proper. The drive representation is too undifferentiated to function as a representation in the psychological sense of the term; it comprises both the idea and the quantum of affect. It can be best pictured as a mixture whose elements can be separated only under the influence of repression; basically, it is closer to the drive. The 'representant,' by contrast, is more 'psychical' than the drive at its source, although less than the representation proper. In Freud's writings (1933 [1932], pp. 73, 145) the primary psychic representation, the 'representant,' has nothing to do with the representation in the sense of idea ('Vorstellung') or, more generally, with any notion implying a separation between the idea and the energic affective element; it is rather a kind of force, or vector, directed from the body to the mind, which can be interpreted as a demand for psychic work.

The 'representants' dwell in what Green calls 'matrices of experience,' which are formed by a process of 'primary symbolization.' In these matrices, affects and ideas are indistinguishable (henceforward, I shall call representations in the sense of ideas, i.e., Freud's 'Vorstellungen,' ideas, while preserving the term 'representation' for its habitual usage, that of representation [of something]). The 'matrices of experience' are formed on the basis of a kind of 'primary logic,' which is expressed in a so-called minimal unconscious semantic (whose rules are detailed by Green through a vast and imaginative array of defense mechanisms and primary process transformations [1977, p. 152]). These mechanisms, or figures, of primary thinking (Green calls them 'psychoanalytic rhetoric') are the means to symbolize states of absence of the object or of chaos (absence of meaning) that cannot be put into words. This area, to Green's mind, is one in need of further research and one in which fresh knowledge is most likely to come up.

The next step in the process of representation of the drives, which Green calls 'secondary symbolization' or 'psychization,' differentiates two kinds of drive representations: affect and idea. The differences between affects and ideas are several:

1. Ideas possess what Green calls a 'double relaying'; i.e., they have both thing- and word-representations. Affects lack such a double relaying; they represent only body states. In fact, affects, according to Green, constitute a bodily language of mnemic traces, and they may be said to be essentially perceptions of movements between pleasure and unpleasure in all their gradations. Affects cannot be represented as something considered outside of themselves; they always turn back upon themselves (see Green's 'retournement,' usually translated as 'reversal,' 1973, p. 304). In this sense, affects have an inherently narcissistic or self-referring quality and are profoundly linked with identificatory processes and with self-perception.

2. Ideas can also exist in the absence of perceptions, in which case ideas are substituted for perceptions (1984, pp. 773, 782); hence they are called 'representations' ('Vorstellungen,' which strongly evokes the imaginative, substitutive—in short, representative—aspect of ideas) in Freud's theory. This means that we can have either perceptions or representations; we can perceive objects in the outer world or entertain thoughts about them. Affects, by contrast, exist without a specific outside referent; they refer, simultaneously or alternately, to both internal and external situations. As Green put it (personal communication, 1985), representations (in the sense of ideas) are *of* something, while affects represent (the person's body) *for* the person; they reflect back on himself. This could be put in yet another way:

3. Affects present the drives to the psyche in a parallel way to ideas, but whereas the latter are additionally represented by words, i.e., by language, affects are not further represented, i.e., substituted or symbolized.

Green regards affects and ideas as homologous in representing the drives, being of equal importance. The erroneous notion that affects are inferior in their conceptual status may stem, in Green's view, from a faulty reading of Freud. Green's overview of Freud's affect theories concludes with the statement that affects became increasingly important in Freud's theory, until finally, in his structural theory (which Green calls, consistently with his approach, the second topographical or last drive theory), Freud definitely reversed the balance between affects and ideas in favor of affects. This important fact has been overlooked in all critical readings of Freud, writes Green. We have the means now to uphold this ignored major shift of emphasis in Freud's theory and to use it productively, on condition that we discard the assumption made by Freud to the effect that "all representations originate from perceptions and are repetitions of them" (1925, p. 237; see my discussion of the problem with this idea in chapter 1). Green considers this assumption erroneous in that it excludes affects, which originate from within, from the domain of representations in the general sense. Today, writes Green, we would accord a much greater role to affects in the transformation and even in the creation of mnemic traces. Not only outer perceptions, but affective traces as well, create representations, even before the psychic apparatus arrives at the stage where it is able to register outer perceptions. The point made here by Green is of tremendous theoretical importance, and I shall return to it later in this study.

This discussion brings us to the issue of the relation between affect and memory, or between affect and reproduction. Affect, according to Freud as interpreted by Green, does not 'belong' to outer perceptions; affect is not an emotional experience in vivo, but the reproduction of one. It is essentially a residue, aroused by repetition, a kind of memory of some experience (see the *Project*, 1895 [1950], p. 320), and it only indirectly refers to, or relies upon, external or fresh impressions. This idea is a central tenet in Green's theory, which relies heavily on Freud's *Project*.

To this conception Green adds the idea that, although affect is essentially a reproduction and a trace, it can have a representation of its own. The hypothesis that an affective trace creates representations is Green's major point of divergence from the later Freud (1923, 1925). Green contends that affective representations present one's body states to oneself; they are a kind of 'emoting' of the body. In this sense, affect is reflexive and even reflective. It reflects on what has been experienced in a delayed manner ('nachtraeglich,' after the fact; 'après coup' in French). Hence, the moment of experience and the moment of meaning or signification never coincide, the latter always being retroactive. In this context, affect is the signification of an experience by the liberation of a desire or of accumulated experience (the term 'liberation' is taken from the world of discourse of the *Project*, and it seems to be a nice way of synthesizing a statement of the early Freud with another, more experience-near term for 'discharge'). By its liberation, the affect comes to signify the experience.

From all this, we can see that affects are much more complex than a cursory glance would indicate. In fact, Green regards this complexity as the major problem in the psychoanalytic conceptualization of affect. He deplores the fact that the concept of affect, which is indeed "highly composite" (Freud, 1916–1917, p. 395), has been grossly oversimplified, and he criticizes American psychoanalytic theories of affect for obliterating many of the finer distinctions arrived at by Freud. These theories, in his opinion, fail to make the basic distinction, for instance, between the 'idea' as an integral part of feelings and what is conventionally called an idea ('Vorstellung,' or representation), an error Green claims to find in Brenner's theory of affect, for instance (for more on this point, see my discussion of Leventhal's theory in Chapter 8). Other, perhaps related, criticisms leveled by Green against these theories are their strong focus on the concept of adaptation, to which affects have a very tenuous relationship in his view, and their pushing affect back to the biological domain, thereby evading the conceptualization of psychic functioning. The perspective offered by this type of theories is coupled, in his view, with an extremely restrictive concept of 'object.' The essence of his argument against object relation theorists is their neglect, in his opinion, of the 'relation' in the object relation; the 'relation,' to Green's mind, is more important than the object per se (1975).

These views expressed by Green are linked with his conviction that psychoanalysis can never be a developmental or general theory; its scope is, and should be, limited to inner psychic reality, that is, to the exclusive dealing with drives (as sources) and with desires (as aims and as objects). After having rejected at length the tenets of ego psychology, Green draws on Kleinian and Lacanian theories as sources of inspiration for the construction of a model that attempts to link affect to external circumstances, to experience and its effects, and to the self in its relation to the object (see the appendix in Green, 1973, pp. 309–46).

RECAPITULATION

To clarify Green's complex approach to affect still further, let me retrace some of the steps in his reasoning. This time I shall base myself mainly on his later works, notably his 1977 paper presented at the 30th International Congress in Jerusalem and on his papers of 1975 and 1984. In the first part of his 1977 paper, Green tries to reach, with a kind of fascination, into the most obscure regions within psychoanalytic theory. Studying Freud's references to affects, he makes the point that, although Freudian theory had accorded an ever greater role to the concept of affect (a fact he claims has been overlooked to an amazing degree), psychoanalytic theory was still left with very serious unresolved problems. Green summarizes them as follows:

1. Owing to certain theoretical considerations, particularly Freud's assumption of a necessary link between all representations and verbal signs (1915), and between representations and external perceptions (1925), Freud was prevented from giving affects a representational status. Such a status, claims Green, is precisely what is needed as a prerequisite for a theory of affect.

2. Throughout his writings, Freud consistently subordinated the subjective, experiential dimension of affects to their energic, 'objective,' quantitative aspect. Consequently, theorizing on the qualitative (subjective) aspect of affect remained greatly neglected.

One way out of these difficulties is to reject affects altogether as unfit for theorizing, as Lacan did. Green rejects this approach as unacceptable, for the reason that linguistic rules and structures can in no way supply us with a satisfying analogue for all mental functioning, which is the aim of psychoanalytic theory as he sees it. Consequently, Green approaches these two major problems (the 'subjective' and the 'representational') in the following way.

First we discuss the treatment of the representational problem. Green begins by postulating that the unconscious consists of 'meaning chains,' which are necessarily nonlinguistic. These are concatenations of various elements that all carry meanings: words and feelings, thing-representations, bodily gestures and signs, and motor actions. All of these participate in a 'polyphony' of meanings orchestrated in the unconscious, in an ongoing 'living discourse.' Here, affect appears in its semantic, intra-communicative function.

In placing affect in the unconscious, which is conceived as the locus of all kinds of representations, Green has put affect in the representational domain in a definite and general manner. Now there remained for him the problem of the specific structure of affect, which to him is indissolubly linked with the drives. In his view, based on some of Freud's definitions of the unconscious, the latter cannot sufficiently explain the links between affects and drives, nor the ever-changing qualities of the affects. To this end, the concept of the id is necessary, says Green, and he suggests that with the aid of the structural concept of the id, which is the seat of the drives, affects can be given structure. Furthermore, in the id, affects can be linked with the continual psychic work (of elaborations and transformations) that the body demands of the psyche through the mediation of the drives.

It may be said that Green's is an id theory of affect, based on the concept of

the drives as the sources of affects, which the affects represent. The concepts
of the id and of the drives are the mechanisms that generate and help us explain
what Green calls the qualitative transformations of the affects, which represent
the demand for psychic work. Linked with this is the view that the role of the
ego is not that of the neutralization of affects, because their transformations are
effected in the id by the drives, but their so-called chaining ('mise-en-chaîne'),
that is, their submission to an organization. The inherent tension between two
basic organizational levels also involves the most profound problems of affect.
The issue is the relationship between the dimension of discharge or force of
affect (the less organized level) and its dimension of meaning (the more organized
level). In this context, the aim of the unconscious is dual; it transforms meaning
into a quality-less, biological quantity and then discharges it, and it also transforms or translates one meaning into another, within the constant chaining of
meaning in the unconscious.

Green suggests that although Freud did not separate the two dimensions of
affect because of his wish to preserve the idea of the complexity of affects, we
could, at this stage of our theoretical development, do so without losing from
view the complexities of the concept. To begin with, he says, we should keep
in mind that the two dimensions, energy or force and meaning or sense, are
ultimately inseparable (see Ricoeur, 1970). Together they constitute, in Green's
poetic words, a "couple linked by a relationship of objective incertitude" (1973,
p. 288). Here Green tries to convey that the manifestation of affects is often
objectively discernible and yet the same time is only partially communicable
(see also 1977, p. 129).

On the level of theory, however, we can clearly and legitimately distinguish
between affect as a force and affect as a meaning bearer (signifier). As a force,
even when it is not disruptive and tempestuous, affect supports the chaining of
representations. It is the force of the affect that starts the association, the linking
of the representations, and propels them forward, and it is this force that supplies
the energy necessary for operating the psychic apparatus. On the other hand,
and at the same time, affect as a carrier of meaning is the agent of the so-called
conjunction and disjunction of the other psychic elements of discourse. In this
role of meaning bearer, affect has the function of what Green calls (under the
influence of Lacan) 'punctuation of the signifier'; it lends the color, the nuances,
and the modulations to the verbal sign. Also, when representations (ideas,
thoughts) are suspended, the flow of meaning continues through the affects,
which then signal the existence of a gap in the sequence of representations.

Green's perspective on affects is profoundly intrapsychic. He seems to conceive of affects as our relationships, our energized relationships, to an experience
and ultimately to ourselves. Affect is seen by Green as a kind of perception of
'otherness' in oneself. This idea, borrowed from Lacan's framework and applied
to the affects, is meant to convey that when in an emotional state (and Green
repeatedly speaks of a person 'in' emotion), a person is beside himself. The
person in such a state glimpses another part inhabiting his self in his inner

surround; he perceives 'the other,' that is, the unconscious, in himself, and it is in the psychoanalytic discourse that this 'otherness' becomes most discernible and poignant.

DISCUSSION

Green's theory of affect is a scholarly, large-scale attempt at a synthesis of many ideas from various sources. Its aim is to provide the concept of affect with a secure theoretical basis and to put it on equal footing with other psychic processes and products of the mental apparatus that carry meaning and do or demand 'psychic work.'

The challenge Green feels should be met in such a task is threefold:

1. To undo the arrest in theorizing on affects that has existed since Freud assumed that only phenomena linked with perception could be considered representations. Freud's postulate did not enable affects to be regarded as dissociated from outer perceptions, to be the representations of anything.

2. To counter Lacan's influence in excluding affects from psychoanalytic theory just because they are not linguistic phenomena.

3. To conceptualize affects in accordance with the broadening scope of psychoanalysis, which now accommodates nonneurotic disturbances of thinking and of mental functioning (as elaborated, for instance, in the work of Winnicott and Bion).

For this purpose, Green investigated the structure of affect within the different phases of psychoanalytic theory. In this view, affect has successively grown in importance over the developing stages of psychoanalytic thinking, in which progressive thrusts were made further into psychic reality, into deeper layers of the mind. Green sees this thrust as moving from external, 'historical' reality through object relations to intrapsychic mental functioning and primary narcissism (1975, p. 9).

Basically, Green considers affects as representations of the drives, on a par with ideas, as postulated by Freud in 1915. He then adds the assumption of the role of the id as being, via the drives, a structuralizing agent of the affects. The ego is seen as binding the affects and putting them within an ongoing chain of meanings, an internal discourse, assumed to be incessantly going on in the unconscious. Given their mercuriality, affects cut across several domains of mental functioning (e.g., the ego, the id).

Green elaborates the idea that affects have their own representations. Affects, in his view, are independent of outer perceptions and represent oneself (particularly one's body-self) to oneself. This is their essential and profound meaning and function. Sometimes, however, the affects exceed a certain threshold and become extremely powerful and disruptive. It is the coupling of force and meaning that accounts for difficult theoretical problems concerning the affects—the fact that affects are both discursive (meaningful and communicative, a kind of sign system) and at the same time peremptory and arousing to the point of disorganization.

Recently, Green has emphasized in his writings a picture of mental functioning within a delimited space. Here he acknowledges the influence of Bion and of the French psychosomatic school (e.g., Marty, de M'Uzan), who are concerned with disturbances of thinking and symbolization. All this has important implications for affect theory, particularly after Green elevated the concept of affect to that of symbol.

8
Recent Trends in Affect Theories
in Psychology

This chapter deals with theories of emotion in psychology. My approach here is different from the one I have chosen toward psychoanalytic theories. The reasons for this difference are two: the first has to do with my unequal interest in the two areas, and the second results from the different character of the theories in each. As the main interest of this book lies in psychoanalysis, the treatment of psychoanalytic theories of affect has been understandably more expanded and explicatory. Psychological theories of emotion serve in this framework mainly as indicators of the directions of thought and types of concepts obtaining today in this adjacent field.[1]

Another point is the different structure of psychoanalytic and psychological theories. Roughly speaking, psychoanalytic theories seem to be in the nature of general, holistic models of mental functioning, whereas psychological theories are based on a more circumscribed view of systems and their functions. To put affect theories in psychoanalysis in an understandable form, one needs to outline the whole, or at least a great part, of the theoretical web surrounding a particular theory. By contrast, in psychology, for historical and for other reasons (e.g., criteria of acceptability of research paradigms), there have always existed rather partitioned areas of investigation and of theorizing; learning, perception, motivation, and, recently, emotion refer to separate realms of knowledge and theory, and each is considered a different domain for investigation.

There is ample evidence indicating that the concept of emotion is being accorded increasing importance in psychological thinking, and the domain of emotions and their study is rapidly expanding. New and more comprehensive theories are being formulated, important symposia (some of them interdisciplinary) are being held, and intensive research is being devoted to the subject. In particular, increasing attention is being given to the adaptive and subjective value of emotions. Many authors have noted that emotions gained significantly more attention in the 1980s than they had, for instance, in the 1960s (see the 17th annual Carnegie Symposium on Cognition, 1982). This fact is attributed to the changing intellectual climate, which no longer allows emotion theories to "remain . . . on the edge of things" (Izard, 1982; A. Cooper [1986] in psychoanalysis also talks about the 'new romanticism' as a zeitgeist, expressing the same idea, namely, that we are witnessing the inception of a general paradigm more receptive to the phenomena of feelings).

It is unfeasible here to attempt to cover all theories of emotion in psychology. There are some reviews of extant emotion theories, such as those of Plutchik (1980), Clark & Fiske (1982), Pliner, Blankenstein, & Spiegel (1979), and Knapp (1987). These reviews are on different levels of sophistication and updatedness, and the interested reader is referred to them. I have chosen here, out of a huge number of models and theories, those theories that seemed to me the most central or typical or that I found useful or cognate to important theories of affect in psychoanalysis.

An initial assessment of some of these theories immediately brings to light an obvious characteristic of theirs. Theories of emotion, like theories in other realms of academic psychology, have been heavily suffused with evolutionary and biologically oriented formulations. These theories have revolved around comparative anatomical and physiological research or investigations of expressive patterns that were supposed to inhere universally in emotions, or they have attempted to define so-called basic emotional reactions to stimuli. Plutchik, Tomkins, Izard, Scott, Pribram, Chance, most of the contributors to Pliner, Blankenstein, and Spiegel (1979), and many more hold such a position, which shall henceforward be called *position A*. One may get the impression, on reading the literature on emotions, that this is the true and most representative face of psychological theories of emotion. When one encounters this type of theory, which is built on simplistic, biologically based conceptions of emotions, after encountering theories of affect in psychoanalysis that are steeped in and aided by powerful and sophisticated concepts such as fantasies, defenses against emotions, and postulated goals of well-being and feeling-homeostasis, one may feel somewhat disappointed with this picture of thought on affect today. It does not look as if this type of psychological theory could offer much by way of enlarging our understanding of the psychodynamic role and the subjectively felt aspect of affects, which are the concern of psychoanalysis.

Another look, however, reveals a vast field with different and more useful—and exciting—ideas and formulations on the concept of affect. Here we no longer have to deal solely with theories and ideas based on premises that are rather irrelevant to those of psychoanalytic theory and practice. This alternative theoretical orientation to emotion in psychology, which I shall call *position B*, is cognitively, socially, and experientially oriented. Most notable among the authors of this trend are Arnold, Lazarus, Leventhal, Mandler, Averill, Scherer, and others.

A quick comparison of these two positions shows that whereas position A uses key concepts such as evolution, drives, and sometimes even instincts, primary innate emotions, and physiological and pharmacological experiments on animals, position B is a discourse and a research enterprise involving such concepts as cognitive appraisals and evaluations, values and interpretations, and social role enactments. It could be said that position A bears an affinity to some metapsychological formulations of the early days of psychoanalysis, such as accumulation and discharge of energy, emotions as innate dispositions that are phylogenetically transmitted and instinctually derived, and so on. On the other hand, the concepts current in position B have an affinity to later psychoanalytic concepts, such as conscious and unconscious fantasy, affect signals and affective values, affect complexes, affective structures, and so on. Position B regards emotions as many-leveled systems or complex 'syndromes' and as being at the same time highly evolved individual structures that transcend wired-in programs. What is similar in both positions, however, is the significance both of them attach to biological substrata and mechanisms and to physiological changes, and sometimes also to the communicative aspect of emotions, although these are placed in a different context in each position. In the light of these basic differences, an axis of division will be drawn between phylogenetically and cognitively oriented emotion theories.

In what follows, I shall try to elucidate some of the main tenets and elaborations in each of the demarcated positions, but my presentation of these positions will not be evenhanded. Animal research, 'emotions' induced in the laboratory, and the tracing of facial or bodily expressive patterns are less interesting for the orientation of this study than, for instance, the way cognitions, beliefs, and fantasies interact with feelings or, to take another example, the contrast between continuity (such as self states, feeling states, the so-called background of safety or anxiety), on the one hand, and interruption, irruption, and impulsivity, and so on, on the other. Having clarified the direction of this chapter, let us begin with what we have called position A.

POSITION A: EVOLUTIONARY THEORIES OF EMOTION IN PSYCHOLOGY

Position A is based on the evolutionary viewpoint; it derives from Darwin's work, which has framed, and still frames, a whole tradition. Darwin asserted that emotions evolved with particular functions, all centered around increasing the chances of survival; survival is enhanced by communicating information via the emotions from one animal to another. Expression and communication of emotions thus increase the probability of adaptive behavior by preparing the organism for action. Thus, within this framework, emotions are basically adaptive and help to organize the animal's behavior in accordance with the demands of the environment.

In this framework, the biology of the emotions is accorded great importance. It is assumed that psychological phenomena cannot be understood without specifying the underlying physiological processes and, if possible, isolating and localizing the structures involved. Proponents of this view see the study of the physiology of emotion as the best road to an understanding of emotion. Within the biology, or rather the physiology, of emotion, a controversy has been going on between so-called peripheralists and centralists; while the former (following the tradition of James) attributed the main sources for emotional behavior to the viscera or the autonomic nervous system, the latter (in line with Cannon's refutation of James's theory and MacLean's brain theory of emotion) regarded emotion as activated and controlled mainly by the cortex. With time, the extremes of both positions were discarded by most theoreticians, and it was realized that both are relevant and contain useful knowledge. The question then became one of the interaction between the two systems—the cortical and the autonomic—in the generation of emotions.

Upon these premises, Robert Plutchik (1962, 1980, 1984) has conceptualized emotions as processes of behavioral homeostasis and fundamental signaling systems that are derivatives of certain prototypical life situations. Plutchik has developed a model of eight basic emotions that are assumed to play a major adaptive role and can be combined in numerous ways to produce manifold observable 'states.' Plutchik uses 'states' in a broad sense to mean not only situations, but also personality traits, coping styles, and defenses.

Plutchik positions these eight basic emotions in a circular model, in which what he considers opposite emotions are placed across from one another, whereas adjacent emotions blend into each other. Plutchik reports that this circular model was obtained and tested by empirical ratings of degrees of similarity and intensity of lexical emotion terms. Notwithstanding the esthetic appeal of Plutchik's construction, one wonders whether the elemental emotions he chooses are not too neatly and arbitrarily packaged; whether transitory or long-standing, automatic or nuanced, all emotional varieties in his classification receive an equal place, without regard for the different mechanisms underlying them and the roles they play. Nevertheless, Plutchik has done important work in reviewing extant emotion theories under the aegis of the evolutionary perspective and in attempting to align other theories of emotion with his own framework, and he has kept in close touch with new theories that are being developed outside his area of theoretical commitment.

Just as Plutchik has defined and updated Darwinian ideas, J. P. Scott (1980), in his systems theory analysis, presents a view that is essentially a refinement of old instinct theories. Scott rejects the view of emotions as mechanical and automatic; instead, he sees them as flexible and differentially adaptive to internal and external circumstances. Emotions, in his view, do not have a single, overarching function but serve many different purposes, and no emotion can be taken as a model for all the other emotions. Scott, like most theoreticians of his type, conceives of a small number of primary emotions, to which new emotions are added only when they prove to be of paramount importance from an evolutionary perspective. According to Scott, emotions are variously linked to the different behavioral systems of the organism, and their functions vary according to the level of systems organization in which they appear. Scott proposes nine classes of social behaviors and assumes that emotions are functionally related to these nine systems. He supports his model with experimental evidence from his research on dogs and other animal experimental data.

Scott claims that there is no hard-and-fast line between emotions and sensations—the two grade into each other and form a continuum—and that there usually are no specific physiological mechanisms or brain localizations responsible for each specific emotion.

Like Plutchik, Scott attempts a systematic ordering of the emotions he regards as most basic. Although his theoretical system impresses one as more sophisticated than Plutchik's, it remains under the exclusive impact of evolutionary ways of thinking, and he makes no substantial distinction between man and animal.

Other authors, such as the ethologist I. Eibl-Eibesfeldt (1972, 1981), regard the expressive patterns of emotions as playing a major role in controlling human relationships. Eibl-Eibesfeldt maintains that certain basic strategies of social interaction are innate and universally observable in human groups. He has conducted extensive studies on small, preliterate societies and found that there are universal facial-expressive movements that are a blend of positive and negative emotions and that act as unconscious signals aimed at maintaining existing social positions. Following Konrad Lorenz, he regards what he calls 'affective expressions' as composed of fixed action patterns. This view subsumes affects under the category that, in ethology, has traditionally been reserved for instincts. In fact, the basic theoretical project of another worker in this perspective, M. Chance (1981), is to draw tight parallels between instincts or their analogues (such as innate releasing mechanisms) and affects. Chance discusses his assumption that fixed action patterns are enacted by children, while in adults they are combined in various ways with verbalizations. He emphasizes the importance of social context (in the sense of crude animal imitation) on affects.

A central figure in the tradition of biological, although this time neurological rather than evolutionary, theories of emotion is Karl H. Pribram (1967b, 1970, 1980, 1984). On the whole, Pribram's is an outspokenly biological orientation to emotions. His views began with a visceral orientation, but experimental results "quickly disabused" him of such a limited view (see Pribram, 1970). Gradually, he developed a more comprehensive position, which incorporated elements from other emotion theories, particularly Nina Bull's attitude theory (1951) and Magda Arnold's appraisal theory (1960, 1970a). In his own view, however, James's, Lange's, Cannon's, and even medieval theories are to a certain extent all represented in today's more comprehensive models. Pribram's main arguments concern brain organization, and he attempts to show that emotions are localized in certain brain regions rather than in the viscera, as James and his followers thought. Following a discussion of midbrain elements that have been identified in emotional behavior, he proposes that the cortex is the central contributor to emotional behavior, and he gives special weight to memory factors. This view of emotion emphasizes the idea that an emotion is an internal event, not an expressive behavior.

At an earlier stage of his thinking Pribram conceived of emotions in terms of plans, as neural programs that are operated when the organism is disequilibrated. In the 1960s and 1970s, Pribram distinguished between motivations or action tendencies ('go' Plans) and feelings proper, which he saw as engendered and terminated in the body on the interruption of some activity ('stop' Plans). At a later stage of his thinking, however, Pribram realized that there exist certain behavioral dispositions or moods (such as depression, which poses a problem for 'Plan theorists' of emotion) that can hardly be conceived of as Plans; rather, they must be seen as organismic states, or 'Images.' These are not planned beforehand, but some outcome is appraised, and the process of appraisal is monitored, i.e., felt. Hence feelings should be conceptualized as Monitors and as being in the nature of Images rather than Plans. These Images are the matrix within which Plans are formed; both the 'go' Plans making up the motivations of the organism and the 'no-go' (stop) Plans of which emotions are constituted are engendered by Images. The fact that Pribram felt compelled to modify his view and regard many emotional phenomena as images, rather than plans, attests to the profound role of imagery, fantasy, and highly individualized momentary decision processes, which must be reckoned with in any theory of emotion, as we shall see later.

In his 1970 paper, Pribram's focus of inquiry shifted from emotions as motivations to stop an ongoing activity toward their subjective dimension. Feelings are now conceived by him as monitors. Pribram now declares that feelings should be admitted as legitimate entities for study.

The most recent Pribram is still different. Recently (see Scherer & Ekman, 1984), Pribram has presented a so-called neurobehavioral analysis of emotion. He now maintains that current neurophysiological data support a multidimensional view of the organization of emotion. Basing his view on neurophysiological findings, Pribram postulates four major dimensions of emotion, underlying each of which he proposes specific neurophysiological localizations and processes. The four dimensions are his (earlier) distinction between affective (emotional) and effective (motivational) feelings, the dimension of arousal and stability, that of specificity and diffuseness of sensations, and the dimension of "self versus world outside."

Closing his last paper, Pribram sees a basic compatibility between his neurological findings and Plutchik's and Ekman's social-expressive empirical findings. In line with his penchant for sweeping syntheses, Pribram looks hopefully at a possible approaching convergence of results of these different research programs.

In his intellectual autobiography, "The Quest for Primary Motives: Biography and Autobiography of an Idea" (1981), Silvan Tomkins, one of the pioneers in the domain of modern affect theory, speaks of his early intuition about the centrality of affect in mental life. At that time, in the early 1940s, such an intuition was a vague and alien idea, lacking any empirical or theoretical base. The field of affect and emotion was in disrepute at that time, he writes. At that period, Tomkins found cybernetics to be helpful in approaching affects, and in the late 1940s he spoke of the role of the affect mechanism as a separate and central coassembly, amplifying other systems.

In 1962 and 1963 (the years of Schachter & Singer's famous experiment) appeared Tomkins's two-volume book, *Affect, Imagery, Consciousness*, in which he expounded his theory of affects as the primary biological motivating mechanisms, which are more urgent than drive deprivation, pleasure, or physical pain. Tomkins shows how what we usually take to be the most basic drives, e.g., breathing, hunger, or sex, are powerless to affect us if they are not accompanied by the fitting affects. It is from the affects that these drives get their sense of urgency and their sometimes desperate quality of need. The drive must be assisted by affect as an amplifier if it is to work at all.

Hence, the affect system is, in Tomkins's view, the primary motivational system because without its amplification nothing else matters, and with its amplification everything else *can* matter.

Affects are separate from the drives. Both drives and affects, which Tomkins sees as involving body responses quite distinct from the other bodily responses they are presumed to amplify, require general, nonspecific arousal, which Tomkins calls amplification. But the drives have insufficient strength as motives without concurrent specific amplification by the affects. The role of affective amplification is to provide the drives with vital information of time, place, and response, i.e., when and where to do what, in case the body does not know how to help itself otherwise. The primacy of the affects is demonstrated, first, by the fact that the drives require amplification from the affects, whereas the affects are sufficient motivators in the absence of drives (one must be excited to be sexually aroused, but not the other way around). To motivate anyone, it is sufficient to arouse one of the innate affects, writes Tomkins. The primacy of the affects as motives over the drives is also demonstrated by the fact that, in contrast to the specificity of the space-time information of the drive system, the affect system has more general properties, which permit it to assume a central position in the motivation of people. The affect system has the generality of time, rather than the rhythmic specificity of the drive system. The affect system also permits generality and freedom of object, intensity, and duration. Compared with the drives, affects may be either much more casual and low in intensity or much more compelling and intensive. The affect system is so flexible that humans are able to oscillate, writes Tomkins, between affect fickleness and obsessive possession by the object of their affective investment. Furthermore, affects can be used to combine with other affects, to intensify or modulate them and to suppress or reduce them. The freedom of the affect system provides it with its basic power to combine with a variety of other components.

In his 1979 paper on script theory, Tomkins attempts to go beyond affect theory into a broader theory of learning and development, memory, and social life. He speaks here about what he calls 'psychological magnification,' the lifelong process of the expansion of one affective scene in the direction of a connected but somewhat different scene, which may be remembered or anticipated through memory, thought, and imagination. The individual's rules for predicting, interpreting, and controlling a magnified set of scenes comprise his script.[2] The most important element in any script is the most intense and enduring affect, the sharpest change within an affect, and the most frequently repeated sequence of such affect and affect changes.

Tomkins is perhaps best known for his study of, and distinction among, eight, and later nine, innate affects. Each of these has a specific role, together comprising all other affects as variations on them. The positive affects, according to him, are interest or excitement, enjoyment or joy, and surprise or startle. The negative affects are distress or anguish, fear or error, shame or humiliation, contempt, disgust, and anger or rage. The differences among them are accounted for by three general variants of a single principle—namely, the density of neural stimulation (the number of neural firings per unit of time). Tomkins considers the three variables of stimulation increase, stimulation constancy, and stimulation decrease as three discrete classes of activators of affect, each of which further amplifies the sources that activate them. Such a set of mechanisms guarantees sensitivity to whatever is new, whatever continues for any extended period of time, and whatever ceases to occur. In Tomkins's view, affects derive their meaning and their experiential quality from the form of their neural stimulation.

Toward the 1980s and onward, Tomkins modified his theory of 1962–1963 in four essential ways. First, he specified that what he means by affect as amplification is not the general arousal type, but specific analogic amplification. Second, he now believes that it is the skin of the face, rather than the face musculature, that is the major mechanism of analogic amplification. This tallies with his shifting his emphasis from the communicational to the motivational dimension of affects. Investigating the motivating properties of what he considers affect analogues, such as pain, sexual sensitivity, and fatigue, Tomkins found that the most compelling states to which a person is vulnerable arise on the surface of the skin; the skin, rather than 'expressing' internal events, was found to command widespread autonomic changes throughout the body, and it is the feedback of the changes in the skin that provides the feel of specific affects.

Third, Tomkins now believes that a substantial quantity of the affect we experience as adults is pseudo, backed-up, affect. He has recently found that the innate affects, being very high-powered, extremely contagious phenomena, are socially controlled in their free expression, and that hence what is being experienced as affect is not the original, directly transmitted and communicable thing, but what he calls pseudo or backed-up affect (1984, p. 192). He believes that the constant affective control to which we are subjected produces some ambiguity about what affect feels like, as a great part of the adult's affect life represents transformations, attenuations, and even reversals of the innate, spontaneous, simple affect response, and often it is difficult to know when someone is showing a 'genuine' affect, controlling it, or showing a pretended affect.[3]

Fourth, Tomkins found that affect amplifies not only its own activator but also the response to that activator. Thus, a response prompted by enjoyment will be a slow, relaxed response in contrast to a response prompted by anger, which will reflect the increased neural firing characteristic of both the activator of anger and the anger response itself.

In his 1981 paper, Tomkins makes several important points concerning the present state of affect theory in psychology. He notes the radical increase in research projects and publications in this domain, which he thinks indicates that "the next decade or so belongs to affect." But he warns against the danger that the field of affect might be co-opted by other fields in psychology. On the other hand, affect, which is a phenomenon that owes its power to "a massed, conjoint variance that has biologically evolved to capture the human being in just this way," has been 'violated' by methodological purity (1981, p. 316). Thus, research investigating facial expression while keeping all other conjoint affective expressions 'constant' practically failed, because affect is by definition a compound of many elements. Another example is Tomkins's microanalyses of the face through high-speed photography with the hope of yielding 'secrets' of affect and human nature analogous to those the microscope has revealed about biological structures. This research also failed, because, as he writes, "at 10,000 frames a second the smile becomes an interminable bore, forfeiting the vital information which can be seen easily by the naked eye or by conventional slow-motion photography" (p. 314).

Tomkins also rejects cognitive appraisal theories of emotion, and he agrees with Zajonc (1980) that feeling and thinking are two independent mechanisms. To his mind, cognitive theories of affect address only the learned activation of affect, whereas arousal of an affect depends potentially on many sources of activation.

The affect mechanism is distinct from the sensory, motor, memory, cognitive, pain, and drive mechanisms; it is a flexible mechanism, potentially (and loosely) matched to other mechanisms, evolved to play various parts in continually changing assemblies of mechanisms. Affect, however, is also an end in itself, says Tomkins. People, in his view, are basically interested in seeing to it that life will be exciting and enjoyable, and he emphasizes that affect and motivation are not necessarily 'about' something.

Tomkins repeatedly tries to show that the affect mechanism 'works' by virtue of three major conjoint characteristics—urgency, abstractness, and generality.

Urgency is, in Tomkins's eyes, the primary function of affect; its purpose is to make one care by feeling. Affect amplifies by increasing the urgency of anything with which it is coassembled. It is similar to the pain mechanism in that its function is to provide an urgent analogue to some event or 'lesion' that "concentrates the mind powerfully." The urgency of affect is further guaranteed by its syndromelike features and by its involuntary characteristics. Affect is a complex response, a syndrome, so organized neurologically and chemically via the bloodstream that the messages that innervate it innervate all parts at once, or in very rapid succession; hence it offers great resistance to control, like a sneeze or an orgasm. Affects are also aroused easily by factors over which the individual has little control.

Another feature of affects is their generality. Affects can combine with many other systems; they are not dependent on particular times (like the drives), on particular body localizations (like pain), or on particular objects. By virtue of their generality affects can readily coassemble not only with the drives but also with memory, perception, thought, action, and other affects.

In its urgency, the affect system 'insists,' so to speak, that matters are increasing rapidly, are decreasing rapidly, or have increased too much. In its generality, the affect system is capable of extreme combinatorial flexibility with other mechanisms, which it can shape and be shaped by, thereby rendering its abstractness more particular and concrete.

Tomkins occupies a special place in affect theory (and is also increasingly referred to in psychoanalysis today). The changes in his work and outlook on affects reflect historical changes in psychology itself.

During the twenty-five years or so of his work, Tomkins has changed his views on a number of issues concerning affects, most of them in the direction of laying greater stress on the internal subjective, experiential, and motivational aspects relative to the communicational and expressive dimensions. The paradigm has now become that of the skin feeding back to the person the experiential, feeling aspect that 'belongs' to him, which may be a disguised or falsified affect, rather than that of the face musculature gesticulating simple, straightforward affects to others.

Discussion

Those emotion theories in psychology that have received their general outlook from Darwinian thought emphasize the expressive and community functions of emotions. The main difficulty with this position is that it espouses an attitude that does not account for the subjective aspect of emotions and that assumes that emotions can be experienced without the experiencing person's awareness of the mechanisms that create them. Seen in this light, the two strands of theory in this group, the expressive (e.g., Izard, Tomkins, Ekman and Friesen, Eibl-Eibesfeldt) and the physiological (e.g., Plutchik, Pribram, Scott, Chance), each has its shortcomings. As Leventhal notes (in Pliner, Blankenstein, & Spiegel, 1979), expressive theories tend to take emotion itself for granted, and psychological research attempts to describe the pattern of motor change accompanying particular feelings or, alternatively, to determine the adaptive value of a given emotional behavior, speculating about the species history that led to its development.

As to physiological theories of emotion, which regard feedback from motor reactions as the critical factor in the experience of feeling, their position is very problematical because their reliance on visceral (or other physiological) mechanisms of arousal to explain emotions has not withstood the test of more systematic research.

Another point in this area of emotion theories concerns the attempts at the classification of emotions, defenses, and personality traits (e.g., Plutchik, 1960, 1962). Clearly, these attempts result in arbitrary, mechanistic taxonomies. Defenses are seen in this context as maneuvers that prevent awareness of painful or disturbing feelings, and experimental attempts are made to detect them by conscious self-assessment, a procedure that misses the essentially automatic and involuntary (unconscious) nature of defenses (which, ultimately, may be perhaps less controllable than the emotions themselves). Also, this procedure may easily produce distortions through the research subjects' wishes to please or to appear socially desirable. Defenses are ranged in these theories in a simplified, neat scheme, one defense positioned against another, one seen as the opposite of the other. In this context, the remark made by Knapp to the effect that "in this, as in other fields . . . polarities, like beauty, may be in the eye of the beholder" (1987) seems very much to the point.

On the whole, the evolutionary ('expressive' and physiological) approach to affects has little to say about the tremendous intricacy and web of interrelations of affects among themselves and between them and cognitions. The rather arbitrary ordering and classification of the emotions, their functions, and the defenses against them do not yet constitute useful knowledge about emotions.

Thus Knapp's optimism in his review of emotion theories in psychology in a psychoanalytic journal (1987) seems unwarranted. Knapp regards theories such as Plutchik's as being heuristically valuable in setting a starting point and posing a challenge to future theoreticians to produce their own theories. As Pribram, an important proponent of biological and physiological perspectives on emotion, said recently himself, such an approach can provide "neither an adequate framework for understanding the complexities of emotional processes nor an outline for understanding the intricacies of the relevant neural apparatus" (1984, p. 13).

It seems that a different approach is needed if fruitful contributions to the understanding of emotions, and particularly to the kind of knowledge about the emotions needed in psychoanalysis, are sought after. Such an approach may perhaps be found in the other major tradition of emotion theories in psychology, which I have called position B.

POSITION B: COGNITIVE THEORIES OF EMOTION
IN PSYCHOLOGY

Common to the theories in this position is their allegiance to so-called cognitive theories of emotion, which in general regard emotions as a product of cognitive activity. Most of these theories (Mandler's theory is an exception) are based on Cannon's (1927; see also MacLean, 1973) criticism of the Jamesian position. Cannon demonstrated empirically that visceral reactions lack a direct, one-to-one relationships with feelings but are instead part of the system involved in maintaining general internal homeostasis; visceral reactions are not sufficiently differentiated, they are too slow and relatively insensitive, and they can be separated from the central nervous system without disrupting expressive motor behavior. In line with this perspective, it was also shown that artificial induction (e.g., by injecting epinephrine) of visceral changes creates the autonomic responses of emotion, yet does not lead to a subjective emotional state. Cannon argued that subjective feelings are generated by interactions between the thalamus and the cortex, so that feelings are brain-determined rather than viscerally dependent, as James (1884) had claimed.

If one accepts Cannon's criticism of James, that visceral reactions are not the source of feeling quality, yet believes that visceral reactions are essential for feelings, the next logical step is to adopt the so-called cognition-arousal perspective on emotion (Leventhal, 1979). This view maintains that emotion as a whole consists of the integration of cognitions of the circumstances eliciting an emotion with autonomic arousal, while the quality of the emotional experience is provided by the content of the cognitive experience. In addition to its empirically justified criticism against visceral action as determining emotion, centralist cognitive theory has received support from the long-recognized fact that situational events play a critical role in the selection of emotional responding, that environmental cues or labels produce or emerge as emotional qualities. In this context belongs the famous experiment of Schachter and Singer (1962). Here it is assumed that, owing to the fact that the state of arousal is diffuse and its meaning unclear, there arises a 'need to know,' to be able to explain the arousal sensations. The aroused individual is said to search his environment for a definition or a causal antecedent of his arousal; when the antecedent cause is identified or labeled, the perception of the cause is itself felt as a particular emotional quality. In this framework it is assumed that although arousal is necessary for emotional experience and is consciously noticed, only the cognitive event is sufficient to create the emotional quality; the experience of different emotions depends on the prior differentiation of the meaning (cognition) of the eliciting situation. Although methodological difficulties have been found with Schachter and Singer's experiment, the view grounding it has been elaborated in many ways to express a very basic idea. The idea is that emotion arises from the way a person construes the actual or anticipated transaction with his environment, that the beliefs or assumptions a person holds about himself and the world determine his emotional responses.

One distinguished proponent of this view is George Mandler (1975, 1981, 1982, 1983). An ardent believer in cognitive psychology, Mandler argues that psychology is now able to provide a general framework for understanding emotions, which would account for the interaction between physiological and symbolic mechanisms. Inspired by Schachter and Singer (1962), Mandler integrates the experience of autonomic events with the cognitive, evaluative analysis of meaning he believes is continuously performed by the mental apparatus. Mandler sees an emotion as determined by three factors: the inner experiencing of ongoing autonomic activity, a constant cognitive analysis of the current state of the person and his world, and the interactions of these cognitive analyses with other cognitive processes. Throughout his writings, Mandler studies the many facets of the relationship between visceral and cognitive activity and views the emotions as generated by a concatenation of these two major components.

Mandler believes that eventually, when the particular generating mechanisms of emotion will be elucidated, the umbrella concept of emotion will become superfluous, in a manner analogous to what has occurred in the psychologies of memory, perception, or thought, which concentrate on processes rather than on definition and have differentiated into more particular areas of investigation.

In his 1975 analysis of emotional experience, Mandler sees physiological arousal as contributing to the gut aspect of emotions—their intensity and 'bodily' feel—while evaluative cognitions deal with the 'mental' feel of emotions—their quality and subjective content. In his view, when autonomic activation and cognitive meaning analysis occur together, they are perceived in a conscious process that is experienced as a single event, which, like other gestaltlike experiences, is different from the sum of its parts.

In Mandler's view, the interruption of the ongoing, mostly automatic evaluative activity of the inner or outer surround constitutes a potent stimulus for autonomic activation. This explanation of how emotion is generated, called by Mandler 'interruption theory' (see the discussion of Pribram, this chapter), is a variety of the conflict theory of emotion, which claims that when ongoing organized thought and behavior are interrupted, autonomic nervous activity ensues.

Mandler elaborated the idea that evaluations imply values. He attempted to characterize the cognitive states that may underlie the use of certain 'emotional' words by reference to desires, expectations, and evaluations, in the hope of eventually building a psychology of evaluative cognitions. His tool in this enterprise is schema theory (1982), according to which new encounters are evaluated against existing schemata, representations of experience that guide action, perception, and thought, and the interaction between an event and a schema determines the perception, understanding, and organization of our environment. The congruity between an event and the relational structure of the relevant schema is assumed to be the basis of judgments of value. Congruity and familiarity are positively evaluated, whereas incongruity and accommodative pressure lead to arousal and to positive or negative evaluative states that generate emotion.

The same idea is also elaborated by Richard Lazarus (1968, 1982, 1984a, 1984b), another central figure in this stream, who maintains that cognitive activity is a necessary condition of emotion. Lazarus believes that the resurgence of a cognitive emphasis in psychology and an increased sophistication concerning the role of biological and cultural elements are the factors that have helped to restore the concept of emotion to the center of attention today. For a person to experience an emotion, says Lazarus, he must comprehend—whether in the form of a primitive evaluative perception or a highly differentiated symbolic process— that what is implicated in a transaction with his environment is his own, personal well-being. This evaluating and comprehending process is called by Lazarus cognitive appraisal. In his view, it is only through the concept of cognitive appraisal, that is, by assuming the existence of individually determined interpretive processes that shape emotional responses, that individual differences in intensity, quality, and fluctuations in emotion can be explained. Without reference to the way a person construes his relationship with his environmental context, there is no way to understand that person, says Lazarus. The person must be regarded as an essentially evaluating organism who searches his environment for cues about what he needs and wants and evaluates each stimulus as to its personal relevance or significance. In other words, Lazarus regards emotion as reflecting a changing person-environment relationship through the person's constant evaluation of his ongoing transactions with the environment.

In his cognitive approach to emotion in the years 1966 and 1968, Lazarus extended Arnold's (1960) use of the concept of appraisal to include reappraisal as well. Emotional responses, themselves a function of a particular kind of cognition, are constantly in a state of flux; they may rapidly change in quality when circumstances force an alteration of the earlier appraisal or when defensive modes of thought lead to the reinterpretation of an individual's experience. Feedback from such a continuous interplay changes the cognitions that shape the emotional reaction. According to Lazarus, cognitive appraisal processes not only determine the quality and intensity of an emotional reaction but also underlie the activities that cope with the emotions thus brought about. These so-called coping activities, in turn, shape the emotional reaction by altering in various ways the meanings of ongoing relationships between the person and his surround; appraisal itself is affected by reappraisal.

The experimental findings produced by Lazarus and his coworkers from the 1960s onward, in the laboratory as well as in natural settings, challenged contemporaneous conceptions of emotion as motivator or drive and called attention to the limitations inherent in the treatment of emotion as an antecedent variable. Lazarus and his associates found that emotions did not have uniform effects; the effects of 'emotional' manipulation depended in part on the personality of the subject, and people could indeed modulate their emotional states volitionally (as measured by self-report and heart rate). These findings pointed to the fact that emotion is a product of personality, will, and circumstance.

Lazarus has also been concerned with the problem of the interdependence of thoughts, emotion, and motivation, after it was realized that the classical nineteenth-century distinction among cognition (reason), emotion (passion), and motivation (conation, or will) no longer holds. Lazarus calls for us to put together the Humpty-Dumpty image of the person in classical philosophy and drive psychology to form a whole person again. He visualizes the relationship of affects, evaluative cognitions, and coping strategies as a sequence consisting of cognitive appraisals, emotion, subsequent information processing, reappraisals, and so on. One may theoretically intervene at any point in such a sequence, designate one phase as an antecedent condition, and then examine its consequences; the sequence that is thus observed is relative to one's point of entry into the process. With alternative punctuations of the sequence, other, even reversed, 'causal' patterns can be observed, all legitimate.

Lazarus has recently conducted a long polemic with Zajonc (1980, 1984a, 1984b; Zajonc, Pietromonaco, & Bargh, 1982), who challenged the assumption that emotion is dependent on cognition and asserted that emotion and cognition spring from totally different systems and are dependent of each other, emotion actually preceding cognitive processing. Lazarus sees Zajonc's arguments as exemplifying a widespread misunderstanding of the modern conception of cognition. Within the older conception the mind was regarded as the analogue of a computer, in which meanings were gathered by the scanning of a display of stimulus elements (bits) in a serial and linear manner. Fitting with such a view of what is meant by 'cognitive' is the belief that emotion is added at the end of a cognitive chain of information processing. A view of cognition as a serial scanning of bits of discursive information entails postulating an independent system to account for the occurrence of rapid, nonreflective emotional reactions. Lazarus sees Zajonc's ideas as doing just this.

In contrast, Lazarus considers humans as meaning-oriented, as constantly evaluating events from the perspective of their well-being and as reacting emotionally to these evaluations. Meaning for Lazarus is not something for which we have to await revelation from information processing; it is potentially given and inheres in the person's personality and memory. To his mind, the early presence of meaning does not mean, as Zajonc claims, that it is detached from or independent of cognitive appraisal, but rather that emotion is never totally independent of cognition, even when the emotional response is instantaneous and nonreflective, provided we regard cognition as not necessarily implying deliberate reflection, rationality, or awareness. Cognitive appraisals that shape our emotional reactions can distort reality as well as reflect it realistically. They do not necessarily have to be rational or to imply awareness of the factors on which they rest, and the numerous experiments on subception (Lazarus, 1956; Lazarus & McCleary, 1951; Poetzel, 1917; Stein, 1980) bear evidence to this fact.

These are Lazarus's points against Zajonc. Some more may be added here, as Zajonc's assertions have aroused much controversy and even confusion among affect theorists in psychology, and as these arguments and ways of thinking concern a momentous topic—the relationship between emotions and cognitions. I think that this issue may determine whether we hold a reductionistically biologistic or, alternatively, a quasi-mystical view of emotions, or whether we shall be able to spell out more refined and properly psychological (as well as psychodynamic) models of emotion in the future. It seems that at least some of the arguments Zajonc adduces in his reply to Lazarus's arguments are based either on inaccurate information or on findings that have recently been empirically refuted, but their detail is outside the scope of this discussion. Suffice it to say, first, that Zajonc seems not to take account of Lazarus's and his associates' extensive empirical work, which supports Lazarus's claims and which, furthermore, seems to accord well with Zajonc's own definition of cognition as some kind of mental work that transforms raw sensory data into a form that may become subjectively available.

Second, the points Zajonc brings as evidence against Lazarus's cognitive theory of the emotions are highly problematic, if not downright false. These points are: the absolute primacy of affective over cognitive reactions, where Zajonc confuses reactions with forms of expression; or Zajonc's holding to the invalid view of separate neuroanatomical structures (see Hadley, 1983; Sackeim, Weinman, Gur, Greenberg, Hungerbuhler & Geschwind, 1982; Scherer, 1984; Whybrow, 1984). Another point is his taking experiments on taste aversion and on preferences for specific stimuli (e.g., tones or polygons) as examples of preferences established without awareness. It seems that, taken as a whole, Lazarus's theory is one of the most important and robust frameworks contemporary academic psychology has provided until now for conceptualizing the emotions.

A different view, which bears an affinity with the cognitive conception of affect discussed here, is that of James R. Averill (Averill, Opton & Lazarus, 1969; Averill, 1980a, 1980b), who regards emotions as social constructions. In his view, emotions are responses that have been institutionalized by society as a means of resolving conflicts within the social system. One of Averill's main contentions is that the traditional view of emotions as biologically primitive is misleading. He suggests that biologically determined responses form a relatively small class of emotional reactions, and their primary importance is that they may be incorporated as elements into other kinds of emotion. Averill conceptualizes emotions as cognitive (information-processing) systems or rules of behavior. He presents a model of social playacting, whereby a person's emotion is determined by the manner in which he interprets his own behavior. In Averill's view, an individual will construe his own behavior as emotional in much the same way as an actor interprets a role, as we say, 'with feeling.' Such a self-interpretation (see also Taylor, 1985) not only involves the monitoring of behavior but also depends on the understanding of how the emotional role fits into a larger drama whose script is written by society. Social roles require active interpretation or appraisal by the individual for their enactment. In contrast to what Averill calls 'cold' perceptual judgments about what is true and what is false, appraisals in his eyes are evaluative; they say whether something is desirable or undesirable, and they do so in a highly personal way. It is this latter feature that makes emotional appraisals so revealing of the individual's personality; if you know what makes a person proud, angry, sad, or fearful, says Averill, you know what that person considers important about himself, including those aspects of his personality that he may not recognize or admit. The appraised object is a meaning imposed on the environment; it is a cognitive construction.

In addition to appraisal and object, there is, in Averill's view, another criterion for the existence of an emotion, and that is the experience of 'passion,' which differentiates emotion from nonemotion. When experiencing an emotion, the individual is undergoing or suffering some change or transformation. To Averill, the experience of passivity is not intrinsic to the emotional response but constitutes another instance of the impact of one's interpretation of one's behavior on one's experience. It is not the bodily feedback per se that determines the intensity of the response but the 'symbolism' associated with physiological arousal to which it is subject that determines the quality of an experience (1980b, p. 62). Depending on the cultural context, a variety of different emotions may be fashioned from the same biological system; conversely, elements from several different systems may be incorporated into a single emotion.

Emotions, according to Averill, are social roles, which require knowing how to apply emotional concepts in a manner appropriate to the situation. A person, like an actor, must not only know his own part and the parts of the others but also understand how the various roles relate to the plot of the play. Emotional roles are controlled by numerous feedback loops from many levels and are learned through internalization. Averill believes that children learn emotions in the same way as they learn social roles, i.e., by 'playing at' feeling the various emotions; together with observations of the emotional behavior of others, this play helps children understand the meaning of emotional roles (see De Sousa, in Rorty, 1980).

In addition to his analysis of emotions in terms of social role playing, Averill presents us with a lucid discussion of motivation and its relation to the emotions. He attempts to develop a conception of motivation that would be applicable to both motivating and motivated properties of emotional syndromes, and he uses Chein's method of hierarchical analysis to that end. This view assumes that the totality of responses forms a hierarchy, with lower-order responses serving as material for higher-order responses, which serve as their purpose or goal. A superordinate act can be considered the motive for an act lower in the behavioral hierarchy if the latter is necessary for the completion of the former. Within this perspective, behavior is defined by reference to some goal. In this way, all behaviors are both motivating (when treated as superordinate acts) and motivated (when treated as subsidiary responses). Averill believes that affects have been traditionally studied as belonging to the category of motivating behaviors (i.e., as motives for other behaviors) rather than as motivated behaviors themselves, i.e., as superordinate goals or purposes to be striven for (see the discussion of

Lazarus, this chapter). Averill believes that the category of affect as a high-order phenomenon determined by many lower-order factors is considerably more important than that of affect as a lower-order phenomenon that determines and motivates other phenomena.

Another important worker in this area, who offers a rather sophisticated theory on the generative mechanisms of emotion, is Howard Leventhal (1974, 1979, 1982, 1984). Leventhal strongly argues against so-called arousal-cognition theories of emotion, and he attacks both components of these theories. Thus he argues that arousal theories of emotion treat emotion with nonemotional mechanisms. In his view, these theories claim (following James) that emotion *is* the perception of bodily or automatic feedback or (following Schachter & Singer) that emotion *is* the integration of autonomic feedback with cognitive events.

Leventhal proposes a perceptual-motor theory of emotion, in which he builds a comprehensive model for the generation of the emotions through specific psychological and neurological mechanisms, which are analogous, in his view, to perceptual mechanisms. Leventhal integrates various experimental data into his hypothesis of a three-stage, recursive model for the creation, experience, and appraisal of emotion.

Upon examining a large amount of evidence on the subject of arousal, Leventhal concludes that arousal has been assigned such an exaggerated role in explaining emotions because of its noticeability during or after emotional episodes. He argues (following Cannon) that arousal is present whenever the organism is preparing for intense activity of *any* kind, and he agrees that arousal accompanies emotion and appears to be more intense with strong and with active emotions, and that the removal of arousal may create substantial changes in emotional experience. But he stresses that there is little evidence to suggest that arousal is essential for emotional experience. There are, moreover, indications that the autonomic system is not essential for emotionally motivated learning in animals; all this negative evidence itself rests, in his view, on considerable unclarities in the definition of arousal (Lacey, 1967; Stein, 1980). Added to this is the finding that sometimes becoming aware of an arousal response may be a condition for *reducing* emotionality. Leventhal concludes that autonomic activity lacks emotional significance, although it usually becomes conditioned to emotional activity and experience over time.

As to the second component in cognition-arousal theories, cognition, here Leventhal takes issue with the hypothesis that the basic role of cognition is to serve as the primary element in defining emotional quality. He tries to show that the role of cognition in emotion is not unequivocally clear, and he suggests that we should distinguish two roles of cognition: as an initiator of emotional experience and as the source of the quality of emotional experience itself. Most emotion theories agree about the first role of cognition, namely, that perception and interpretation of the environment and internal 'imagery' and ideas initiate emotional processing. That is not the same, writes Leventhal, as arguing that cognition itself is the feeling quality. The pleasure, insult, or threat value of a situation is conveyed by cognitive appreciation or understanding, but the emotional quality and experience generated by that understanding depend on an additional response mechanism other than situational cognition and autonomic or bodily arousal. Something else is needed for an emotion, and arousal and cognition are not enough.

To Leventhal's mind, the real problem confronting the psychology of emotion is the need to develop a model describing the mechanisms for the construction of feelings. He proposes a processing model for the construction of emotional experience, in which emotional construction is described as a process consisting of a series of stages. First, there is a perceptual-motor stage, which also includes the mechanisms that create an experience of emotion; following this stage is a planning-action stage, in which emotional and non-emotional information is used for planning and constructing overt action. According to Leventhal, the output of this process, a combination of emotional experience and behavior and instrumental action, feeds back into the stimulus setting, so that responses can alter the conditions eliciting the emotion and become information for further emotional responding; Leventhal calls this the appraisal stage (cf. Lazarus, 1984a). Leventhal views this sequential feedback process as a regulatory system that aims at sustaining a particular organism-environment fit.

According to this theory, emotion is created in the first stage; it is the perception of the eliciting stimulus, to which an expressive motor reaction is added. It involves the reception and interpretation of the stimulus situation and the construction of a subjective emotion, that is, an emotional representation of the situation. The second stage deals with the generation and execution of action plans to cope with (that is, to alter or control) the perceived situation and the emotional reaction to it. The third stage involves setting criteria and evaluating the outcome of the efforts at coping. Leventhal visualizes this three-stage system as rapidly cycling through the stages of representation, coping, and appraisal, while each of the latter two stages can influence both the perception and emotion aspects of the representation. The perception of a situation produces an automatic, expressive motor reaction by the schematic (memory) and the expressive (motor) systems. This automatic output goes to the facial system to produce expressive change and is then compared to the volitional motor pattern generated by the individual's 'conceptual' emotional response to the situation. Feelings arise when the spontaneous motor system discharges (feeds forward) into the voluntary motor system. This process occurs before motor activity is registered in the face. The fit or lack of fit between the two response processes, the expressive-motor and the facial-expressive, is the main signal for the conscious perception of emotion.

Leventhal rejects the possibility of the existence of emotion without cognition in most situations in life, provided that cognition is broadly defined, so as to include perceptual, non-verbal clues. He shares the assumption of other theorists operating in a Darwinian framework (such as Ekman, Izard, or Tomkins), who view emotion as a fundamental, independent property of experience. From this perspective, he says, the quality of emotion can be determined by organized activity in neurochemical and motor areas of the central nervous system and not necessarily by higher-level (verbal) cognitive processes. Consequently, Leventhal, like Lazarus, disagrees with Zajonc, who speaks of emotions without cognitions. In his view there are only a very few cases in life where this degree of independence of emotion from cognition can be seen (e.g., in early infancy or in the case of drug use). Leventhal argues that Zajonc uses an arbitrary definition of cognition when Zajonc appeals for a separation of cognition and emotion, and he contrasts Zajonc's theory with his own perceptual-motor theory, which sees emotion as intimately intertwined with various types or levels of cognition. He argues that the complexity of the emotional processing system requires that we distinguish between different types of cognition and recognize that we cannot answer questions about the linkage of emotion to cognition if we treat cognition and emotion as unitary constructs. There are several types of processes that may be called 'cognitive,' and parallel to them are several types of processes in the system that generates emotion. We should also remember that these systems are complex and flexible and can produce seemingly contradictory outcomes. In his view, single-issue hypotheses will provide little understanding of emotional processes. In this belief, he joins many modern thinkers on affects, such as Tomkins, Scherer, and others.

Leventhal mentions two of the functions of emotions that he feels have been given relatively little attention until now. The first is the function of emotions as gauges (Pribram calls them monitors) that provide an ongoing, moment-to-moment readout of the state of the organism as it is engaged in problem solving. The second function of emotions that has been neglected until now is integration across the levels of the processing hierarchy. Emotions play a critical role in organizing the regulatory system so that its coping stage meshes with the demands of the environmental representation. The three systems involved in the three-stage processing of emotion—the cortical, the schematic-perceptual, and the primitive sensory-motor processes—are used in the service of a common goal, self-regulation.

Leventhal's theory offers some ideas that may be applicable to psychoanalytic conceptualizations. I shall list only some of the issues here, such as his treatment of the interrelationship between voluntary and involuntary emotion-generating processes (the mechanisms of feedforward and feedback of 'emotional' information between motor and cerebral systems); the concept of schematic or affective memory, which may be of interest to the question of unconscious feelings (see Stern's RIGs [1985]); findings and formulations concerning the processes of intensifying or reducing of emotional experience; and discussion of the pervasive tendency, long known in psychoanalysis and here empirically established, to attribute the causes of emotion to others rather than to oneself. These various points have been mentioned here cursorily for lack of space, in order to indicate that there are some potentially fruitful ideas for a psychoanalytic theory of affect to look at. Also interesting is the convincing case Leventhal makes against advocates of expressive theories of emotion (e.g., Izard, 1971; Tomkins, 1962, but not the later Tomkins), who claim that expressive motor activity plays the essential role in the creation of feelings, in other words, that simple feedback from expressive facial muscles is the source of subjective experience.

Discussion

In the formulations recently put forward in theories of emotion represented under what I have called in this study position B, cognitive and social theories come together. Cognitive theories in psychology elaborate key concepts such as frames, scripts, and representations (Fodor, 1981, 1983; Schank & Abelson, 1977; Tomkins, 1979) while social theories speak of roles and attribution (Heider, 1971; Kelly, 1955; Weiner, Russell & Lerman, 1978). Common to both realms of theory is the concept of situation, or environment, as it is represented in the individual and interpreted by him and as it is evaluated or compared according to some social or cognitive value system or schema. In the following discussion, I shall look at these two streams as they mark the terms and concepts used to explain emotion.

A central characteristic of the theories discussed in position B is the profound role they give to appraisal or evaluative judgment in emotion. It was Magda Arnold (1960) who first developed emotion theory in terms of appraisal, asserting that appraisal is a ubiquitous, intuitive, and automatic process going on all the time, through which we judge what is good and pleasurable and what is bad and unpleasurable around us. Even appraisals that require some memory of past encounters either are based on past approach/avoidance scenarios or invoke the judgment of good or bad as something given. For Arnold, the knowledge of good and evil is inborn and apparently lodged in the cortex of the limbic lobe (1960, p. 34). Pribram acknowledges his indebtedness to her, as do Lazarus, Kanner, & Folkman (1980), but other theorists as well have elaborated emotion theories in terms of the concept of appraisal. Lazarus and his associates (e.g., Lazarus, 1984a; Lazarus, Averill, & Opton, 1970) have made extensive use of the concept of appraisal that is based on the assumption of an immediate, unmediated apprehension of meaning. Mandler (1982) asserts that evaluation and appraisal are judgments that cannot be grounded in consensually established sets of features or attributes of the objective target event, but rather depend on what he calls relational, structural characteristics that require some match between the event and the inner schemata or personal expectations of the observer himself. All these formulations lead in the direction of the greater importance of the personally variable and subjective factor as compared with the simple, 'objective,' public, environmental stimulus. The effect is a revolutionary shift in conceptualizing both persons and their emotions.

The weight given to the subjectively cognitive dimension of emotion ties in with another feature of these theories, namely, their reliance for explanation on some variant of schema theory to account for the mechanisms underlying the processes generating emotion, their 'deep structure.' Leventhal defines emotion

as "a form of tacit or intuitive knowledge, a given in experience." Schemata
are seen as crucial for creating the tacit knowledge embodied in the emotions,
and schemata are essential for conceptually going beyond situational perception,
expressive reaction, or autonomic response. Many workers within this framework
have reached the conclusion that there is no way of dealing with the more complex
problems of emotional behavior without a theory of the underlying mechanisms
of emotion that allows us to anticipate and account for the highly subjective and
apparently conflicting outcomes. Prior to the ascendancy of this conception, the
domain of emotion consisted of multiple, separate hypotheses about what generates emotion, such as feedback, cognition, or arousal. These theories, which
were based on single hypotheses, lacked the power to analyze the difficult
problems of emotion. Schema theory as a species of a theory of mental representations (see Hadley, 1983) makes it possible to lead various emotional manifestations back to an underlying generating mechanism that in some way includes
the personal history of the individual. A schema is a complex inner structure
that includes many elements of past experience and learning at a level related
to the general development of the individual having the schema. Most importantly, a schema also contains values, which are assumed to greatly influence
and color ongoing transactions and experiences. In this context, beginnings are
made to apply Piagetian schema theory to the emotions (see Ciompi, 1988;
Thompson, 1985).

The increasing explanatory ambition and power that recent theories of emotion
have come to possess are also reflected in recent attempts to explain the notion
that connects emotion inseparably with the experience of passivity and of over-
whelmingness. Historically, the powerful, passive experience of passion was
accounted for by relating emotions to biologically primitive ('instinctive') reactions, by emphasizing the role of the autonomic ('involuntary') nervous system
in the mediation of emotion, or by assuming that emotions are basically non-
cognitive ('irrational') responses. In contrast, the present tendency in cognitive
theories of emotion is to propose a different explanation for this well-known
phenomenon. It is asserted (see in particular Averill, 1980a; but also Solomon,
1976, in philosophy and Schafer, 1983, in psychoanalysis) and it was empirically
found (see Krystal, 1988; Lazarus, 1982, 1984a) that emotions are much more
voluntarily controllable than had been assumed and that the experience of passion
and passivity depends on expectation and sometimes even on linguistic use (see
Schafer, 1976).

9
The Relevance of Recent Trends in Theories of Emotion in Psychology and Infant Studies to Psychoanalytic Affect Theory

Both psychoanalysis and psychology, with all their differences in perspective and theoretical framework, are at present strongly concerned with the concept and phenomenon of affect. In psychology, the paradigm has been laboratory research and also, more recently, experiments in naturalistic conditions, including infant research. Emotions are manipulated, assessed by various measures (Emde, 1980; Gaensbauer, 1982; Lazarus, Kanner & Folkman, 1980; Leventhal, 1982; Plutchik, 1980; Scherer, 1984) and classified according to some coordinates of approach-avoidance (Plutchik & Kellerman, 1981). Alternatively, their neuroantomical (Arnold, 1970; Pribram, 1984) and neurochemical (Whybrow, 1984) bases are investigated, facial and postural expressions of emotion are systematically gauged (Ekman, 1984; Izard, 1977; Tomkins, 1962–1963, 1981), and models are abstracted from these. In psychoanalysis, efforts to understand the emotions are two-pronged: on the one hand, attempts are made to consider necessities of theoretical consistency, updating, and reorganization (Green, 1977; Kernberg, 1976, 1982, 1984; Noy, 1982; Sandler, 1972, 1983), and on the other hand, forays are made into clinical phenomenology of the affects with all their intrapsychic and interpersonal vicissitudes and nuances (Green, 1977; Krystal, 1975, 1978, 1988; Lachman & Stolorow, 1981; Lewin, 1965; Peto, 1967; Schafer, 1964; Socarides, 1977).

Many factors have contributed to the present situation, in which the broadest and strongest interface between psychoanalysis and psychology is obviously the domain of affects. One can simply say that the crucial importance of affects is now being recognized in both disciplines. In psychology, the stage has been reached where the concept of cognition has been broadened and deepened, and only a short step was required to realize that the new and more sophisticated conception of cognition must involve emotions. In psychoanalysis, on the other hand, affects have always had a central place by virtue of their motivational and defense-inducing power and by their serving as the most reliable and important phenomenon in the clinical situation. One of the central problems in the history of psychoanalysis was that conceptual psychoanalytic tools had yet to be found and applied to this basic empirical knowledge.

At present, a lively mutual borrowing of terms and a deep interpenetration of ideas are going on in psychoanalytic and psychological theories of emotion. Let us begin by pointing out some aspects that have been imported from psychoanalysis into psychology. Following this, some potential or actual contributions from psychology to psychoanalysis will be explored.

There are writers in psychology who have expressed recognition of the fact that psychoanalytic theory has inspired both research and theory construction in psychology and theoretical thinking in psychosomatic medicine. They believe that psychoanalysis has demonstrated that what is involved in all emotions is conflict and also that it is important to realize that some or all aspects of an emotion are as a rule unconscious. These writers also see psychoanalytic theory as having helped to eliminate a bothersome problem in psychology, namely, what comes first in an emotional reaction, the feeling or the bodily change. Psychoanalysis provided an answer by asserting that both feeling and bodily change arise concomitantly out of a common source, namely, from an unconscious evaluation of a state or a situation, be it from the common matrix of the drive or from an underlying unconscious fantasy (Plutchik, 1980).

On a more specific level, the prototypical psychoanalytic concept of defense has gained ascendancy in psychological theories of emotion (Plutchik & Kellerman, 1981). Emotional defenses have at last been accepted in psychology as constantly operating, ubiquitous phenomena. Consequently, efforts have been made to construct personality and diagnostic profiles assumedly based on various defense mechanisms, where defense mechanisms are defined as typical ways of handling emotions. But these classificatory systems consist of preliminary and cumbersome taxonomies, arbitrarily composed and lacking a unifying underlying rationale that could have made them cohere into a well-argued dynamic system.

Another aspect of the infiltration into psychology of ideas that grew on the soil of psychoanalysis is illustrated in a recent collection of papers on emotion that is part of a series in personality and social psychology called *Emotions, Relationships, and Mental Health* (edited by P. Shaver, 1984). This collection rides on the upsurge of interest in the subject of close relationships, "the crucible in which powerful emotions are formed" (p. 7). The leading trend in these papers is exemplified by the translation of psychological concepts into terms taken mostly from the domain of the emotions. Thus, stress is called here 'negative emotion,' and coping is given the name of 'emotion work' (Thoits); also, emotional expression and catharsis are accorded great value in these papers (e.g., Scheff, Tavris), which, it should be noted, sum up respectable academic work, rather than publicize fashionable cathartic therapies. So-called emotional relationships are discussed and studied (de Rivera; Mark & Folger), and so is 'emotional support,' which is considered here as immunizing against physical illness as well as against acting 'weirdly' (Hansson; Jones & Carpenter; Laudenslager & Reite).

What seems more pertinent for our perspective, however, is the issue of the relevance and the actual or potential contributions to psychoanalytic theories of affect accruing from psychology. Here prospects seem exciting. A small but significant indication of the growing interpermeability of psychoanalysis and psychology is the very use of the term 'emotion,' which has been mainly featured in psychology and which is now being used in psychoanalysis alongside the term 'affect.' A recent example is Knapp's 1987 review of some contemporary contributions to the study of emotions in psychoanalysis.

It would seem that psychoanalytic theory could benefit from some formulations and conceptions in psychology. Some initial attempts have recently been made to integrate findings or issues in psychology into psychoanalytic theory. The most notable examples are those of Kernberg (1976, 1982, 1984), who maintained that he attempted to integrate into his affect theory findings from ethology and neurophysiological research, and Noy (1982), who tried with his proposed affect theory to address questions about affects that he felt had been left unresolved in psychological theories as well.

Undoubtedly, most theoreticians in psychoanalysis are appreciative of the great difficulties inherent in putting together a well-informed theory of affect that does not violate empirical findings and that is capable of encompassing at least a great part of the numerous clinically observed phenomena. It seems, however, that many theoreticians of affects in psychoanalysis are stuck somewhere among efforts to amend Freud's last, mainly structural theories, to reformulate general principles of mental functioning, to continue fighting the concept of the drives and to try to sum up the affects in the psychoanalytic situation according to some vague or arbitrary organizing grid or model.

Thus, Kernberg retains the drive concept and uses it in his theory as a construct unequivocally linked with affects. In this process, the concept of the drive becomes something very different from the concept used and elaborated in psychoanalysis so far. In Kernberg's thought, the concept of drive denotes something akin to a behavioral disposition (cf. the original sense of 'Affekte' in German, that of dispositions, Laplanche & Pontalis, 1973). Affects, according to Kernberg, have the status of a superordinate system, a metaplan or master plan for action (this is comparable to the role ascribed to affects in Noy's theory). The question that poses itself in this case concerns Kernberg's policy of talking in terms of, and committing himself to, binary plans, i.e., libidinal or pleasurable and therefore positive, and aggressive or unpleasurable and hence automatically negative plans. On the one hand, Kernberg's arrangement bypasses the grave problems plaguing Freud's last dual drive theory (see Kaywin, 1966; Loewald, 1970; see also Stern, 1985), problems that point to the inadvisability of dividing all experience into positive and negative parts, thereby losing other dimensions and differentiations of affects. On the other hand, Kernberg's theory in a sense ignores the growing 'psychologization' and 'emancipation' of the affects so evident in recent psychoanalytic literature (see Emde, 1983; Sandler & Sandler, 1978, 1985; Schafer, 1979; Stern, 1985, and others) in that, although his theory makes the affects the building blocks of mental structures, affects in his theory ultimately become drives.

Another theoretician of affect theory, Pinchas Noy, seems to rely mostly on outdated psychological theories, be they theories of motivation, psychsomatics, or emotion (this point was discussed at length when dealing with his work in chapter 3).

The same problem is to be found in Knapp's 1987 extensive review of recent publications on emotion, where he has likewise failed to distinguish between superseded or refuted theories of emotion and newer, comparatively more informed ones. Moreover, Knapp has neglected the crucial importance of the cognitive factor and (ironically for a psychoanalyst) the subjective perspective, choosing for discussion mainly theories couched in evolutionary terms. In addition, this extended review suffers from many inaccuracies.

The most serious attempts in the direction of assimilating psychological knowledge into psychoanalytic thinking are apparently being made at present in the area of infant research and theorizing. The most outstanding names here are Robert Emde (1980, 1981, 1983, 1984) and Daniel Stern (1985). Psychoanalysis seems to cry out for a more satisfactory integration between its theoretical and clinical domains. The field of infant research seems to hold a promise for one aspect of such a large-scale integrative bridging of the gap, through linking the so-called clinical (clinically reconstructed) infant with the (experimentally and naturalistically) 'observed' infant (Lichtenberg, 1987; Stern, 1985).

Emde and Stern have conducted extensive research within the framework of developmental psychology; the former uses systems theory concepts prevailing in this field, while the latter tries to frame his empirical and theoretical work within a theory of multiple, evolving senses of the self. Stern has imported a great variety of conceptions and new angles into psychoanalysis. Both Emde and Stern have opened new vistas for the understanding of affects in psychoanalysis; both combine knowledge from developmental theories and from empirical observations gathered in psychology with psychoanalytic knowledge, and both blend materials from several fields and organize them into comprehensive models of affect development, organization, and subjective experience in early life. It remains to be seen what their work implies about affects in later life. On the other hand, there are some very serious points of contradiction between their outlooks and the views held in psychoanalysis today, whose discussion cannot be undertaken here. In any case, Emde, Stern, their associates, and other workers in this area (e.g., Demos, 1982, 1987; Lichtenberg, 1983, 1987; Solyom, 1987; Trevarthen, 1984) are still exceptions, and their ideas have not yet been sufficiently assimilated into affect theory.

Having looked at some points of import from psychoanalysis to psychology and vice versa, I should like to discuss a more global issue—the changes taking place concomitantly in psychoanalysis and psychology, changes that by their simultaneous occurrence acquire the meaning of being mutually validating. Briefly, the story here is that of affects as they become (at least for adults) liberated from the drives and from notions of physical arousal (anxiety, exertion) and attached to notions of subjective value and evaluation. As the interest of this study lies more in psychoanalysis than in psychology, greater stress will be laid on the contributions from psychology that seem relevant and potentially fruitful for a psychoanalytic theory of affects, rather than the other way around.

To begin with, the parallel between the transition in psychoanalysis from biological instincts to the more psychical drives (see Rapaport, 1953) and a similar transition in psychology, where conflict theory has come to replace instinct theory, is striking.[1] But this was only the first step. In 1970, Magda Arnold wrote that:

Psychologists found themselves unable to continue accepting instincts as valid psychological categories. Influenced by learning theory, most psychologists refused to recognize instinctual patterns that owed nothing to learning. They acknowledged the driving force of instinct but denied that it was a vital force producing inherent patterning. Thus the concept of instincts was replaced by that of drives, that provided the push for any motivated action, and emotion became the bodily upset or excitement produced by the collision of drives. The conflict theory of emotion came into vogue—which focused attention to the emotions of fear and anger but failed to account for positive emotions, or even negative emotions like hate (p. 170).

This quote shows that the first step had been taken but that it was not enough. In psychology, the concept of instinct was replaced by that of the drive, while in psychoanalysis the instinct was a borderline concept between the somatic and the psychical evolved into the (instinctual) drive, seen as the psychic representative of the bodily drive or need. Following this, something happened to the concept of drive itself, and what happened is clearer in psychology than in psychoanalysis.

That the notion of drive is closely linked to the notion of arousal has been accepted in both psychology and psychoanalysis, although the link was put in somewhat different terms by theoreticians in the two disciplines. In psychoanalysis, the drive has been conceptualized as some energy-seeking discharge (Freud, 1915a), the derivatives of which were called affects; sometimes affects were even equated with the energy itself. Later, the drive was described as being cyclic and peremptory (Rapaport, 1960; G. Klein, 1976). In psychology, the concept of arousal became synonymous with that of emotion and later even replaced it (Duffy, 1957). In both areas, the concept of drive or arousal became fused and confused with the concept of affect. Later, the concept of arousal in psychology broadened with the discovery of nonspecific, diffuse activating systems in the central nervous system, a discovery paralleled by findings that showed that arousal is ubiquitous and accompanies all physical and most mental activities. These developments in knowledge resulted in the concept of arousal losing the foremost importance it had in explaining emotions. A good example is the change that took place in the thought of Robert Plutchik, the biologically and evolutionary minded theoretician, who had in the past relied on arousal as the explanatory basis for the affects. He recently expressed the opinion that the concept of arousal has relevance, at best, to a few basic emotions (fear, anger, and joy), that it cannot describe the bodily states that may be associated with mixed emotions (such as greed, guilt, envy, and remorse), and that, moreover, for most emotions there are no obvious changes in arousal levels at all and, conversely, that arousal can also be elicited with activities other than emotions.

Now that the explanatory importance of the drive concept has decreased and subjective factors have gained ascendancy in psychological theories, the question in psychology became: What concept would replace the drive as a motivator that could at the same time reflect the unique determining force of subjectivity? Furthermore, what is the relationship between emotion and motivation? These questions were being asked because some writers in psychology believed that emotions and motives should be distinguished and differentiated from each other (see Arnold, 1960; Leeper, 1948; Plutchik, 1980; Solomon, 1976; Solomon & Corbit, 1974; but cf. Tomkins, 1980, 1984). The separation of emotions and motives proves, however, to be a very difficult task. Traditionally, emotions and motives were distinguished in psychology and in early psychoanalysis in terms of the difference in the stimuli that arouse motives (and what was called motives usually meant the drives) and those that arouse emotions. The classical distinction said that physiological inner stimuli or states (notably of absence or lack) arouse motives in a cyclic or rhythmic fashion, whereas external stimuli arouse emotions. Thus, emotions are said to be externally oriented, whereas motives are internally directed, and whereas motives are cyclic and dictated by bodily needs, emotions are more flexible and less dependent on stimuli (Scherer, 1984; Tomkins 1979).

In psychoanalysis the view of the relations between motives and affects has not been much simpler than in psychology. Here affects are increasingly equated with motives by being endowed with motivational power (Kernberg, 1976; G. S. Klein, 1976; M. Klein, 1945; Sandler, 1972), as opposed to the former views, in which affects were clearly distinguished from motives, which were seen as generally coterminous with the drives (Hartmann, 1927; Noy, 1982; Rapaport, 1953).

A different conception of what a motive is that could replace the concept of the drive as the motive and that has a more plausible relation to emotion is value. The concept of value has attained central importance in many recent affect theories, both in psychoanalysis (Sandler, 1985) and in psychology (Mandler, 1982). The routes to this concept were many and various, but there is a surprising convergence toward the same conception from different quarters. One of the sources of this development has been the growing realization that the subjective element in emotion cannot be conceptually ignored anymore. Some developments in philosophy, particularly in the philosophy of science (e.g., Davidson, 1980; Polanyi, 1958; Rorty, 1979; Wittgenstein, 1953), promise to offer conceptual tools for future use concerning subjectivity and subjective values. Philosophical ideas have their impact sometimes in an extremely mediated way; they are in the air, so to speak, and very often they become absorbed, unwittingly and sometimes belatedly, into the conceptual repertoire of theoreticians, be they psychoanalytic or others.

The focal issue embraced by the concept of value is the idea that the personal subjective value (or meaning) of a situation for a person affects his feelings as well as his acts and choices. Sandler, in his 1985 paper, speaks of motivation in terms of affective value. He defines 'affective value cathexis' as a feeling state with which a particular mental representation is invested, which is a measure of its positive or negative attractiveness, of its value for the person (or, in Sandler's words, for the ego). Affective value determines priorities of motivation. The point is that with this concept, the personal value that situations or objects hold for a person is not only taken into account but regarded as determining his motivations. Mandler too, calls to his aid the concept of personal value in trying to answer the question of what it is about taste that is indisputable and what is in the 'eye' of the beholder that confers beauty, threat, attraction, or other feeling-evoking attributes (1982).

This view logically leads to the contention that feelings, by telling the person what he values, at the same time tell about the person who feels them. Charles Taylor, an important contemporary philosopher, writes in 1985 that feeling is determined by the 'import' of a situation for a person, by which he means that experiencing a given emotion always involves experiencing it as bearing a certain import for oneself. Through this import we can understand the person as subject, through understanding the sense of the situation for him, what he values, and what matters to him. Saying what an emotion is like for a person involves making explicit not only the sense of the situation it incorporates but also the kind of being the person who experiences it is, through what is of value to him and how it is so.

Linked with the concept of value and underlying it is the concept of evaluation or appraisal, the process of which is assumed to be constitutive of emotion. In this context, the psychological terms 'evaluative judgments' (Mandler) or 'cognitive appraisals' (Arnold, Lazarus) are more developed and worked out than Brenner's 'ideas,' which are posited as one of the two components of affect (the other being bodily sensations).

This new terminology clearly touches on the cognitive dimension of affects. The concepts elaborated by psychologists concerning what may be described as the cognitive side of affect seem to express a belief in the tight connection between affect and cognition. This may be even more than a connection; there is a discernible trend to view feelings and knowledge as being together in the nature of one global process with different faces or phases. Such a view transcends the simplistic juxtaposition of ideas and sensations, or thoughts and feelings, a juxtaposition and a separation with an affinity to dualistic or atomistic, Cartesian or Lockean conceptions. In psychoanalysis, this separation of ideas ('representations') and affects was useful at the time it was made, for it exposed the vicissitudes of affects and ideas under repression that lead to the different neurotic syndromes. But many analysts have since then expressed the need for these separated concepts to be put together again, so that their basic unity should no longer be ignored but rather worked on. Lazarus's description of how the link between the person and the situation is appraised and emotionally reacted to, following which the new reaction is appraised and likewise emotionally reacted to, and Leventhal's sophisticated theory (based on considerable empirical underpinnings) and discerning treatment of levels of cognition in relation to emotion, are captivating and relevant.

These models fit in with a more complex view of emotions, according to which emotions are seen as both stimuli and reactions, and they partially fit in with Melanie Klein's implicit conception of what I have called emotional 'clusters' or syntactic chains. These models also echo Green's (Lacanian) conception of concatenations of meanings. Common to all these different conceptions is the idea of emotions as generating reactions to themselves, reactions that further activate emotions, fantasies, attitudes, and acts.

The fact that feelings are extremely complex structures in themselves had already been glimpsed by Freud in the 1920s, but the idea was articulated in psychology and by developmentalist researchers in psychoanalysis only in the 1970s and onward. We are talking here about the momentous shift that has taken place from viewing emotions as sheer arousal, even as the vital 'amplifiers' of activity and experience (Tomkins), to regarding emotion in psychology as a multidimensional process (Leventhal), a syndrome (Lazarus, Averill), or a construct (Plutchik). The conceptual upheaval in the theory of emotions is very clearly illustrated in Plutchik's latest book (1980), in which he writes:

In my 1962 book on emotion, I defined emotion as a patterned bodily reaction . . . which is brought about by a stimulus. This definition is . . . limited in that it emphasizes only the functional language of emotions . . . [whereas] an emotion can be described in terms of multiple languages that include subjective feeling, cognitions, impulses to action, and behavior. A fuller but more complex definition must take these elements into account.

He then presents his later definition of emotion as

an inferred complex sequence of reactions to a stimulus . . . [which] includes cognitive evaluations, subjective changes, autonomic and neural arousal, impulses to action, and behavior designed to have an effect upon the stimulus that initiated the complex sequence. These complex reaction patterns may suffer various vicissitudes, which affect the probability appearance of each link in the chain.

Furthermore, he notes that even this complex definition is not sufficient, in that it indicates the functions of emotions but does not explicitly comment upon the nature of the stimuli that initiate the chain of reactions called an emotion, the meaning, or inferred cognitive evaluation, of a stimulus.

Implied in the view of emotions as complex structures with their own generating mechanisms is the refocusing on emotion as a consequence, a complex reaction, so that attention is given to the determinants of the emotion proper (Lazarus, 1984a, 1984b; Leventhal, 1982; Mandler, 1982; Scherer, 1984). A cognitive conception of emotion as a consequence of other processes emphasizes the active 'cognitive work' inherent in an emotional reaction and highlights the role of the person (or his ego [Sandler] or self [R. Stern]) in the perceptual and cognitive work he constantly produces in relation to his inner and outer surround.

Thus, psychology is trying at present to tackle the difficult problem of the subjective and personal element, so central in emotions, through seeing emotion as a cognitive, appraising event. This approach may open the door to what is called in psychoanalysis the internal world, with its fantasies, inner presences, and stored learning experiences, which determine our emotions and make them intelligible.

A major addition to this basic view of the affects is the interpersonal dimension of affect communication, affect attunement, and emotional contact, a dimension that has been much elaborated in psychoanalytic thought since Freud. Infant research has been concerned with the subtle and powerful emotional communications going on between infant and caretaker and has attempted to define and separate the components and to find the mechanisms responsible for these exquisitely tuned and complex processes of emotional communication. In this context Gaensbauer (1982) writes that the establishment of an adequate psychoanalytic theory of affect is contingent upon a full understanding of the nature of emotional development during the earliest years of life, and "the direct observation of infants and young children has been a very necessary complement to retrospective reconstruction and has made invaluable contributions to our current knowledge" (p. 29).

There is a growing realization of the profound importance of the caregiver-infant relationship and of the role played by emotional signaling that communicates needs, intentions, and satisfactions and motivates and provides indications and reinforcement not only for need satisfaction but also for learning, loving, and exploring. The emotional availability of the caregiver in infancy is considered the central growth-promoting feature of the early rearing experience (Emde, 1980, 1988; Spitz, 1965; Stern, 1985). The states of 'we'-ness (Stern), 'referencing' (Emde), 'matching' and affect 'attunement' (Stern) are ubiquitous and continuous phenomena vital for mental development. Affect attunement is a highly complex, nonverbal process that relies on the cross-modal perception (perception across different sensory modalities) in another person of certain forms (e.g., intensity, duration, rhythm), which are transformed into feelings. These processes go on between mother and infant and, to various extents, between any two people who relate to each other. Psychotherapy and psychoanalysis make much use of affect attunement and affect resonance, which are the first steps in the process of empathy. Some of the more precise and detailed formulations made on the basis of infant-caregiver interactions may, it is hoped, be assimilated into psychoanalytic affect theory.

Continuous affect attunement between mother and infant, or between two other persons, proceeds with discrete affects as well as with what D. Stern has called 'vitality affects.' The conception of the existence and knowledge of rules of functioning of a continuous stream of feelings ('vitality affects') is intriguing and adds a whole new dimension of affect theory. This may provide us with a beginning of an articulation of what it is that is ineffable in feelings.

10
Conclusions and New Directions

Having reviewed and discussed various major theories of affect separately, we may now bring our results together in terms of the central themes and problems running through them. From the multifaceted theoretical work on affects, an attempt will be made in this chapter to carve out a general picture that may serve as a map for finding one's way among the numerous trends and formulations existing in this domain and for discerning more clearly the most salient points and issues in the field. Accordingly, theories of affect discussed here will be overviewed in terms of the problems they address. In the first part of this chapter I shall take stock of what has been achieved so far in the domain of affect theory; in the next part I shall tease out the main issues and points of agreement or contention among various affect theories; the concluding part will deal with new directions of thought and fresh paths recently taken concerning affects, which seem to be fruitful for the future.

Beginning with Freud, we have seen that although in his view affects had a double usage, that of body states and of subjective feelings, only the first usage was incorporated into his theory in 1915. The subjective aspect of affects remained outside the theory even when the drive-derivative conception was replaced by the conception of affects as ego functions and as signals in 1923 and 1926. The problem of the subjective and experiential side of affects could not be solved theoretically by Freud for several reasons. One of them had to do with the fact that his metapsychology was characterized in terms of energy, forces, and drive cathexes. Another reason derived from the very fact that affects were still regarded as basically drive derivatives, with no autonomous status and representations of their own.

On the other hand, in the very early days of psychoanalysis, that is, before

1915 and particularly before 1900, Freud established feelings as the sources of behaviors, symptoms, and defense mechanisms. In a sense, he later 'went astray,' as Landauer (1938) and others pointed out, by losing sight of the crucial importance of affects, as he was absorbed in his endeavor to conceptualize mental phenomena through drives and structures underlying feelings and experience. Already in his topographical theory (although not in clinical practice) Freud had felt compelled to deny affects unconscious and even preconscious status, a status that could be given only to the biological drives or to the repressed and preserved ideas. This practically meant that affects lost their proper psychodynamic status to a phenomenological explanation that could not encompass unconscious levels and hence cannot belong to the psychoanalytic domain. In Freud's structural theory affects could not have representations of their own because of his a priori definition of representations as stemming from external perceptions, whereas affects were seen as internal perceptions. The years 1920 and 1926 marked Freud's return, even if indirectly, to the task of developing affect theory through loosening the tie of affects to the drives and to the id. But that development was only one step in his theory.

Both at the beginning and at the end of Freud's thinking on affects, his psychodynamic explanations were embedded in biological terms. Freud's successors elaborated and advanced his last theories against this biological background, and in some aspects of their work they succeeded in breaking through the biologically inspired frame. In retrospect, it can be seen that much of the work on affects done after Freud was aimed at continuing and promoting the severance of affects from the drives as their sources and the reinstatement of the autonomy and centrality of affects. This came close to Freud's formulations in the first phase of his theory, in which affects served as basic explanatory constructs, fitting with their place in the clinical situation, the differences being that at this later stage the component of psychic energy was left out. Instead, attempts were made to account for the centrality of affects by tracing the multiple relationships among ego, instincts and affects, affects and objects, and affects that trigger, relieve, or cause other affects.

Within ego psychology, efforts were focused on the relations between the ego and the affects, which involved the issues of the taming of affect and of the ego's being overwhelmed by traumatic affect, particularly anxiety. The concepts of thresholds, somatization and desomatization, and the structuralization of affects, as well as the general question of whether affects belong to the ego or to the id and whether and in what cases affects are ego functions or id forces, tension or discharge phenomena, occupied a central place in this kind of theorizing about affects.

Melanie Klein, for her part, directed her efforts at Freud's 1920 dual drive theory, which to a great extent dealt with the vicissitudes of feelings and their corresponding parts of the self and internal objects, while Wilfred Bion elaborated notions of processing raw emotional data into thoughts and knowledge, seeing mental health in terms of the fundamental need to contain the emotions. Bion's theory was intended, among other things, to develop and add to Melanie Klein's theory the notion of containment of feelings, the dimension of self-awareness, and obligation to truth, i.e., psychic reality and intrapsychic knowledge. Bion, however, was concerned mainly with knowledge and truth and stressed the asensual quality of psychic experience. Bion's language of processing emotional experience into growth-promoting materials for the mind was framed in core metaphors of space and metabolism. I have suggested that Melanie Klein's theory can very profitably be viewed as a descriptive theory of strong emotions—a view that solves many of the conceptual difficulties of this theory. Klein's thinking on emotions contains some deeply perceptive insights, but it cannot serve as a general theory of affect, as her thinking does not adequately deal with emotions other than strong ones, such as the calmer or more subtle emotions. Almost unwittingly, the instincts in Klein's writings came to stand for affects—a kind of solution to the question of the relationship between drives and affects.

A very different solution to the problem of the relationship between drives and affects was offered by Joseph Sandler. He argued that affects are not exclusively tied to the drives, but are motivated by such factors as the state of functioning of the mental apparatus and the relationship of the self with its internal objects. Affects are seen in his theory as conveying values to the person who experiences them, and this is their motivational role. Sandler's concepts of the present and past unconscious (1983, 1984) and of the layering of fantasies (1986) came as a reply to the need to replace or to supplement structural issues and solutions with more complex, topographical notions about mental structure and functioning.

Otto Kernberg aimed at anchoring affects in psychoanalytic theory itself, so as to do justice to their importance in the clinical situation. His way of doing this was by elaborating the role of affects in linking drive theory, object relations theory, and structural theory. Affects are conceived in his theory as the links between self and object representations and as the seeds out of which all other mental structures develop; affects are seen as the earliest experiences with oneself and with objects. Psychic 'molecules' or units, made of self, object, and affect, are considered the primary elements, which are said to become integrated later with the superstructures of the drives and with the three structures of ego, id, and superego. Kernberg feels that the problem with affect theory is the removal of affects from their biological bedrock (caused by Freud's separation of drives, drive cathexes, and affect cathexes), and he therefore aimed at getting the affects closer to the drives; drives became in his theory affect derivatives, thereby changing their original meaning.

André Green has been interested in extending affect theory to clinical syndromes other than the neuroses (to which he believed Freud's affect theories mainly applied). Green elaborated the semantic function of affects and attempted to show that affects too have representations in the unconscious and in the id. In Green's theory, affects are seen as being part of the ever present unconscious chain of signifiers in the unconscious and as representing one's body to oneself.

A different theoretical outlook and different problems pervade theories of emotion in psychology. I have grouped recent theories into those that present models of affect expression and communication on the basis of evolutionary assumptions (Plutchik, Eibl-Eibesfeldt, Pribram, Tomkins) and those addressing the cognitive, perceptive, and subjective dimensions of emotions (Mandler, Lazarus, Zajonc, Averill, Leventhal). I have argued that the latter group of theories may be of assistance to psychoanalytic knowledge by virtue of their emphasis on internal mechanisms that generate subjective experience rather than on biological programming and prepatterned types of external emotional expression and communication, their development of notions such as the cognitive dimension of emotions, and their incorporation into their explanations of the subjective values of the person experiencing the affect.

New infant research has brought forward theories that seek to illuminate the genetic, adaptive, and communicational aspect of affects. In this domain, born of the coming together of developmental psychology and psychoanalytic theory and research, affects are seen mostly as pre-programmed patterns for making contact with the outer world and with caretakers and, by extension, with other human beings, through the expression of various needs and states of awareness. In this framework, emotions are generally seen as developing from fixed biological patterns into psychological, intrapsychic means of discernment of the environment, other persons, and oneself. Exciting findings point to the role of affects in fostering self-experience and self-development.

This short overview of the various endeavors to develop the concept and theory of affect in psychoanalysis and outside it will now be followed by a series of propositions, culled from the preceding chapters of this study, that may be useful for teasing out a picture representing the standing of affect theory today, mainly in psychoanalysis. These propositions will be enumerated briefly, to be expanded later on.

1. Thanks to the work of Rapaport, Jacobson, Kaywin, Noy, Sandler, Kernberg, Applegarth, and many others, theories purporting to explain affects in terms of psychic energy are definitely no longer tenable.

2. Explanations of affects in terms of drives have proved to have a very limited usefulness, if any (G. S. Klein, 1976; Sandler, 1971; see also Holt, 1976).

3. A concept that was traditionally used to explain emotions in psychology and that is a homologue of the concepts of psychic energy and drives in psychoanalysis is arousal. This concept has likewise been convincingly dismantled as an encompassing explanation for affects in psychology (Kernberg, 1980, 1982; Lazarus, 1982; Leventhal, 1982, 1984; Lewin, 1965; Plutchik, 1980, 1984).

4. Signal theories of affect have largely replaced the energy or drive theories of affects in psychoanalysis and are still held today in various forms (Brenner, 1982; Emde, 1980, 1988; Jacobson, 1971; Krystal, 1975; Schur, 1967, 1969; Zetzel, 1965). Signals can be preconscious or unconscious, and signal theory has been one of the answers to the paradox of unconscious feelings, i.e., 'unfelt feelings.'

5. Affects are regarded as having representations of their own, probably inherently dwelling in the body and rooted in bodily motor-affective schemata (Green, 1973, 1977, 1984; Lichtenberg, 1987; Shevrin, 1978; Stern, 1985).

6. According to some theories, feelings are part of an ongoing, mostly unconscious concatenation of signifiers (Green, 1973, 1984).

7. Some theories emphasize the self-generative nature of feelings by implicitly or explicitly assuming kinds of 'feeling chains' or 'feeling cycles' (Jones, 1929; Melanie Klein, 1935, 1946). Complexes of behaviors can be comprehended as 'emotional syllogisms' (G. S. Klein, 1976; Alexander, 1935).

8. Affects cannot be separated from cognitions (Lichtenberg, 1987; Mandler, 1975, 1982; Novey, 1959, 1961; Stern, 1985). Affects supply valuable and vital knowledge of personal significance to the person who experiences them (Lazarus, 1982, 1984a, 1984b; Sandler, 1985b; Taylor, 1985; and writers on countertransference, e.g., Heimann, 1950; Little, 1951; Racker, 1957; Searles, 1955, 1979; Winnicott, 1947, 1960). Thus, affects are themselves a kind of cognition or knowledge; in a way, they are interpretations of the environment and of the person to himself. A related point is the mutual relationship of affect and thought: thought influences, changes, or reinforces feeling, and feelings in turn generate thoughts that fit with them; the relationship is reciprocal.

9. Feelings touch on issues of motivation and are sometimes identified with motives (Kernberg, 1980, 1982; Melanie Klein, 1937, 1945; Riviere, 1936; Sandler, 1972, 1985b) and sometimes distinguished from them (Noy, 1982, and most writers in psychology). Various theories regard affects as primary, as shaping experience, behavior, and self and object representations, that is, as motivating, whereas other theories (sometimes even the same ones) treat affects as secondary, as reactive to situations, dependent on the differentiation of self and object representations, expressing self states or the state of functioning of the mental apparatus (Basch, 1976a, 1981; Kohut, 1971, 1977; Sandler, 1972, 1985b), that is, as being motivated by all these causal factors.

10. The last point is linked with the view that affects fulfill a double function: they are both goals to be striven toward (such as attaining well-being or pleasure) and signals on the road to the goal. The system is not linear but has so-called circular causality, in which affects are 'set points' in a feedforward and feedback process.

11. The circular, nonlinear relationship between affects and motives should not be confused with the basic assumption in psychoanalysis that affects in a sense exist from the beginning of life and are the bedrock and the building blocks of mental structures (Kernberg, 1976), of object relations (Klein, 1933; Sandler & Sandler, 1978), and of the self (Demos, 1987; Emde, 1983; Stern, 1985). This point can be divided into the following two statements:

12. Affects have an indissoluble, primary, formative relationship to objects or their representations. Affects color all object relationships (Emde, 1980, 1988; Kernberg, 1976, 1982; Sandler & Sandler, 1978); the emotional availability of the other is recognized as a basic need (Emde, 1980, 1988); and affects are said by some theories (e.g., Melanie Klein, 1937, 1945; Riviere, 1936) even to create, in a sense, internal objects.

13. Affects nourish and organize the self, while simultaneously expressing the self; affects

contribute to the sense of self, and they testify to the person's actual value system (Basch, 1981; Emde, 1983; Kernberg, 1982; Sandler, 1985b; Schwartz, 1987; Stern, 1985). Recent findings tend to stress the importance of positive emotions in development and in 'affect attunement' (Emde, 1988; Stern, 1985).

14. The cardinal issue of unconscious affect has undergone various attempts at clarification: (a) within signal theory; (b) within a modified conception of metapsychology and metatheoretical thinking (see Anscombe, 1981; G. Klein, 1976; Schafer, 1976, 1979); (c) stressing the domain of the preconscious to encompass much that is considered unconscious, including unconscious feelings (see Hampshire, 1983a; Sandler, 1983, 1985b); and (d) in connection with the concept of self, or selfhood.

15. The last point concerns the mutual dependency between general psychoanalytic theory and affect theory. This study has approached affect theory as it was influenced in its various stages of evolution by developments in psychoanalysis. At this point, I shall take a cursory look at the influence and implications of affect theory on psychoanalytic theory; the fuller elaboration of this idea, an outline of psychoanalytic theory as dictated by findings and elaborations in the study of affect, is a task for the future.

Points 1, 2, and 3 deal with the emancipation of affects from their historical dependence on psychic energy, arousal, and drive. These points specify what affects are *not*, or what they are no longer considered to be. Points 4 to 8 deal with the complex structure of affects, their representations, and their modes or rules of functioning. These points involve the signal and perceptual function of affects, indicating that feelings can be no less unconscious than other mental processes, that they are also, perhaps basically and most of the time, signals. These points also offer ways of seeing how affects work in general and in relation to each other. It is maintained that feelings have their own representations and even types of memories, a fact that makes them into certain kinds of cognitions, evaluations, or perceptions. Points 9 to 13 pertain to the motivational, developmental, and object-relational role of affects. Of these, points 9, 10, and 11 speak of what I have called the double function of affects: memories and motives, on the one hand, and goals to be attained, on the other. Points 12 and 13 deal with the fundamental fact that affects are indissolubly tied, in fact part of, self and object or, on a more theoretical level, that affects are linked with self and object representations and are thus absolutely necessary for psychic development. Finally, points 14 and 15 touch on psychoanalytic affect theory, on psychoanalytic theory in general and some of their mutual implications. In the following pages, these points will be discussed, with more attention given to the issues that have received less elaboration thus far.

This study has touched on diverse criticisms against explanations of affects in terms of psychic energy (see Basch, 1976b; Holt, 1965; Rosenblatt & Thickstun, 1970). One of the pioneers in this area was Louis Kaywin (1960), whose work has been largely neglected, and it may be appropriate to mention it here. On the basis of a survey of various statements on instincts made by Freud, as well as contemporary biochemical, genetic, and embryological theories, Kaywin concluded that the concept of psychic energy in psychoanalysis is unnecessary and that thinking about energy qualitatively, as 'libidinal,' 'aggressive,' or 'neutral,' leads to great difficulties. In his work, Kaywin tried to move from speaking in libidinal terms to speaking in terms of affect. But Kaywin is just one of many thinkers who have worked to get the concept of psychic energy out of current psychoanalytic thinking (see Applegarth, 1971; see also Kernberg, 1976; Sandler, 1972; and others). There have been proposals to substitute the concept of meaning, 'psychic value,' or psychic significance (Basch, 1976b) for that of psychic energy. Meaning is a relational, not a nominative, term; meaning measures aspects of the relationship between sender and receiver (while energy is a measure of caloric exchange in the molecular order or else a metaphor for intensity or power).

The next two points deal with the relationship between drives and affects. In this context, Brierley (1937), Jacobson (1971), Kaywin (1960), Kernberg (1976), Sandler (1972), and others should be mentioned. The diverse studies and ideas found in these works point to the conclusion that the use of the concept of drive in the sense of energy is an untenable conception. In contrast, the use of the concept of drive as a compound of affect representations (Kaywin, 1960), or structured self and object representations linked by affects (Kernberg, 1976), features largely in modern affect theory. An early advocate of this line of thought, which has effected a reversal of the direction leading from drives to affects, is again Kaywin, who in 1960 posited that affects, which he saw as 'tonal precipitates,' that is, as representations of pleasurable and unpleasurable experiences, build up into 'reaction patterns,' which is the name he gave to instincts. The same idea, put somewhat differently, has also been articulated by Kernberg, whose thought is much better known (see chapter 6). Within his model, the concept of drive has acquired the meaning of a disposition, a motive for action or behavior that has been built up through numerous affective experiences accumulated with (external and internal) objects.

According to most contemporary authors (with the exception of Brenner, 1982, and some other ego psychologists and also with the exception, although in a different manner, of Green, 1973), affects are no longer regarded as drive derivatives, at least not exclusively so. Instead, affects are considered as coming from many other sources (which are not even termed 'sources,' in line with the recent trend in psychoanalysis of speaking more in terms of aims and determinants than in terms of sources of the drives), such as other feelings and object-related fantasies (Sandler & Sandler, 1978), or are regarded as shaping internal objects (Brierley, 1937; M. Klein, 1945), or, alternatively, feelings and raw experiences are regarded as material for psychic processing (Bion, 1962). Some authors even consider affects themselves to be the building blocks of the drives (Kaywin, 1960; Kernberg, 1976). In addition, findings from infant research point to the significance of affective synchrony in the affectively charged and channeled dialogue between mother and infant. These findings and the explanations that frame them likewise tend to replace older explanations of infant behavior in terms of drive gratification and pressures (Emde, 1980; Lichtenberg, 1987; Stern, 1985).

Concomitantly with the waning of the conception of affects as drive derivatives emerged the conception of affects as essentially signals. Signal theory has been discussed at length in the writings of Schafer (1976), Schur (1955, 1960, 1968a), and Brenner (1982) and needs no repeating here. It is increasingly accepted now that affect signals change—mostly unconsciously—the way a person thinks, feels, and acts. Not only strong passions, affect storms, or moods have the power to transform an experience and one's view of reality; signals do as well.

Since signals are mostly unconscious, the paradox of unconscious feelings seemed to have found a certain solution. The reasoning here is that signals are ego functions and, as such, are closer to perception or to 'thoughtlike awareness,' and hence can be unconscious (panel, 1968). The paradox of 'unfelt feeling' (Hampshire, 1983a) now becomes analogous to that of the famous 'preperceiver's paradox' in psychology or to Freud's (1923) treatment of the seeming contradiction hiding in the concept of an unconscious defense. In other words, feelings do not have to be in the nature of a full and open experience; rather, they may be momentary perceptions or apperceptions of a situation by rapid and subliminal (see Lazarus, 1982, in psychology) or 'gyroscopic' (Sandler & Sandler, 1984, in psychoanalysis) scanning for its personal meaning. This most basic issue of unconscious feelings will be picked up again in a later part of this chapter.

The increasingly recognized autonomous status of affects led investigators to probe into their ways of functioning from the most diverse perspectives, be it their self-generative (Melanie Klein, 1937, 1945; Jones, 1929), syntactic (Green, 1973, 1977), or syllogistic (Alexander, 1935) nature. Melanie Klein has described vicissitudes of feelings and has given us a portrait, unsurpassed in its power, of how strong feelings, such as envy, hate, or love, arouse other feelings and thus generate whole chains of feelings. In her view, the dynamics of feelings are the primary elements and motives of psychic life and development. Jones (1929) writes in a similar vein. He likewise sees feelings as bringing in their wake other feelings, which are the outcome, corollary, or defense against the former, as seen in the clinical situation. Franz Alexander's paper, "The Logic of Emotions and Its Dynamic Background" (1935) deals with what he calls 'emotional syllogisms,' that is, emotional connections that seem to us self-evident from our daily introspective experience. Alexander even goes so far as to say that our psychoanalytic concepts are based on these tacitly accepted emotional connections, and he uses the Oedipus complex as an example of a chain of such syllogisms (p. 400). The formulation of these syllogisms strongly resembles what I have called Melanie Klein's 'feeling chains' (chapter 4). Alexander says that although we are familiar with many such syllogisms from our daily experience, there are others discovered by psychoanalysis that are not self-evident. Alexander thinks that "the emotional logic of unconscious processes, though similar to the logic of conscious processes, is not entirely identical with the latter" (p. 401), but he goes on to elaborate this point into finer discriminations between conscious and unconscious processes. Forty years later, George Klein was to write that

emotional comprehension becomes a primary objective in therapy. . . . [Emotional comprehension] implies experiencing a meaning at the level of its unconsciously affective core—namely, as an emotional syllogism [which is] a rule or a premise, expressing the logic of affective values, which guides behavior and thought. . . . Comprehension involves experiencing this syllogism in its emotional aspect (1976, p. 99).[1]

From the effort to understand the way affects work, there is but a small step to the cognitive dimension of affect, which is, as I have shown (see particularly chapters 4, 5, 7, and 8), a very powerful notion in contemporary thinking on affect. The notion that our thoughts are steeped in feelings and have meaning for us only if they are accompanied by feelings and, on the other hand, the idea that feelings derive from and depend upon contents and fantasies (mostly of self in interaction with objects) are now taken as evident in psychoanalytic thinking (see Krystal, 1988). Put together, these two premises, which are based on substantiated evidence, lead to the conception that ties together affects and cognition, and sees them as separable only theoretically for purposes of certain conceptualizations, and in life only under unusual circumstances (such as intoxication, altered states of consciousness, or certain psychopathological conditions).[2] The power of the underlying feelings determines what meaning will be given to a thought, an act, a dream, or a metaphor that is connected with or taps these feelings (Rose, 1988, p. 169); or, as Modell (1984) put it, in psychoanalysis meanings depend more on affects than on words.

The emphasis on the cognitive or value- and meaning-laden aspect of feelings has been supported by the recent 'cognitive revolution' in psychology (see, e.g., Mandler, 1975), in which cognition has come to be seen as carrying an incomparably broader meaning than had been assumed before. Not only have affects been adjoined to ordinary normal mental functioning, but personal factors, such as beliefs, expectations, motives, and commitments, which influence attention and appraisal, have been increasingly reckoned with and investigated to see in what ways we actively select and shape experience and mold it to our own requirements. Within this new conception of cognition, cognitive processing, including perception, is seen as a multisystem and multistep operation comprising many feedback mechanisms. These feedback mechanisms process the new perception by comparing and confronting it with the associations it evokes; it is then evaluated and given meaning by parts of the mind that are only partially conscious. It has been experimentally proven and is now widely accepted in cognitive psychology that sensory 'raw material' is analyzed in semantic depth and on the basis of biases toward specific emotional content. Perception involves complex perceptual discriminations and various choices and decisions without consciousness (Dixon, 1971; Shevrin, 1978; Stein, 1980). The meaning of all this is that emotionally relevant meanings (connotations) can be triggered by inputs whose full-fledged understanding or decoding has not yet been achieved. These are new developments in psychology. Psychoanalysis, for its part, has been using concepts of fantasies, self and object representations and relationships, introjects, and so on—all concepts that combine thoughts and feelings. Both disciplines agree that emotion is never totally independent of cognitions, even when the emotional response is instantaneous and nonreflective. Meaning, in the sense of personal significance for well-being, is always an essential component of emotional reactions.

Recognizing the complexity of affective structures gives us a better grasp on their developmental and (object) relational significance. The works of Novey (1959, 1961), Schmale (1964), Krystal (1975, 1988), Lachman & Stolorow (1981), and Basch (1976c, 1981), as well as Mahler, Pine & Bergman (1975), contain or imply developmental theories of affect that consider the emergence, differentiation, and verbalization of affect to be dependent on the differentiation of self and object representations. Kernberg (1976, 1980), Sandler (1972) and Sandler & Sandler (1978), on the other hand, posit affects as building or linking self and object representations. In the latter theories, affect has a formative value in fostering the differentiation of self and object representations. Both groups recognize the reciprocity of the relationship between affect and self-and-object (or, as Stern calls it, self-with-object); infant researchers speak of the role of affect as absolutely necessary for attachment and for development in general, whereas theoreticians like Sandler, Kernberg, and others show, particularly in their clinical writings, how feelings depend on the person's developmental stage. A different stress is laid in the two domains on the question of whether affects depend on the structuring of self and object representations, or whether affects are there from the beginning, while self and object representations are built and differentiated through the affects. This difference may be a result of different vantage points; the first group of thinkers refer to observations of affects mostly in infants and children or in war neurotics, that is, directly and under natural conditions, whereas the latter authors were guided by theoretical considerations and by clinical reconstructive experience. When one observes the individual from a developmental angle, particularly the development of the self and of object relations, it is striking to what an extent affect depends on the maturation of cognition or object relationships. On the other hand, when retrospectively reconstructuring a person's history and past object relationships, one becomes alert to the fact that all relationships, to the self as well as to the object, are embedded in and imbued with feelings of different sorts.

Affects not only establish links between self and object but are profoundly important in consolidating and nourishing the self. Demos (1982), Emde (1983), Stern (1985), and others all say, though in different ways and from different vantage points, that feelings, if affirmed, organize the self-experience. George Klein writes:

A . . . key tenet of clinical psychoanalytic theory concerns the formative influence of pleasure experience and anxiety in the development of self-identity and in the structuring of motives. . . . Both might be said to refer to states of selfhood, complementary to each other. Just as anxiety is informative of estrangement, denoting threat or conflict, pleasure is informative of accord with well-being, of things and objects acquiring values of approachability and desirability" (1967, p. 18).

Krystal (1988), on his part, has developed a genetic theory of affect, in which he posits that it is in adolescence that a most important point of affect maturation is reached, permitting the consolidation of self representations.

The recognition of the vital role affects have for the consolidation and sustenance of the self appeared relatively late, and the recency of the discussions on this topic testifies to this fact. The latest writings speak of feelings as self-regulators (Emde, 1983) and 'self-invariants' (Stern, 1985), terms indicating the recognition that affects possess a kind of experiential continuity that makes them the safeguards of the sense of self. According to several authors, notably self psychologists and some infant researchers, the 'self' does not exist at the beginning of life; insofar as the infant's self exists as an idea, it is a product of the mother's mental production—the self of the child that is in the mind of the parents is only a virtual self. Most important among the infant's needs that have to be fulfilled by his caretakers is their response to and the stimulation of the child's affective reactions to them. Basch (1981) writes that when a concept of self becomes a possibility for the child, he has already been permanently influenced by the affectively toned learning experiences that he has encoded in the early sensorimotor transactions with his parents and other caretakers. These affectively weighted, information-processing memories or schemata form the basis of the self and serve as a sieve through which future experience is strained.

This bears on a further contrast between two vantage points. One considers affects as the bedrock, the matrix, of all experiences of the self in relationship with his objects (Sandler, 1972; Sandler & Sandler, 1978) and also of experiences that are later to become the drives (Kernberg, 1976, 1980). The other view holds that affects become real feelings (of and for self and other) only with the maturation and differentiation of (self and object) representations, which make it possible for feelings to be symbolized and reflected upon rather being reflex-like, preprogrammed phenomena.

This may be another instance of what I have called the 'double-edgedness' of affect. In psychoanalysis, feelings play a double role; feelings are goals, in that it is assumed that we strive to feel good, safe, and whole (and in pathological cases, to feel hurt, enraged, or helpless), and they are also signals that indicate whether we are coping with a danger situation or whether we have attained the state we desire. This conception of the double-edgedness of affect best fits a systems theory in which there is no simple linear sequence of events, but so-called circular causality. In such a conception, whether affects are signals or indicators or whether they are goals or end points depends on the point at which one chooses to enter. In other words, affects are a kind of set point in a self-regulating system of dynamic equilibrium; affects, in this framework, are pointers of well-being. Feeling states provide information about one's situation and values (see Sandler, 1971, 1985b), and certain feeling states (well-being) are goals to be striven for (Sandler & Sandler, 1978). Thus, what on one level is motivating may be motivated on another level, and affect is hence both motivating and motivated. Affects may be seen as short- or long-range plans and commitments that motivate action, and, on the other hand, affects may be aroused or motivated by almost any factor (see Tomkins, 1979, 1984).

One of the great discoveries of psychoanalysis in its early days was that feelings are motivating in a very complex and mostly hidden, sometimes cunning, manner. Much of Freud's work at that time could be said to be aimed at showing the ways and the extent in which feelings stood behind symptoms. Later it was shown that feelings motivate not only symptoms but also defenses. Then came a time when light was thrown on the aspect of feelings as motivated; to the psychoanalytic conception that feelings lie hidden beyond symptoms was added the view that behind feelings there are ideas, fantasies, and, in more recent days, object representations and relations to them and to the self. Feelings themselves came to be seen as shaped and toned by the contours and tints of internalized object relationships. A still more recent interest of psychoanalysis lies in the investigation of the person's relationship to his affects and feelings; that is, the way an individual feels about his feelings and handles them determines and is determined by his character. Some interesting though scattered work has been done on this idea (see Krystal, 1988; Schafer, 1964; Sifneos, 1975; and the countless clinical descriptions in the literature).

The dimension of emotion as motivated (by the representation or judgment of internal and external situations) is also addressed in cognitive theories of emotion in psychology, in which the antecedent conditions for emotions are being studied at present. In the psychoanalytic situation, too, the analyst usually helps the patient to see why the patient feels the way he does. This means going from the affects (which are there already or whose emergence the analyst facilitates through interpretation) to their motives, the royal road to which is the transference and the countertransference; the analytic process never ends with the mere expulsion or expression of feelings. Even when the analyst proceeds from utterances, thoughts, or contents of fantasies to the feelings underlying them, he will always strive to reach the next stage in this cycle, that of recovering the meaning behind the feelings, that is, the things that brought them about.

This point has bearings on the relationship of affects to the self. Basically, psychoanalysis regards feelings as tools for the person who 'has' them, keys and indicators for the understanding of meaning. When a person is aware of his having an affect, he feels himself, so to speak; he has intimate, unmediated awareness of himself. As Krystal writes, "To the experience of an emotion we must add the experience of 'having' an emotion" (1988, p. 6)—how one interprets and reacts to having an affect becomes an important part of one's identity.

As we have seen, many authors have pointed to the inseparable link between self and affect development. Stern (1985), for instance, sees the affects as the most constant and unchanging mental element throughout life, and he therefore calls them self-invariant and sees them as building the self and the sense of self. Emde's (1983) recent concept of the affective core of the self is another example. In contrast, Krystal (1988) says that the establishment of a discrete self representation is the fundamental event in affect development, and he goes to great lengths to show how affects in the mature adult should optimally be experienced as belonging to the self. He considers affects to be in essence 'extended self-manifestations' in the sense that feelings are responses to one's self-evaluation (p. 356). Kohut directly links a healthy, cohesive self with certain characteristic feelings and feeling states. Kohut's self psychology was marked from its beginning by sensitivity to feeling states of the self and between the self and the self object. Sandler's term 'the child within' is an evocative metaphor for infantile parts of the self that have to be reclaimed with the help of the provision of feelings of safety and well-being by a responsive other. Much of Melanie Klein's writings concern processes of dissociation and splitting from the self of feelings, together with parts of the self. Thus, the self grows on the affects, and the more it is able to contain them and to own them, the stronger it becomes. Krystal describes how one comes to acquire insight, comfort, and familiarity with affects as states of oneself.

What makes possible tolerance of painful affects without dissociating them from the self experience is the ability to modify them periodically for some short period of gratification or respite. This is akin to the process of mourning, which is in essence an oscillation between the painful consciousness of the loss and the experience of blotting out, or temporary denial, in which renewed strength is gathered to face the pain of loss. Mourning is accomplished when the painful event is assimilated into one's self representation.

Defending against affects is conceived in modern psychoanalysis as more complicated than repression in the usual sense. When an affect becomes intolerable, what happens is not the repression of some content or quantity that presses for discharge; it is rather a change of awareness. It is the exclusion of affect from the experience of belonging to the self, a process in the nature of a dissociation. The exclusion of affect from selfhood goes together with the projection of the affect onto objects, or with experiencing it as alien, either in the form of physiological phenomena or as moods. The point is that this change of awareness may occur in a state of consciousness (G. Klein, 1976; Krystal, 1975, 1988). Thus, it is not enough to detect the signs of emotion in a person; just having an emotion does not prove that the subject is aware of having it and is able to name or use it as a signal for himself. Sometimes an experience can be conscious yet repressed in a functional sense, that is, defended against. What is not recognized as part of the self representation is found to be functionally repressed, even if it retains the quality of consciousness (Krystal, 1988, p. xii). In repression, what is lacking is not consciousness—or at least effects in consciousness of a repressed content, or representation—but self-relatedness, ownership, responsiveness to feedback that would lead to experiencing the meaning of the behavior. Thus, making unconscious ideas conscious does not necessarily lift repression unless those ideas are also made self-conscious, that is, made "part of the 'I' " (Freud, 1933). In addition to consciousness, or self-consciousness, there is consciousness of an 'I' (Cavell, 1988). Retranslating Freud's 'Ich' into 'I' (rather than 'ego') brings out the closeness of this term to the concept of the self and self experience. In this context, the work of George Klein is pertinent. He writes that repression is not of a memory (content) but of the meaning of the memory. And meaning is significance for the self. Klein defines repression as a gap in understanding. To undo a repression, then, means to bring about comprehension, to perceive a link that the person had not seen before, and to reach a new level of understanding (1976, p. 248).

This is a new conception of affects, particularly unconscious affects, and of defenses against affects. In this view, affects are defended against when they are alienated from the self, deprived of the recognition of selfhood. According to this conception, defended affects are affects that are experienced not as belonging to one's self but as alien to one form (e.g., physiological attacks) or another (coming from the object, not from oneself). When affects are defended against, they and their related cognitive aspects are experienced as part of external reality (Novey, 1959) or as belonging to the object (Melanie Klein, 1937, 1946; Krystal, 1988). The distinction between conscious and unconscious gives way to that between belonging to the self and being alienated from it; emotions that are not experienced as belonging to the self should be seen as essentially defended against. Basically, self and affects develop in a dialectical manner; an enhanced self and better-differentiated self and object representations enable the person to experience affects on a higher developmental level, with more discernment and nuancing, and, conversely, more articulated and developed affects strengthen and consolidate the self and enhance the differentiation between self and object.

Stolorow, Brandschaft, & Atwood (1987), when discussing self psychology, write that its emphasis on the centrality of self-experience in both psychological development and pathogenesis has the singularly important implication "that it leads inevitably to a theoretical shift from the motivational primacy of instinctual drive to the motivational primacy of affect and affective experience" (p. 66; see also Basch, 1983). Thus, there are some indications that there may be a great theoretical shift toward the paradigm of the self and affects, where affective states are seen as enhancing differentiation and consolidation of the self, rather than the paradigm of the ego vis-à-vis the drive, i.e., controlling or using them.

The subject of unconscious affect has remained problematical in psychoanalysis. The question of unconscious affect is at a juncture of some basic problems in psychoanalytic theory, such as the nature of affect, feelings or emotions (the experiential dimension of affect), the status of defense in relation to the topographical unconscious, and so on. The problem of unconscious experience, which is at the base of the question of unconscious affect, can be addressed through several arguments.

One of these arguments concerns the fact, supported by the work of almost every worker in the field, that points to the affect being what may be called a syndrome or a 'cluster concept' (see Kaplan, 1958; Sandler, 1983). A 'cluster concept' is defined through multiple criteria, and it does not have to fulfill all of them in order for it to apply. These criteria, in the case of affect, are bodily changes, which may be objectively measured and/or subjectively felt; facial expressions, which may be observed by another person and/or experienced by the person himself; certain thoughts accompanying the feeling (sometimes called its content); the feelings themselves, which are the most subjective and ineffable component in an affect; and urges to do something about these feelings.

According to this view, we may call a phenomenon an affect if it fulfills most, but not necessarily all, of the criteria for its occurrence. We may call a phenomenon an affect if it involves bodily changes, facial expressions, even particular thoughts, but without the awareness of any feeling accompanying these occurrences. In such a case, we are justified in saying that we are dealing with unconscious feelings, in the sense that the affect is there, but the experiential side of it, the feelings, is not experienced, although the feelings may be perceived by some other person than the one having the affect. This also explains why it is appropriate to use the more experience-distant term 'affect,' which reflects the importance of the psychoanalytic discovery of unconscious feelings, as contrasted with the inadequacy of common usage, based on direct introspection or direct reference (which does not allow for paradoxes like 'unfelt feelings,' 'unexperienced experience,' 'unemotional emotion,' or the like). In this sense, 'affect' refers to emotional phenomena irrespective of their relation to consciousness. Thus, affect as a mental state may have many of the characteristic features of emotions, in particular their effects in modulating behavior, but may lack the feature of being phenomenologically manifest. Anscombe (1981) says that the concept of affect accounts for the psychoanalytic assumption that the changes in behavior and thought mediated by these mental processes are more central and essential than the manifestation of emotion as experience. Hence, on this obvious level, we are justified in calling an affect unconscious, when its feeling aspect is not consciously experienced.

This does not mean, of course, that feelings are necessarily stored somewhere 'inside' in a concrete, immutable form. Such an idea would parallel the fallacy that unconscious affects must be 'deep down,' a fallacy to which Freud submitted when he assumed that consciousness is on the surface of the psyche (1923, p. 19).

One of the most important theoreticians in psychoanalysis, Roy Schafer, has criticized this spatial metaphor. Schafer reasoned that since feelings cannot be stored in space, they are not things, and they are neither locatable inside nor discharged to the outside.

Schafer, however, took his argument further and thereby has touched on some of the most crucial and much debated issues in psychoanalytic theory today, such as the question of the viability of a metapsychology in psychoanalysis, the specifically psychoanalytic concept of the dynamic unconscious, and unconscious affects.

Schafer's ideas are elaborated around the question of whether we need a metapsychology or whether, as he and George Klein before him claimed, we would be better off without this theoretical superstructure. In discussing Schafer's arguments, I shall rely mostly on Anscombe's (1981) critique of Schafer's action language, in which he shows how Schafer's theory, one of the most systematic attacks against psychoanalytic metatheory, is most problematic when he applies it to the emotions. We shall also see that Schafer's treatment of the emotions has the result, in the last analysis, of undermining one of the most important contributions of psychoanalysis, the dynamic unconscious.

Anscombe argues that in order to proceed with his project of replacing metapsychology with a more immediately clinical set of concepts, Schafer could not allow for any mental phenomena that could not be accounted for in the language of human action. Emotions, in this respect, pose a particular difficulty on account of their being relatively passive phenomena. But it is the very fact that feelings may overwhelm the person that calls for a theory explaining the cases when a person is not master of himself. Schafer's theory cannot account for the unique, specific experience we all have of emotions as potentially unconscious and overwhelming. There must be a meta-theory, if emotions are not to be considered as a kind of conscious action, which they are in Schafer's clinical theory. Emotions are relatively passive phenomena consisting of active experiencing, not active doing or thinking. Thus, in a paradoxical way, accounting for the nonvoluntary, subjective, even passive aspect of the emotions implies the necessity of a metatheory that would speak of an unconscious as something altogether different from what is conscious.

To Schafer, the criterion for an emotion is the use (see Wittgenstein, 1953) people make of the word denoting it, rather than the fact that the experience of one emotion is different from that of another emotion. In maintaining, however, that emotions refer not to inner experiences but to ways of acting, Schafer is compelled to conclude that emotion is voluntary and a matter of choice like any other conscious action. In this way, Schafer's theory precludes an unconscious that is different and discontinuous from what is conscious.

The very failure of Schafer's model of the emotions as potentially available actions—the untenability of such a position about affects—logically calls for the need for a metapsychology, in the sense of a theory that can account for the "things a person cannot do" (Anscombe, 1981, p. 225). An observational account without a metaclinical or metapsychological theory is inadequate because it cannot account for the phenomenon of unconscious feelings. Thus, one aspect of the study of affect in psychoanalysis is its provision of at least one convincing argument for the necessity of a metapsychology in psychoanalysis, a theory that will account for those experiences and manifestations that cannot be explained by considering unconscious phenomena as just another 'dislocated' (Freud, 1893–

1895) or 'faultily observed' (Schafer, 1976) version of conscious phenomena. The existence of unconscious affects testifies to the fact that we cannot refer in the analytic dialogue only to a person's conscious communication or experience, but there must be a theory of (metaclinical, underlying) mechanisms. Structural theory itself turned to the explanation of mechanisms or structures on inferring the existence of unconscious guilt.

Anscombe reminds us that there are things a person cannot do, particularly in psychopathological states, where there are 'gaps in personhood' and where feelings are sometimes stronger than the person himself, and for these things we need a theory. Such a theory will have to account for the fact that unconscious mental phenomena are both intentional and involuntary (Eagle, 1980) or have conscious consequences but leave gaps in understanding (G. Klein, 1976).

RECAPITULATION

In this study I have traced different kinds of work on affects in theory and research, and I have come up with a picture in which affect emerges as a very central concept and as a phenomenon that can and must be discussed and given a place in theory in its own right. The affective phenomenon exists in all kinds of defending, defensive, conflicted, and motivating states; it forms the bedrock of clinical practice, and, in the final analysis, it is profoundly linked with the self; however, theorizing about it has proved extremely difficult.

Two major problems concerning affects in Freud's theory that have made it difficult to conceptualize them in the past have been solved within certain frameworks. The 'drive view' of affects was corrected by Joseph Sandler, among others. Sandler divided and delimited different phases of Freud's theory and attempted to uncover the importance for mental functioning of such concepts as signals and wishes, and the profound motivational importance of feelings such as safety and well-being, depression and shame. Feelings, in his theory, are signals in the deepest sense. They are the true pointers to the experienced state of the person; they are the only way of knowing, in the sense that all our knowledge comes from experiential input to our mental apparatus; and they are pursued for their own sake because of their strong reinforcing value (in this sense, there is some affinity between Sandler's line of thought and that of Tomkins, 1962–1963, 1979).

Other works had further implications, leading to a 180-degree revolution in psychoanalytic theory, namely, the attempt to replace the drives by affects. Affects display many characteristics that are similar to those of the drives. Affects have links with the body, and they are immediate, biologically built-in, external signaling devices that later become more and more 'interiorized,' refined, signal-like, and (consciously or unconsciously) experiential. As Basch (1986) reminds us, instinct theory was pure speculation on Freud's part and had nothing to do with anything actually uncovered through the psychoanalytic method. The fact that we *feel* 'driven' to engage in one or another kind of behavior does not necessarily entail that we are pushed by drives. Basch stresses the massive, varied evidence indicating that Freud's hypotheses concerning development and mental functioning were in error and that alternative, experimentally more valid explanations are now available. Thus, the most recent lines of thought (Sandler, 1985b; Tomkins, 1979, 1984; in a sense, Aylwin, 1985) regard the affects themselves as possessing the 'driving' and driven, peremptory and 'amplified' characteristics attributed in the past to the drives; occasionally it is even suggested that the drives are overall configurations built on units of affects linked to self and object representations (Kernberg, 1980).

Once affects were given motivational status of their own, independently of the drives, another major problem made itself felt: their problematical cognitive status. We have seen that affects were considered fluid quantities without structure or representation. This view led several important thinkers (e.g., Freud, 1923; Hartmann, 1939a; Lacan, 1977) to deny affects a theoretical status of their own and to exclude them from theory altogether. This problem was addressed by André Green (1973), who has worked out an articulate model of affect representations and has attempted to spell out their nature and way of operating. Green posits a continuous, unconsciously functioning chain of heterogeneous signifiers, among which are also the affects. He believes that affects belong to the body, representing the body to oneself, yet at the same time have an inherently semantic function; they are signifiers.

Green built up his conception, among other things, on a tour de force, in which he rejected Freud's basic and long-accepted belief that only external perceptions may have representations. Instead, Green maintained that affects do not have to originate from external perceptions in order to have representations. This idea tallies with many observations, notably those of Piaget, who showed that mental life begins not with perception but with the activation of sensorimotor schemata. It also tallies with much of infant research, which shows that affective life begins with expressive motor patterns that serve as signaling devices to the exterior.

These theoretical developments made affects independent of the drives and of external perceptions. But then it was found that affects did not fit comfortably within structural theory, which, as has become increasingly clear, is "not enough" (see the international congress, Montreal, 1987, e.g. Sandler, 1988). Evidence for this situation is the fact that theories of affect in ego psychology seem to be greatly lacking in their treatment of affective phenomena, in particular their feeling aspects (see chapter 3). The debate on whether affects belong to the id or to the ego (Green, 1973; Rangell, 1968; J. Sandler with A. Freud, 1985) has lost much of its interest, owing to the increasing difficulty of un-equivocally differentiating between the ego and the id (see G. Klein, 1976; Schafer, 1976). The conception of affects as drive phenomena to be controlled

(Rapaport, 1953), even tamed (Fenichel, 1941), by the ego, collapsed in view of newer conceptions of the drives as complex, structuralized entities (see Kaywin, 1960; Kernberg, 1980; Schafer, 1976). On the other hand, the view that feelings are sensations plus contents (Brenner, 1982), or behavioral programs inspired by primary process thinking (Noy, 1982), meets with difficulties on account of the clash between an underlying computer model and a model of wishful thinking divorced from reality. Added to this, there has accumulated a wealth of empirical (clinical and developmental) findings that point to the utmost importance of affects in shaping object relations and in sustaining and developing a sense of self.

What are we left with, then? Taking a very broad perspective, we can see that all attempts to build a psychoanalytic theory that do not grant affects a central place have foundered. Thus, the 'drive' view had to be changed and improved, time and again, by Freud, Sandler, Kernberg, Basch, and many others. The 'language' view (Lacan) proved a failure, and the 'action' view (Schafer) did not fare much better. Many theories rose and fell or, rather, were found to be lacking, whereas affects remained the orienting pole. Freud's first theory, the trauma model, was an affect theory complicated later in the topographical model by the concept of drive. His second topographical (the structural) theory received its impetus, as is well known, from the problem of unconscious guilt. This theory involved the tripartite model, which proved fruitful for a time by emphasizing aspects that had been ignored before. Structural theory, however, focused on ego functions and on drives to the exclusion of affects, and it turned out to be too simple and mechanistic to house feelings and experience with objects, although it gave us the concept of signal. Later models, such as object relations theories and Kleinian theory, were also somehow inspired by affective phenomena: object relations theory by phenomena of love, object-seeking, and attachment and Kleinian theory by aggression and anxiety.

The effort to find a level of discourse for the affects is difficult and many-sided, and only the first steps of the discussion have been taken here. In any case, there are three general theoretical issues that, as a result of this study, seem most relevant at this stage. The first concerns the need for a metaclinical (metapsychological) theory to account for 'gaps in personhood,' i.e., for experience that does not belong, and may never come to belong, to the self experience of a person. The second point pertains to considerable innovations made in psychoanalysis once the first and second topographical theories proved inadequate to account for clinical phenomena. Changing concepts, such as defense, the unconscious, and development in terms of self and object representations, are clear examples. The third point touches on the plentiful evidence in the area of infant research, to which psychoanalysis is beginning to lend an ear. This evidence progressively articulates the evolving links of the affects with the self, through the vital mediation of the caretaking object. These are important points with which we have to contend in the future in improving our affect theory.

IMPLICATIONS FOR TREATMENT

Feelings carry the multiple roles of evaluating, shaping, connecting, motivating, and reinforcing learning. There are 'appropriate' and 'inappropriate' feelings (inappropriate feelings are appropriate to some other contents).[3] In addition, there are 'organized' and confused, primitive and differentiated, nuanced, rich and warm, alienated and bizarre feelings (e.g., Jacobson, 1971).

Seen from this perspective, the fulcrum of pathology is not the existence of negative affects per se (as some ego psychologists seem to claim) but an 'inappropriate' or discordant—repressive or submissive, defensive or otherwise intolerant—relationship of the person to his feelings. This is the critical factor in assessing psychodynamics and psychopathology, and we can see in the literature the manifold possible relations persons have with their feelings, such as containment (Bion), tolerance (Zetzel, Krystal), mastery (Fenichel), use as a source for action and thought and understanding, or evacuation (Bion), denial and projection (Freud, Melanie Klein, etc.), hatred of feelings (Bion), trauma and paralysis (Krystal, Furst), 'affectualization' (Rangell), erotization (Chasseguet-Smirgel), and so on. In a sense, psychoanalytic therapy is emotional 'education,' the fostering of emotional growth and emotional courage (to know and to own what one feels, even if it be unpleasant, painful, or puzzling, and to be aware of a whole gamut of nuanced, changing feelings). This education can be made possible through creating an atmosphere that is a priori conducive to tolerance for all kinds of feelings, through facilitating feelings of safety, mutuality, and emotional matching between the two participants, and through close attention and sensitivity to the feeling states both patient and analyst bring to bear on their therapeutic relation. This in turn bears on psychoanalytic technique, which has been profoundly influenced by developments in the theory of affects.

In psychoanalysis it is explicitly or tacitly assumed that treatment revolves around the core of affect, that what is most critical and curative in analysis always involves affects (see Joseph, 1985; Krystal, 1988; Pulver, 1987).[4] Both insight theories and relationship theories of cure are linked with affects in the sense that insight must be affective as well as cognitive and that object relationships are always affective. With all these assumptions, it becomes clear that a profound change has taken place in the treatment paradigm in psychoanalysis; it is no longer (interminable) chimney sweeping (where affect is regarded as essentially pure quantity) and no longer making the unconscious conscious and acquiring insight (where affects are seen as the topographical by-products of the drive). Treatment now mostly consists in approaching painful feelings so as to be able to tolerate them in order to be in touch with one's self or to transform them, not mechanically, through discharge, but by connecting them with oneself and endowing the situation that evoked the affect with a different meaning and thereby changing its accompanying affect; this in turn transforms the self. We can see here the close link among affect theory, theoretical statements about the nature of affect, and the understanding of what is curative in psychoanalysis. In the same spirit, the rules for interpretation have changed. In the past, they were worded as "start at the surface"; "interpretation of resistance precedes interpretation of content" (Fenichel, 1941). These rules were grounded on the metapsychological conceptions of the first and second topographical layerings and divisions of the mental apparatus. Today, the rules of interpretation are construed with constant reference to the subjective, experiential moment of the individual. Interpretation is seen to "elucidate the nature of . . . the psychic structures that organize the patient's subjective experiences in general and thematize the transference relationship in particular" (Atwood & Stolorow, 1984, p. 46). Feelings are inherently reflexive in the sense that they 'fall back' upon the person who 'has them' (Green, 1973), they say something, they communicate to oneself about oneself and one's situation (Lazarus, 1984a; Sandler, 1985; Taylor, 1985), and they are also transmitted to the other person, a fact most concentratedly used in the transference-countertransference exchange. Thus, the therapeutic endeavor is now seen in terms of understanding and re-organizing the patient's feelings within his subjective world.[5]

Notes

CHAPTER 1. FREUD'S WRITINGS ON AFFECT

1. The totalizing effect of emotions is discussed by Matte-Blanco (1988), by Sartre (1948), and by others.

2. See Eagle (1987) and Schafer (1980) concerning the fallacy of assuming that unconscious material is statically stored and retrievable in its untouched, original form. See also chapter 10.

3. 'Feelings' has been offered as a translation for the German word 'Empfindungen,' which means 'sensations.' Feelings and sensations are sometimes synonymous in English, but they are only rarely interchangeable in German. It should be pointed out here that several authors distinguish between feelings in the sense of affects and feelings in the sense of sensations. Thus, the philosopher of mind McGinn (1982) distinguishes between what he calls 'sensations' and 'propositional attitudes,' the latter including affects. Ramzey and Wallerstein (1958) also formulate a carefully documented distinction between affects and sensations (and on the basis of this distinction they differentiate between bodily pain and mental pain, including its later derivatives, fear and anxiety). What emerges from most discussions on the subject is that a feeling quality need not necessarily be accompanied by bodily sensations, and sensations may be seen as a category in themselves. (See Stern, 1985, and particularly Krystal, 1988, on the 'detachability' of sensations of pleasure and unpleasure from the affects.)

4. In contrast, Dahl suggested (panel, 1982) that it was the absence of a theory of affect that led Freud to introduce the structural model of the mind.

5. In French, the close relationship between repression and suppression may be seen in the use of 'refoulement,' meaning repression, whereas the French 'repression' means suppression (see, e.g., Laplanche & Pontalis, 1973).

6. See the *Project*, where Freud speaks of two forms of unpleasure, which correspond to traumatic and signal anxiety, respectively; in the first, as a result of trauma, unpleasure

is freshly released by the secretory neurons, and in the second, the increase of tension registers in the ego (1895 [1950], pp. 320, 358).

CHAPTER 3. EGO PSYCHOLOGY AND THE AFFECTS

1. This last subclass is adapted from Scheler's classical classification of feelings (1927, in Hartmann, 1964).

2. The concept of threshold was extensively used (e.g., for explaining unconscious affects) in a panel on affect theory in psychoanalysis held by the American Psychoanalytic Association in 1982.

3. A similar approach had been assumed by McDougall (1928) in his famous instinct-affect theory, in which each instinct was assumed to be coupled with a specific affect. Schur's suggestion of an instinct to avoid danger, which is a related idea, was aptly criticized by de Rivera (1977), while Brenner (1982) put it even more strongly, saying that the assumption of an instinct to avoid danger resolves most of the intrinsic problems of anxiety without needing Freud's theory of anxiety.

4. This view calls to mind Noy's theory of affect, which assumes three major solutions to psychic conflict: psychosomatic illness (reminiscent of Brenner's primary unpleasure), depression, or anxiety.

5. The subject of transformation was discussed at length in chapter 1, where it was shown that it almost disappeared after the theoretical developments of 1920, 1923, and 1925.

6. Other thinkers, e.g., Lewin (1965), Novey (1961), Ross (1975), and Schur (1968a), also stressed the close connection of affects and ideas, but, in Brenner's view, they all failed to include ideas as part of the affects.

7. The view of affects as discharge processes is found in Freud's second theory of affects of 1915 and in Rapaport's 1953 paper, while the view of affects as tension phenomena is expounded mainly in Freud's 1894 essays and in Brierley's 1937 paper on affects. Compare these views with the James-Lange theory (1885) as a kind of discharge theory versus Cannon's (1911) as a kind of tension (homeostatic) theory.

8. See the etymological root of the word 'Affekt' in German (Laplanche & Pontalis, 1973, p. 13).

9. Peto (1967) applied the distinction between intersystemic and intrasystemic affects to clinical phenomena in general, and to the subtle moment-to-moment occurrences in the analytic session in particular. By observing these affective tensions, he also gauged the patient's ego strength and use of affects. Another application of this idea is found in Piers & Singer's (1953) distinction between guilt and shame, according to whether the tension is between ego and superego (guilt) or between ego and ego ideal (shame).

10. A similar idea was expressed by J. C. Fluegel in his book *Studies in Feeling and Desire* (1955; see in particular the chapter entitled "L'appetit vient en mageant"). Fluegel discusses what he calls self-sustaining (motivated, pleasurable) activities and analyzes the factors that account for their termination. He calls "the fundamental paradox of homeostasis" the fact that in the very process of seeking to relieve our needs we are creating ever fresh ones (p. 91).

11. Jacobson's intuition had to await the work of Silvan Tomkins, who, in his affect theory (1962–1963, 1970, 1984), gave the factors of changes in the level of stimulation a central role in determining not only pleasure and unpleasure but the differences between the main affects (see chapter 9).

12. In line with this idea stands Krystal's valuable work, published in a series of papers gathered recently in a book (1988) on affect tolerance and other dimensions of affective experience from a clinical standpoint. Krystal acknowledges his work as being inspired by Zetzel's (1949) observations on the capacity to bear anxiety.

13. Noy does say that when the ego is strong enough it can use anxiety and depression as signals, but as signals that indicate that something is wrong or does not function appropriately. Such a view involves extreme or marginal cases, rather than seeing anxiety and depression as signs of normal processes, such as mourning or developmental crises.

CHAPTER 4. AFFECTS AND POSITIONS: MELANIE KLEIN, WILFRED BION

1. There are papers in the psychoanalytic literature on dynamics of particular emotions, many of which are collected in Socarides (1977); however, Melanie Klein's monograph *Envy and Gratitude* is a classic in the field.

2. "Klein's [view of the drives is that of] antithetical, object-related passions" (Greenberg & Mitchell, 1983, p. 142).

3. For explicatory texts on Bion's thought, see Grinberg, Sor, & De Bianchedi (1975), Grotstein (1981), and Meltzer (1978).

4. See Novey (1959), who forcefully, although in a different vein, argues for the identity of knowing and feeling.

CHAPTER 5. AFFECTS AS FEELING STATES AND AS VALUE FUNCTIONS: JOSEPH SANDLER

1. See Green's similar, more detailed argument (chapter 7).

2. Hartmann himself mentioned in this context Max Scheler's philosophical theory of values, which are, according to Scheler, perceived through our emotional response to them. Scheler's theory may be regarded as a precursor to Hartmann's and Sandler's theories of value.

CHAPTER 7. THE FRENCH SCHOOL: ANDRÉ GREEN— A DISCOURSE ON AFFECTS

1. For Lacan, "truth," rather than knowledge, is the supreme aim and intention of psychoanalytic thought (Green, personal communication; see also Lacan, 1977, pp. 74, 286).

2. If affect as meaning carrier connotes an idea and may suggest an intellectualistic theory of affect, which certainly was not Green's intention, let me quote here one of his aphoristic assertions on affect. He says that "affect is the flesh of the signifier and the signifier of the flesh" ("L'affect est la chair du signifiant et le signifiant de la chair"); the allusion is to Merleau-Ponty (Green, personal communication).

CHAPTER 8. RECENT TRENDS IN AFFECT THEORIES IN PSYCHOLOGY

1. Recent burgeoning affect theories in philosophy, some of which are naive, some promising (e.g., de Sousa, 1987; Rey, 1980; Rorty, 1980; Solomon, 1976, 1980; and others), are outside the scope of this book.

2. Compare this to Stern's concept of RIGs (1985, p. 97) and de Sousa's paradigm scenarios.

3. See Schafer's discussion of "sincere and pretended emotion" (1976, pp. 324–29).

CHAPTER 9. THE RELEVANCE OF RECENT TRENDS IN THEORIES OF EMOTION IN PSYCHOLOGY AND INFANT STUDIES TO PSYCHOANALYTIC AFFECT THEORY

1. One may find fruitful ideas in other disciplines provided one is careful not to transgress the 'rules of the game,' i.e., the methods of investigation and their underlying assumptions in each discipline. More specifically, one must keep in mind that psychoanalysis is mainly interested in psychodynamics and mental conflict, while psychology in its present state seems to aim at elucidating the generative mechanisms of behavior and, recently, of experience as well. If, however, one holds that both disciplines are interested in obtaining a theory of the mind, then the possibility of traffic of knowledge between them is open. This bears on a related question, namely, whether psychoanalysis should be seen as a separate domain (see Sherwood, 1969) and investigations should rely solely on what Brenner calls 'psychoanalytic data' (1982), so that data or the ideas based on them obtained from other sources are seen as irrelevant to psychoanalytic thinking. This issue is also related to the question of whether psychoanalysis should be seen in an exclusively hermeneutical framework or not. The present study is obviously opposed to such a separatism, but the methodological arguments underlying it are outside its scope (for a clarifying discussion of these issues, see, e.g., Eagle, in Stern, 1987).

CHAPTER 10. CONCLUSIONS AND NEW DIRECTIONS

1. We are so used to thinking in terms of feelings habitually causing other feelings that we hardly ever notice the fact that we are dealing with feeling chains or syllogisms. Thus, for example, we know that narcissistic feelings, such as idealization, grandiosity, devaluation, fear of dependency, and so on, induce shame, whereas impulsivity, sexual (incestuous) feelings, and rage induce guilt, feelings that signify danger lead to anxiety, and so on.

2. See Lewin's discussion of whether there is 'pure' feeling (1965).

3. In this context, see Sachs, who claims:

Between any person's emotions or affects and the causes or causal objects thereof, there always obtains an actual proportionality or real appropriateness, no matter how discrepant or incongruous those relations may appear to be, and regardless of the person's mental condition, that is, irrespective of whether Freud would deem him psychotic, neurotic, or normal. [He goes on to say that Freud] treated all anomalies of emotion . . . as only ostensible, taking it . . . for granted that beneath . . . those incongruities there is an unconscious but real congruity (1974, p. 146).

4. Pulver (1987) quotes Joseph (1984), who hypothesized that analysts of various theoretical persuasions are all working out the same unconscious affects and fantasies in the transference, even when they approach them on different levels of development or with different metaphors, since all these levels reverberate with each other anyway. He suggested that the different theories are metaphoric variants of the same affective truth.

5. Hillman (1961) strongly makes the point that feelings are healing per se, not only because of discharge/catharsis, but because they reorganize, create, arrange, and dismantle the old and static.

References

Abraham, K. (1921). Contributions to the theory of the anal character. A short study of the development of the libido in the light of mental disorders. In *Selected Papers of Karl Abraham*, trans. D. Bryan & A. Strachey. New York: Basic Books, 1953, pp. 370–92.

———. (1924). A short study of the development of the libido viewed in the light of mental disorders. Ibid., pp. 418–501.

Alexander, F. (1935). The logic of emotions and its dynamic background. Int. J. Psychoanal., 16: 399–413.

——— & French, T. M. (1946). *Psychoanalytic Therapy: Principles and Applications*. New York: Ronald Press.

Amacher, P. (1964). *Freud's Neurological Education and Its Influence on Psychoanalytic Theory*. Psychol. Issues, vol. 4. New York: Int. Univ. Press.

Anscombe, R. (1981¹). Referring to the unconscious: A philosophical critique of Schafer's action language. Int. J. Psychoanal., 62: 225–42.

Apfelbaum, B. (1966). On ego-psychology: A critique of the structural approach to psycho-analytic theory. Int. J. Psychoanal., 47: 451–75.

Applegarth, A. (1971). Some comments on aspects of the theory of psychic energy. J. Amer. Psychoanal. Assn., 19: 379–416.

Arlow, J. A. (1952). Ego psychology and instinctual studies. Annual Survey of Psychoanal., 3: 76–88.

———. (1977). Affects and the psychoanalytic situation. Int. J. Psychoanal., 58: 157–70.

Arnold, M. B., ed. (1960). *Emotion and Personality*. New York: Columbia Univ. Press.

———, ed. (1968). *The Nature of Emotion: Selected readings*. Middlesex, England & Baltimore: Penguin.

———, ed. (1970a). *Feelings and Emotions*. The Loyola Symposium. New York: Academic Press.

————. (1970b). Perennial problems in the field of emotions. In *Feelings and Emotions*, ed. M. B. Arnold. New York: Academic Press.

————. (1980). Emotion and anxiety: Sociocultural, biological, and psychological determinants. In *Explaining Emotions*, ed. A. O. Rorty. Berkeley: Univ. of Calif. Press, pp. 37–72.

Atwood, G. E. & Stolorow, R. D. (1984). *Structures of Subjectivity*. Hillsdale, NJ: Lawrence Erlbaum.

Averill, J. R. (1980). Emotions and anxiety: Sociocultural, biological, and psychological determinants. In *Explaining Emotions*. ed. A. O. Rorty. Berkeley: Univ. of Calif. Press.

————. (1981). A constructivist theory of emotion. In *Emotion: Theory, Research and Experience*, ed. R. Plutchik & H. Kellerman. New York: Academic Press, pp. 305–39.

————, Opton, E. M., Jr. & Lazarus, R. S. (1969). Cross-cultural studies of psychophysiological responses during stress and emotion. Int. J. Psychol., 4: 83–102.

Aylwin, S. (1985). *Structure in Thought and Feeling*. London: Methuen.

Balint, M. (1939). Early developmental stages of the ego. Int. J. Psychoanal., 30: 265–73.

Basch, M. F. (1973). Psychoanalysis and theory formation. Ann. Psychoanal., 1: 39–52.

————. (1975). Perception, consciousness and Freud's Project. Ann. Psychoanal., 3: 3–20.

————. (1976a). The concept of affect: A re-examination. J. Amer. Psychoanal. Assn., 24: 759–77.

————. (1976b). Psychoanalysis and communication science. Ann. Psychoanal., 4: 385–419.

————. (1976c). Theory formation in chapter VII: A critique. J. Amer. Psychoanal. Assn., 24: 61–100.

————. (1981). Psychoanalytic interpretation and cognitive transformation. Int. J. Psychoanal., 62: 151–76.

———— (1983). Empathic understanding: a review of the concept and some theoretical considerations. J. Amer. Psychoanal. Assn., 31: 101–26.

———— (1986). Clinical theory and metapsychology: Incompatible or complementary? Psychoanal. Rev., 73: 261–71.

Bernfeld, S. (1944). Freud's earliest theories and the school of Helmholtz. Psychoanal. Q., 13: 341–62.

Bibring, E. (1941). The development and problems of the theory of instincts. Int. J. Psychoanal., 22: 102–31.

Bion, W. R. (1962). *Learning from Experience*. London: Marsefield.

———— (1963). *Elements of Psychoanalysis*. London: Marsefield.

———— (1967). *Second Thoughts*. London: Marsefield.

———— (1970). *Attention and Interpretation*. London: Marsefield.

Blanck, G. & Blanck, R. (1974). *Ego Psychology: Theory and Practice*. New York: Columbia Univ. Press.

Bowlby, J. (1960). Grief and mourning in infancy and early childhood. Psychoanal. Study Child, 15: 9–52.

———— (1969). *Attachment and Loss*: Volume 1, Attachment. New York: Basic Books.

—— (1973). *Attachment and Loss*: Volume 2, Separation, Anxiety and Anger. New York: Basic Books.

Brenner, C. (1953). An addendum to Freud's theory of anxiety. Int. J. Psychoanal., 34: 18–24.

—— (1973). Psychoanalysis: Philosophy or science. In *Psychoanalysis and Philosophy*, ed. C. Hanly & M. Lazerowitz. New York: Int. Univ. Press, pp. 35–45.

—— (1974). On the nature and development of affects: A unified theory. Psychoanal. Q., 43: 532–56.

—— (1975). Affects and psychic conflict. Psychoanal. Q., 44: 5–28.

—— (1982). *The Mind in Conflict*. New York: Int. Univ. Press.

—— (1987). Notes on psychoanalysis by a participant observer. J. Amer. Psychoanal. Assn., 35: 539–56.

Breuer, J. & Freud, S. (1893–1895). *Studies on Hysteria*, S.E. 2, London: Hogarth Press.

Brierley, M. (1937). Affects in theory and practice. Int. J. Psychoanal., 18: 256–68.

—— (1951). *Trends in Psychoanalysis*. London: Hogarth Press.

—— (1969). 'Hardy perennials' and psychoanalysis. Int. J. Psychoanal., 50: 447–52.

Brody, S. (1982). Psychoanalytic theories of infant development and disturbances: A critical evaluation. Psychoanal. Q., 51: 526–97.

Bull, N. (1951). The attitude theory of emotion. Nerv. & Ment. Disease Monographs, No. 81.

Calhoun, C. & Solomon, R., eds. (1984). *What Is an Emotion?* Classic Readings in Philosophical Psychology. Oxford: Oxford Univ. Press.

Cannon, W. B. (1927). The James-Lange theory of emotions: A critical examination and an alternative theory. Amer. J. Psychol., 39: 106–24.

—— (1936). *Bodily Changes in Pain, Hunger, Fear and Rage*. New York: Appleton-Century-Crofts.

Cavell, M. (1985). The self and some related issues: A philosophical perspective, parts 1 & 2. Psychoanal. & Contemp. Thought, 8: 3–44.

—— (1987). A response to Otto Kernberg's "The dynamic unconscious and the self." In *Theories of the Unconscious and Theories of the Self*, ed. R. Stern. Hillsdale, NJ: Analytic Press, pp. 58–69.

—— (1988). Interpretation, psychoanalysis, and the philosophy of mind. J. Amer. Psychoanal. Assn., 36: 859–79.

Chance, M. A. (1981). An ethological assessment of emotion. In *Emotion: Theory, Research and Experience*, ed. R. Plutchik & H. Kellerman. New York: Academic Press, pp. 81–111.

Cheren, S., ed. (1987). *Psychosomatic Medicine. Theory, Physiology and Practice*. New York: Int. Univ. Press.

Ciompi, L. (1988). *The Psyche and Schizophrenia: The Bond between Affect and Logic*. Cambridge, MA: Harvard Univ. Press.

Clark, M. S. (1982). A role for arousal in the link between feeling states, judgments, and behavior. In *Affect and Cognition*, ed. M. S. Clark & S. T. Fiske. Hillsdale, NJ: Lawrence Erlbaum.

—— & Fiske, S. T., eds. (1982). *Affect and Cognition*. The 17th Annual Carnegie Symposium on Cognition. Hillsdale, NJ: Lawrence Erlbaum.

Cooper, A. (1986). Psychoanalysis today: Old wine in new bottles. Presented at the annual meeting of the Amer. Psychoanal. Assn., May 1986.

Dahl, H. (1979). A new psychoanalytic model of motivation. Psychoanal. & Contemp. Thought, 1: 373–408.

Darwin, C. (1965). The Expression of Emotions in Man and Animals. Chicago: Univ. of Chicago Press. (Originally published 1872).

Davidson, D. (1963). Actions, reasons and causes. J. Philos., 60: 685–700.

—— (1980). 'Mental Events' and 'The Material Mind.' In Essays on Actions and Events. Oxford: Clarendon Press.

—— (1982). Paradoxes of irrationality. In Philosophical Essays on Freud, ed. R. Wollheim & J. Hopkins. Cambridge: Cambridge Univ. Press, pp. 289–305.

Demos, E. V. (1982). Affect in infancy: Physiology or psychology? Psychoanal. Inq., 1: 533–74.

—— (1987). Affect and the development of the self: A new frontier. In Frontiers in Self Psychology, ed. A. Goldberg. Hillsdale, NJ: Analytic Press, pp. 27–53.

De Rivera, J. (1977). A Structural Theory of the Emotions. Psychol. Issues, Monograph no. 40, 10(4). New York: Int. Univ. Press.

—— (1984). The structure of emotional relationships. In Emotions, Relationships, and Mental Health, ed. P. Shaver. Beverly Hills, CA: Sage.

De Sousa, R. (1980). The rationality of emotions. In Explaining Emotions, ed. A. O. Rorty. Berkeley: Univ. of Calif. Press, pp. 127–52.

—— (1987). The Rationality of Emotion. Cambridge: MIT Press.

Dixon, N. F. (1971). Subliminal Perception: The Nature of a Controversy. London: McGraw-Hill.

Duffy, E. (1957). The psychological significance of the concept of "arousal" or "activation." Psychol. Rev., 64: 265–75.

Eagle, M. (1980). A critical examination of motivational explanation in psychoanalysis. Psychoanal. Contemp. Thought, 3: 329–80.

—— (1987). The psychoanalytic and the cognitive unconscious. In Theories of the Unconscious and Theories of the Self, ed. R. Stern. Hillsdale, NJ: Analytic Press, pp. 155–90.

Eibl-Eibesfeldt, I. (1972). Similarities and differences between cultures in expressive movements. In Nonverbal Communication, ed. R. A. Hinde. London: Cambridge Univ. Press, pp. 297–314.

—— (1981). Strategies of social interaction. In Emotion: Theory, Research and Experience, ed. R. Plutchik & H. Kellerman. New York: Academic Press, pp. 57–80.

Ekman, P. (1984). Expression and the nature of emotion. In Approaches to Emotion, ed. K. R. Scherer & P. Ekman. Hillsdale, NJ: Lawrence Erlbaum, pp. 319–343.

—— & Friesen, W. V. (1975). Unmasking the Face. Englewood Cliffs, NJ: Prentice-Hall.

Ellenberger, H. (1970). The Discovery of the Unconscious. New York: Basic Books.

Emde, R. N. (1980). Toward a psychoanalytic theory of affect. In The Course of Life: Psychoanalytic Contributions Toward Understanding Personality Development. Vol.I: Infancy and Early Childhood, ed. S. I. Greenspan & G. H. Pollock. Washington, DC: NIMH, pp. 85–134.

—— (1981). Changing models of infancy and the nature of early development: Remodeling the foundation. J. Amer. Psychoanal. Assn., 29: 179–219.

—— (1983). The prerepresentational self and its affective core. Psychoanal. Study Child, 38: 165–92.

————— (1984). Levels of meaning for infant emotions: A biosocial view. In *Approaches to Emotion*, ed. K. R. Scherer & P. Ekman. Hillsdale, NJ: Lawrence Erlbaum, pp. 77–108.

————— (1988). Development terminable and interminable I: Innate and motivational factors from infancy. Int. J. Psychoanal., 69: 23–42.

————— & Robinson, J. (1979). The first two months: Recent research in developmental psychobiology and the changing view of the newborn. In *Basic Handbook of Child Psychiatry, Vol. 1*, ed. J. Call & J. Noshpitz. New York: Basic Books.

Fenichel, O. (1939). Early stages of ego development. In *The Collected Papers of Otto Fenichel*. New York: Norton.

————— (1945). *The Psychoanalytic Theory of Neurosis*. New York: Norton.

Fluegel, J. C., ed. (1955). *Studies in Feeling and Desire*. London: Duckworth.

Fodor, J. A. (1981). *Representations: Philosophical Essays on Mind and Psychology*. Cambridge, MA: Bradford/MIT Press.

————— (1983a). Imagery and the language of thought. In *States of Mind*, ed. J. Miller. New York: Pantheon Books, pp. 82–98.

————— (1983b). *The Modularity of Mind: An Essay on Faculty Psychology*. Cambridge, MA: Bradford/MIT Press.

Fonagy, P. (1982). The integration of psychoanalysis and experimental science: A review. Int. Rev. Psychoanal., 9: 123–46.

French, T. (1937). Adaptation to reality in terms of the repetition compulsion. Psychoanal. Q., 6: 54–61.

Freud, A. (1936). *The Ego and the Mechanisms of Defense*. London: Hogarth Press.

————— (1952). Studies in passivity. Part 2: Notes on a connection between the states of negativism and of emotional surrender. In *The Writings of Anna Freud*, Vol. 4. New York: Int. Univ. Press, pp. 256–69.

————— (1954). Problems of infantile neurosis: A discussion. Psychoanal. Study Child, 9: 16–71.

————— (1963). Regression as a principle in mental development. Bull. Menninger Clinic, 27: 126–39.

————— (1965). *Normality and Pathology in Childhood*. New York: Int. Univ. Press.

————— (1966–1970). *The writings of Anna Freud*, vol. 7. New York: Int. Univ. Press.

————— (1970–1980) *The Writings of Anna Freud*, vol. 8. New York: Int. Univ. Press.

————— (1977). The principal task of child analysis. In *The Writings of Anna Freud*, Vol. 8. New York: Int. Univ. Press, pp. 96–109.

Freud, S. (1888). Hysteria. S.E. 1, pp. 37–59.

————— (1892). Sketches for the 'Preliminary Comm.' of 1893. S.E. 1, pp. 147–53.

————— (1892, 1893). A case of successful treatment by hypnotism. S.E. 1, pp. 115–28.

————— (1892–1899). Extracts from the Fliess papers. S.E. 1, pp. 173–280.

————— (1893 [1888–1893]). Some points for a comparative study of organic and hysterical motor paralysis. S.E. 1, pp. 155–71.

————— (1894). The neuropsychoses of defense. S.E. 3, pp. 41–67.

————— (1895 [1950]). Project for a scientific psychology. S.E. 1, pp. 281–394.

————— (1896). Further remarks on the neuro-psychoses of defense. S.E. 3, pp. 157–85.

————— (1900). The interpretation of dreams. S.E. 4 & 5.

————— (1904). On psychotherapy. S.E. 7, pp. 255–68.

————— (1905a). Fragments of an analysis of a case of hysteria. S.E. 7, pp. 1–121.

—— (1905b). Three essays on the theory of sexuality. S.E. 7, pp. 123–241.

—— (1907a). Delusions and dreams in Jensen's *Gradiva*. S.E. 9, pp. 1–95.

—— (1907b). The sexual enlightenment of children. S.E. 9, pp. 129–139.

—— (1909). Analysis of a phobia in a five-year-old boy. S.E. 10, pp. 1–149.

—— (1915a). Instincts and their vicissitudes. S.E. 14, pp. 109–39.

—— (1915b). Repression. S.E. 14, pp. 141–57.

—— (1915c). The unconscious. S.E. 14, pp. 159–215.

—— (1916–1917). Introductory lectures on psychoanalysis. S.E. 16 & 17, pp. 13–463.

—— (1917). Mourning and melancholia. S.E. 14, pp. 237–58.

—— (1918 [1914]). From the history of an infantile neurosis. S.E. 17, pp. 1–122.

—— (1920). Beyond the pleasure principle. S.E. 18, pp. 1–63.

—— (1923). The ego and the id. S.E. 19, pp. 1–65.

—— (1924). The economic problem of masochism. S.E. 19, pp. 155–71.

—— (1925). Negation. S.E. 19, pp. 235–40.

—— (1926). Inhibitions, symptoms and anxiety. S.E. 20, pp. 75–173.

—— (1930). The Goethe prize. S.E. 21, pp. 207–11.

—— (1933 [1932]). New introductory lectures on psychoanalysis. S.E. 22, pp. 1–182.

—— (1937). Constructions in analysis. S.E. 23, pp. 255–69.

—— (1940 [1938]). An outline of psychoanalysis. S.E. 23, pp. 139–207.

Furman, E. (1985). On fusion, integration and feeling good. Psychoanal. Study Child, 40: 81–110.

Gaensbauer, T. J. (1982). The differentiation of discrete affects: A case report. Psychoanal. Study Child, 37: 29–66.

Gedo, J. & Goldberg, A. (1973). *Models of the Mind*. Chicago: Chicago Univ. Press.

Gill, M. (1963). *Topography and Systems in Psychoanalytic Theory*. New York: Int. Univ. Press.

Gill, M. M. & Klein, G. S. (1964). The structuring of drive and reality. Int. J. Psychoanal., 45: 483–98.

Glasser, M. (1986). Identification and its vicissitudes as observed in the perversions. Int. J. Psychoanal., 67: 9–18.

Glover, E. (1939). The psychoanalysis of affects. In *On the Early Development of Mind*, ed. G. Glover. New York: Int. Univ. Press, 1956.

—— (1945). Examination of the Klein system of child psychology. Psychoanal. Study Child, 1: 75–118.

Green, A. (1967). Le narcissime primaire: structure et état. L'Inconscient, 1: 127–57.

—— (1973). *Le discours vivant*: La conception psychanalytique de l'affect. Presses Universitaires de France.

—— (1975). The analyst, symbolization and absence in the analytic setting. Int. J. Psychoanal., 56: 1–22.

—— (1977). Conceptions of affect. Int. J. Psychoanal., 58: 129–56.

—— (1984). Reflexions libres sur la representation de l'affect. Rev. Franc. Psychanal., 49: 773–88.

—— (1986). *On Private Madness*. New York: Int. Univ. Press.

Greenberg, J. R. & Mitchell, S. A. (1983). *Object Relations in Psychoanalytic Theory*. Cambridge: Harvard Univ. Press.

Grinberg, L., Sor, D. & De Bianchedi, E. T. (1975). Introduction to the work of Bion. Pertshire: Clunie Press.

Grossman, W. I. & Simon, B. (1969). Anthropomorphism: Motive, meaning, and causality in psychoanalytic theory. Psychoanal. Study Child, 24: 78–113.

Grotstein, J. F., ed. (1981). *Do I Dare Disturb the Universe?* London: Caesura.

Hadley, J. (1983). The representational system: A bridging concept for psychoanalysis and trauma physiology. Int. Rev. Psychoanal., 10: 13–30.

————— Hampshire, S. N. (1983a). Notions of the unconscious mind. In *States of Mind*, ed. J. Miller. New York: Pantheon Books, pp. 100–115.

————— (1983b). *Morality and Conflict*. Cambridge, MA: Harvard Univ. Press.

Hansson, R. O., Jones, W.H., & Carpenter, B. N. (1984). Relational competence and social support. In *Emotions, Relationships, and Mental Health*, ed. P. Shaver. Beverly Hills: Sage.

Hartmann, H. (1927). Understanding and explanation. In *Essays on Ego Psychology*. New York: Int. Univ. Press, 1964, pp. 369–403.

————— (1939a). *Ego Psychology and the Problem of Adaptation*. New York: Int. Univ. Press.

————— (1939b). Psychoanalysis and the concept of health. Int. J. Psychoanal., 20: 308–21.

————— (1950). The application of psychoanalytic concepts to social science. Psychoanal. Q., 19: 385–92.

————— (1959). Psychoanalysis as a scientific theory. In *Psychoanalysis, Scientific Method and Philosophy*, ed. S. Hook. New York: Int. Univ. Press, pp. 3–37.

—————. (1964). *Essays on Ego Psychology*. New York: Int. Univ. Press.

—————, Kris, E. & Loewenstein, R. M. (1946). Comments on the formation of psychic structure. Psychoanal. Study Child, 2: 11–38.

Hayman, A. (1986). On Marjorie Brierley. Int. Rev. Psychoanal., 13: 338–92.

Hebb, D. O. (1946). Emotion in man and animal: An analysis of the intuitive processes of recognition. Psychol. Rev., 53: 88–106.

—————. (1972). *A Textbook of Psychology*. Philadelphia: Saunders.

Heider, F. (1971). *The Psychology of Interpersonal Relations*. New York: Wiley.

Heimann, P. (1950). On counter-transference. Int. J. Psychoanal., 31: 81–84.

Hillman, J. (1961). *Emotion*. Northwestern Univ. Press.

Holt, R. (1965). Freud's biological assumptions. In *Psychoanalysis and Current Biological Thought*, ed. N. S. Greenfield & W. C. Lewis. Madison: Univ. of Wisconsin Press, pp. 93–121.

—————, ed. (1967). *Motives and Thought*. New York: Int. Univ. Press.

————— (1976). *Drive or Wish? A Reconsideration of the Psychoanalytic Theory of Motivation*. Psychol. Issues, Monograph 9. New York: Int. Univ. Press.

Isaacs, S. (1943). The nature and function of fantasy. In *Developments in Psychoanalysis*. ed. M. Klein, P. Heimann, S. Isaacs, & J. Riviere. London: Hogarth Press, 1952.

Izard, C. E. (1971). *The Face of Emotion*. New York: Appleton-Century-Crofts.

————— (1977). *Human Emotions*. New York: Plenum Press.

————— (1978). On the ontogenesis of emotions and emotion-cognition relationships in infancy. In *The Development of Affect*, ed. M. Lewis & L. A. Rosenblum. New York: Plenum Press.

—— (1982). Comments on emotion and cognition: Can there be a working relationship? In *Affect and Cognition*, ed. M. S. Clark & S. T. Fiske. Hillsdale, NJ: Lawrence Erlbaum.

Jacobson, E. (1953). Affects and psychic discharge processes. In *Drives, Affects, Behavior*, ed. R. Loewenstein. New York: Int. Univ. Press, pp. 38–66.

—— (1957). On normal and pathological moods: Their nature and functions. Psychoanal. Study Child, 12: 73–113.

—— (1964). *The Self and the Object World*. New York: Int. Univ. Press.

—— (1967). *Psychotic Conflict and Reality*. New York: Int. Univ. Press.

—— (1971). *Depression*. Comparative Studies of Normal, Neurotic and Psychotic Conditions. New York: Int. Univ. Press.

James, W. (1884). What is an emotion? Mind, 9: 188–205.

—— (1892). *Textbook of Psychology*. London: Macmillan.

—— (1950). *The Principles of Psychology*. New York: Dover. (Originally published 1890.)

Joffe, W. G. & Sandler, J. (1965). Notes on pain, depression and individuation. Psychoanal. Study Child, 20: 394–424.

Jones, E. (1920). Recent advances in psychoanalysis. In *Papers on Psychoanalysis*, 3rd ed. London: Balliers-Tindall & Cox, 1923.

—— (1929). Fear, guilt and hate. Int. J. Psychoanal., 10: 383–98.

—— (1948). *Papers on Psychoanalysis*. London: Marsefield Reprints.

Joseph, B. (1978). Different types of anxiety and their handling in the analytic situation. Int. J. Psychoanal., 59: 223–28.

—— (1985). Transference: The total situation. Int. J. Psychoanal., 66: 447–54.

Kanzer, M. (1971). Psychoanalytic perspectives in theory and practice. In *The Unconscious Today: Essays in Honor of Max Schur*, ed. M. Kanzer. New York: Int. Univ. Press, pp. 13–32.

Kaplan, A. (1958). *The Conduct of Inquiry: Methodology for Behavioral Science*. San Francisco: Chandler Publishing Co.

Kaywin, L. (1960). An epigenetic approach to the psychoanalytic theory of instincts and affects. J. Amer. Psychoanal. Assn., 8: 613–58.

Kelly, G. A. (1955). *The Psychology of Personal Constructs*. New York: Norton.

Kernberg, O. F. (1976). *Object Relations Theory and Clinical Psychoanalysis*. New York: Aronson.

—— (1980). *Internal World and External Reality*. New York: Aronson.

—— (1982). Self, ego, affects and drives. J. Amer. Psychoanal. Assn., 30: 893–917.

—— (1984). New perspectives in psychoanalytic affect theory. Unpublished manuscript.

Klein, G. S. (1976). *Psychoanalytic Theory: An Exploration of Essentials*. New York: Int. Univ. Press.

Klein, M. (1927). Symposium on Child Analysis. In *The Writings of Melanie Klein*, Vol. 1, ed. R. Money-Kyrle. London: Hogarth Press, 1981, pp. 186–98.

—— (1930). The importance of symbol formation in the development of the ego. Ibid., pp. 219–32.

—— (1933). The early development of conscience in the child. Ibid., pp. 248–57.

—— (1935). A contribution to the psychogenesis of manic-depressive states. Ibid., pp. 262–89.

—— (1936). Weaning. Ibid., pp. 290–305.

—— (1937). Love, guilt and reparation. Ibid., pp. 306–43.

—— (1940). Mourning and its relation to manic-depressive states. Ibid., pp. 344–69.

—— (1945). The Oedipus complex in the light of early anxieties. Ibid., pp. 370–419.

—— (1946). Notes on some schizoid mechanisms. In *The Writings of Melanie Klein.* Vol. 3, ed. R. Money-Kyrle. London: Hogarth Press, 1984, pp. 1–24.

—— (1948). On the theory of anxiety and guilt. Ibid., pp. 25–42.

—— (1952). On the origins of transference. Ibid., pp. 48–56.

—— (1957). Envy and gratitude. Ibid., pp. 176–235.

—— (1960). On mental health. Ibid., pp. 268–74.

Knapp, P. H. (1987). Some contemporary contributions to the study of the emotions. J. Amer. Psychoanal. Assn., 35: 205–48.

Kohut, H. (1971). *The Analysis of the Self.* New York: Int. Univ. Press.

—— (1977). *The Restoration of the Self.* New York: Int. Univ. Press.

Krueger, F. (1968). The essence of feeling. In *The Nature of Emotion*, ed. M. B. Arnold. Baltimore: Penguin, pp. 97–108.

Krystal, H. (1974). The genetic development of affects and affect regression. Ann. Psychoanal., 2: 98–126.

—— (1975). Affect tolerance. Ann. Psychoanal., 3: 179–220.

—— (1978). Trauma and affects. Psychoanal. Study Child, 33: 81–116.

—— (1982). Alexithymia and the effectiveness of psychoanalytic treatment. Int. J. Psychoanal. Psychother., 9: 353–88.

—— (1988). *Integration and Self-Healing: Affect, Trauma, Alexithymia.* Hillsdale, NJ: Analytic Press.

Kulovesi, Y. (1931). Psychoanalytische Bemerkungen zur James-Langeschen Affekttheorie. Imago, 17: 392–98.

Lacan, J. (1977). *Ecrits.* Paris: du Seuil.

Lacey, J. R. (1967). Somatic response patterning and stress: Some revisions of activation theory. In *Psychological Stress: Issues in Research*, ed. M. H. Appley & R. Trumbull. New York: Appleton-Century-Crofts, pp. 14–44.

Lachman, F. M. & Stolorow, R. D. (1981). The developmental significance of affective states: Implications for psychoanalytic treatment. Ann. Psychoanal., 9: 215–29.

Landauer, K. (1938). Affects, passions, and temperament. Int. J. Psychoanal., 19: 388–415; also in Imago, 22: 275–91, 1936.

Landenslager, M.L. & Reite, M.L. (1984). Losses and separations: Immunological consequences and health implications. In *Emotions, Relationships, and Mental Health*, ed. P. Shaver. Beverly Hills: Sage.

Laplanche, J. & Pontalis, J. B. (1973). *The Language of Psychoanalysis.* Trans. D. Nicholson-Smith. New York: Norton.

Lazarus, R. S. (1956). Subception: Fact or artifact? A reply to Eriksen. Psychol. Rev., 63: 343–47.

—— (1968). Emotions and adaptation: Conceptual and empirical relations. In *Nebraska Symposium on Motivation*, ed. W. J. Arnold. Lincoln: Univ. of Nebraska Press.

—— (1982). Thoughts on the relations between emotion and cognition. Amer. Psychologist, 37: 1019–24.

—— (1984a). Cognition, emotion and motivation: The doctoring of Humpty-Dumpty. In *Approaches to Emotion*, ed. K. R. Scherer & P. Ekman. Hillsdale, NJ: Lawrence Erlbaum, pp. 221–38.

—— (1984b). The primacy of cognition. Amer. Psychologist, 39: 124–29.

————, Averill, J. R. & Opton, E. M. (1970). Toward a cognitive theory of emotions. In *Feelings and Emotions*, ed. M. B. Arnold. New York: Academic Press, pp. 207–32.

————, Kanner, A. D., & Folkman, S. (1981). Emotions: A cognitive-phenomenological analysis. In *Emotion: Theory, Research and Experience*, ed. R. Plutchik & H. Kellerman. New York: Academic Press, pp. 189–217.

————, R. S. & McCleary, R. A. (1951). Autonomic discrimination without awareness: A study of subception. Psychol. Rev., 58: 113–22.

Leeper, R. W. (1948). A motivational theory of emotion to replace 'emotion as disorganized response.' Psychol. Rev. 55: 5–21.

Leventhal, H. (1974). Emotions: A basic problem for social psychology. In *Social Psychology*, ed. C. Nemeth. Chicago: Rand McNally.

———— (1979). A perceptual-motor processing model of emotion. In *Perception of Emotion in Self and Others*, ed. P. Pliner, K. R. Blankenstein & I. Spiegel. New York: Plenum Press.

———— (1982). The integration of emotion and cognition. In *Affect and Cognition*, ed. M. S. Clark & S. T. Fiske. Hillsdale, NJ: Lawrence Erlbaum.

———— (1984). A perceptual motor theory of emotion. In *Approaches to Emotion*, ed. K. R. Scherer & P. Ekman. Hillsdale, NJ: Lawrence Erlbaum, pp. 271–92.

Levin, K. (1978). *Freud's Early Psychology of the Neuroses: A Historical Perspective*. Hassocks, Sussex: Harvester Press.

Lewin, B. D. (1965). Reflections on affect. In *Drives, Affects, Behavior*, Vol. 2, ed. M. Schur. New York: Int. Univ. Press, pp. 23–37.

Lichtenberg, J.D. (1983). *Psychoanalysis and Infant Research*. Hillsdale, NJ: Analytic Press.

———— (1987). Infant studies and clinical work with adults. Psychoanal. Inq., 7: 311–30.

Limentani, A. (1977). Affects and the psychoanalytic situation. Int. J. Psychoanal., 58: 171–82.

Little, M. (1951). *Transference Neurosis and Transference Psychosis: Toward Basic Unity*. London: Free Association Books.

Loewald, H. W. (1971). On motivation and instinct theory. Psychoanal. Study Child, 26: 91–128.

McDougall, W. (1923). *Outline of Psychology*. New York: Scribner.

———— (1928). Emotion and feeling distinguished. In *Feelings and Emotions: The Wittenberg Symposium*, ed. M. L. Reymert. Worcester, MA: Clark Univ. Press, pp. 200–205.

McGinn, C. (1982). *The Character of Mind*. Oxford: Oxford Univ. Press.

Mackay, N. (1981). Melanie Klein's metapsychology: Phenomenological and mechanistic perspectives. Int. J. Psychoanal., 62: 187–98.

MacLean, P. D. (1973). Phylogenesis. In *Expression of the Emotions in Man*, ed. P. H. Knapp. New York: Int. Univ. Press.

———— (1977). On the evaluation of three mentalities. In *New Dimensions in Psychiatry: A World View*, vol. 2., ed. S. Arieti & G. Chrzanowski. New York: Wiley.

Mahler, M. S. (1961). On sadness and grief in infancy and childhood. Psychoanal. Study Child, 16: 322–51.

———— (1966). Notes on the development of basic moods: The depressive affect. In *Psychoanalysis—A General Psychology: Essays in Honor of Heinz Hartmann*, ed. R. M. Loewenstein, L. M. Newman, M. Schur, & A. J. Solnit. New York: Int. Univ. Press, pp. 152–68.

────── (1974). Symbiosis and the vicissitudes of individuation. In *The Selected Papers of Margaret Mahler*. New York: Jason Aronson, pp. 277–97.
──────, Pine, F. & Bergman, A. (1975). *The Psychological Birth of the Human Infant*. New York: Basic Books.

Mandler, G. (1975). *Mind and Emotion*. New York: Wiley.
────── (1981). Affect, emotion and other cognitive curiosities. Symposium on Cognition, Carnegie-Mellon Univ., no. 17.
────── (1982). The structure of value: Accounting for taste. In *Affect and Cognition*, ed. M. S. Clark & S. T. Fiske. Hillsdale, NJ: Lawrence Erlbaum.
────── (1983). The nature of emotion. In *States of Mind*, ed. J. Miller. New York: Pantheon, pp. 136–53.

Mark, M.M. & Folger, R. (1984). Responses to relative deprivation: A conceptual framework. In *Emotions, Relationships, and Mental Health*, ed. P. Shaver. Beverly Hills: Sage.

Marty, P. & de M'uzan, M. (1963). La Pensee Operatoire. Rev. Franc. Psychanal., 27: suppl., pp. 345–56.

Matte-Blanco, I. (1988). *Thinking, Feeling and Being*. London: Routledge.

Meltzer, D. (1978). *The Kleinian Development*. Part 3: The Clinical Significance of the Work of Bion. Pertshire: Clunie Press.

Mitchell, S. A. & Greenberg, J. R. (1983). *Object Relations in Psychoanalytic Theory*. Cambridge, MA: Harvard Univ. Press.

Modell, A. H. (1963). The concept of psychic energy. J. Amer. Psychoanal. Assn., 11: 605.
────── (1984). *Psychoanalysis in a New Context*. New York: Int. Univ. Press.

Novey, S. (1959). A clinical view of affect theory in psychoanalysis. Int. J. Psychoanal., 40: 94–104.
────── (1961). Further considerations on affect theory in psychoanalysis. Int. J. Psychoanal., 42: 21–31.
────── (1985). *The Second Look: The Reconstruction of Personal History in Psychiatry and Psychoanalysis*. New York: Int. Univ. Press.

Noy, P. (1969). A revision of the psychoanalytic theory of the primary process. Int. J. Psychoanal., 50: 155–78.
────── (1982). A revision of the psychoanalytic theory of affect. Ann. Psychoanal., 10: 139–86.

Panel (1952). The psychoanalytic theory of affects, rep. L. Rangell. J. Amer. Psychoanal. Assn., 8: 300–315.

Panel (1967). Psychoanalytic theory of affect, rep. L. B. Loefgren. J. Amer. Psychoanal. Assn., 16: 638–50.

Panel (1968). Psychoanalytic theory of the instinctual drives in relation to recent developments, rep. H. Dahl. J. Amer. Psychoanal. Assn., 16: 613–37.

Panel (1974). Toward a theory of affects, rep. P. Castelnuovo-Tedesco. J. Amer. Psychoanal. Assn., 22: 612–25.

Panel (1982). New directions in affect theory, rep. E. P. Lester. J. Amer. Psychoanal. Assn., 30: 197–212.

Peto, A. (1967). On affect control. Psychoanal. Study Child, 22: 36–52.

Piaget, J. (1937). *The Construction of Reality in the Child*. New York: Basic Books, 1954.
────── (1954). Les relations entre l'affectivité et l'intelligence dans le developpement mental de l'enfant. Paris: Centre de Documentation Universitaire.

————— (1973). The affective unconscious and the cognitive unconscious. J. Amer. Psychoanal. Assn., 21: 249–61.

Piers, G. & Singer, M. B. (1953). *Shame and Guilt: A Psychoanalytic and Cultural Study*. Springfield, IL: Charles C. Thomas.

Pliner, P., Blankenstein, K. R. & Spiegel, I., eds. (1979). *Perception of Emotion in Self and Others: Advances in the Study of Communication and Affect*. Vol. 5. New York: Plenum Press.

Plutchik, R. (1960). The multifactor analytic theory of emotion. J. Psychol., 50: 153–71.

————— (1962). *The Emotions: Facts, Theories and a New Model*. New York: Random House.

————— (1966). The psychophysiology of individual differences, with special reference to emotions. Annals New York Academy of Sci., 134: 776–81.

————— (1970). Emotions, evolution and adaptive processes. In *Feelings and Emotions*, ed. M. B. Arnold. New York: Academic Press.

—————, ed. (1980). *Emotion: A Psychoevolutionary Synthesis*. New York: Harper & Row.

————— (1984). Emotions: A general psychoevolutionary theory. In *Approaches to Emotion*, ed. K. R. Scherer & P. Ekman. Hillsdale, NJ: Lawrence Erlbaum, pp. 197–220.

————— & Kellerman, H., eds. (1981). *Emotion: Theory, Research and Experience*. New York: Academic Press.

Poetzel, O. (1917). The relationship between experimentally induced dream images and indirect vision. Trans. J. Wolff, D. Rapaport & S. Annin. Psychol. Issues, 1960, 3, Monograph 7: 41–120.

Polanyi, M. (1958). *Personal Knowledge*. London: Routledge & Kegan Paul.

Pribram, K. H. (1967a). Emotion: Steps toward a neuropsychological theory. In *Neurophysiology and Emotion*, ed. D. C. Glass. New York: Rockefeller Univ. Press.

————— (1967b). The new neurology and the biology of emotion: A structural approach. Amer. Psychologist, 22: 830–38.

————— (1970). Feelings as monitors. In *Feelings and Emotions*, ed. M. B. Arnold. New York: Academic Press.

————— (1980). The biology of feeling and emotion. In *Emotion: A Psychoevolutionary Synthesis*, ed. R. Plutchik. New York: Harper & Row.

————— (1984). Emotion: A biobehavioral analysis. In *Approaches to Emotion*, ed. K. R. Scherer & P. Ekman. Hillsdale, NJ: Lawrence Erlbaum, pp. 13–38.

————— & Gill, M. M. (1976). *Freud's "Project" Re-Assessed*. New York: Basic Books.

Pulver, S. E. (1971). Can affects be unconscious? Int. J. Psychoanal., 52: 347–54.

————— (1987). Epilogue: How theory shapes technique: Perspectives on a clinical study. Psychoanal. Inq., 7: 289–99.

Racker, H. (1957). *Transference and Countertransference*. London: Marsefield.

Ramzey, I. & Wallerstein, R. S. (1958). Pain, fear, and anxiety: A study in their interrelationships. Psychoanal. Study Child, 13: 147–89.

Rangell, L. (1955). On the psychoanalytic theory of anxiety: A statement of a unitary theory. J. Amer. Psychoanal. Assn., 3: 389–414.

————— (1967). Psychoanalysis, affects and the 'human core.' Psychoanal. Q., 36: 172–202.

———— (1968). A further attempt to resolve the "problem of anxiety." J. Amer. Psychoanal. Assn., 16: 371–404.

———— (1978). On understanding and treating anxiety and its derivatives. Int. J. Psychoanal., 59: 229–36.

Rapaport, D., ed. (1950). *Emotions and Memory.* New York: Int. Univ. Press.

———— (1953). On the psychoanalytic theory of affects. Int. J. Psychoanal., 34: 177–98.

———— (1960). On the psychoanalytic theory of motivation. In *Nebraska Symposium on Motivation*, ed. M. R. Jones. Lincoln: Univ. of Nebraska Press.

———— & Gill, M. M. (1960). The points of view and assumptions of metapsychology. Int. J. Psychoanal., 15: 153–62.

Ricoeur, P. (1970). *Freud and Philosophy: An Essay on Interpretation.* New Haven: Yale Univ. Press.

Riviere, J. (1936). On the genesis of psychical conflict in early infancy. Int. J. Psychoanal., 55: 397–505.

————, ed. (1952). *Developments in Psychoanalysis.* London: Hogarth Press.

Rorty, A. O., ed. (1980). *Explaining Emotions.* Berkeley: Univ. of Calif. Press.

Rorty, R. (1979). *Philosophy and the Mirror of Nature.* Princeton: Princeton Univ. Press.

Rose, G. J. (1988). *Trauma and Mastery in Art and Life.* New Haven: Yale Univ. Press.

Rosenblatt, A. & Thickstun, J. (1970). A study of the concept of psychic energy. Int. J. Psychoanal., 51: 265–78.

Ross, N. (1975). Affects as cognition: With observations on the meanings of mystical states. Int. Rev. Psychoanal., 2: 79–93.

Rubinstein, B. B. (1980). The problem of confirmation in clinical psychoanalysis. J. Amer. Psychoanal. Assn., 28: 397–417.

Sachs, D. (1974). On Freud's doctrine of the emotions. In *Freud: Philosophical Essays*, ed. R. Wollheim & J. Hopkins. Cambridge: Cambridge Univ. Press, pp. 92–105.

Sackeim, H. A., Weinman, A. L., Gur, R. C., Greenberg, M., Hungerbuhler, J. P. & Geschwind, N. (1982). Pathological laughing and crying: Functional brain asymmetry in the experience of positive and negative emotions. Arch. Neurol., 39: 210–18.

Sandler, J. (1960a). The background of safety. Int. J. Psychoanal., 41: 352–65.

———— (1960b). On the concept of the superego. Psychoanal. Study Child, 15: 128–62.

———— (1962). Psychology and psychoanalysis. Br. J. Med. Psychol., 35: 91–100.

———— (1967). Trauma, strain and development. In *Psychic Trauma*, ed. S. Furst. New York: Basic Books.

———— (1972). The role of affects in psychoanalytic theory. In *Physiology, Emotion and Psychosomatic Illness*. CIBA Foundation Symposium 8. Amsterdam: Elsevier.

———— (1974). Psychological conflict and the structural model: some theoretical and clinical implications. Int. J. Psychoanal., 55: 53–62.

———— (1983). Reflections on some relations between psychoanalytic concepts and psychoanalytic practice. Int. J. Psychoanal., 64: 35–45.

———— (1985a). *The Analysis of Defence.* New York: Int. Univ. Press.

———— (1985b). Towards a reconsideration of the psychoanalytic theory of motivation. Bull. Anna Freud Centre, 8: 223–44.

———— (1986). Reality and the stabilizing function of unconscious fantasy. Bull. Anna Freud Centre, 9: 177–94.

———— (1987). The past unconscious, the present unconscious and the vicissitudes of guilt. Int. J. Psychoanal., 68: 331–42.

Sandler, J. & Freud, A. (1985). *The Analysis of Defense: The Ego and the Mechanisms of Defense Revisited.* New York: Int. Univ. Press.

Sandler, J. & Joffe, W. G. (1966). On skill and sublimation. J. Amer. Psychoanal. Assn., 14: 335–55.

———— (1969). Towards a basic psychoanalytic model. Int. J. Psychoanal., 50: 79–90.

Sandler, J. & Rosenblatt, B. (1962). The concept of the representational world. Psychoanal. Study Child, 17: 128–45.

Sandler, J. & Sandler, A.-M. (1978). On the development of object relationships and affects. Int. J. Psychoanal., 59: 285–96.

———— (1983). The 'second censorship,' the 'three box model' and some technical implications. Int. J. Psychoanal., 64: 413–25.

———— (1984). The past unconscious, the present unconscious, and interpretation of the transference. Psychoanal. Ing., 4: 367–99.

———— (1986). The gyroscopic function of unconscious fantasy. In *Toward a Comprehensive Model of Schizophrenic Disorders*, ed. D. B. Feinsilver. Hillsdale, NJ: Analytic Press, pp. 109–23.

————. (1988). Psychoanalytic technique and "Analysis terminable." Int. J. Psychoanal., 69: 335–46.

Sartre, J. P. (1948). *The Emotions: A Sketch of a Theory*, trans. B. Frechtman. New York: Philosophical Library.

Schachter, S. (1966). The interaction of cognitive and physiological determinants of emotional state. In *Anxiety and Behavior*, ed. C. D. Spielberger. New York: Academic Press.

———— (1970). Assumption of identity and the peripheralist-centralist controversies in motivation and emotion. In *Feelings and Emotions*, ed. M. B. Arnold. New York: Academic Press.

———— & Singer, J. E. (1962). Cognitive, social and physiological determinants of emotional state. Psychol. Rev., 69: 379–99.

Schafer, R. (1964). The clinical analysis of affects. J. Amer. Psychoanal. Assn., 12: 275–99.

———— (1976). *A New Language for Psychoanalysis.* New Haven: Yale Univ. Press.

———— (1979). *Language and insight.* New Haven: Yale Univ. Press.

———— (1980). Narration in the psychoanalytic dialogue. Crit. Inq., 7: 29–53.

———— (1983). *The Analytic Attitude.* London: Hogarth Press.

Schank, R. C. & Abelson, R. P. (1977a). Scripts, plans and knowledge. In *Thinking*, ed. P. M. Johnson-Laird & P. C. Wason. Cambridge: Cambridge Univ. Press.

———— (1977b). *Scripts, Plans, Goals and Understanding: An Inquiry into Human Knowledge Structures.* Hillsdale, NJ: Lawrence Erlbaum.

Scheff, T.J. (1984). The taboo on coarse emotions. In *Emotions, Relationships, and Mental Health*, ed. P. Shaver. Beverly Hills: Sage.

Scheler, M. (1912). *The Nature of Sympathy.* Hamden, CT: Archon Books, 1972.

Scherer, K. R. (1984). On the nature and function of emotion: A component process approach. In *Approaches to Emotion*, ed. K. R. Scherer & P. Ekman. Hillsdale, NJ: Lawrence Erlbaum, pp. 293–318.

———— & Ekman, P., eds. (1984). *Approaches to Emotion.* Hillsdale, NJ: Lawrence Erlbaum.

Schmale, A. H. (1964). A genetic view of affects, with special reference to the genesis of helplessness and hopelessness. Psychoanal. Study Child, 19: 287–310.

Schur, M. (1953). The ego in anxiety. In *Drives, Affects, Behavior*, ed. R. Loewenstein. New York: Int. Univ. Press.

———— (1955). Comments on the metapsychology of somatization. Psychoanal. Study Child, 10: 119–64.

———— (1958). The ego and the id in anxiety. Psychoanal. Study Child, 13: 190–220.

———— (1960). Phylogenesis and ontogenesis of affect- and structure-formation and the phenomenon of repetition compulsion. Int. J. Psychoanal., 41: 275–87.

———— (1964). Symptom formation and character formation. Contribution to discussion of prepublished papers. Int. J. Psychoanal., 45: 147–50.

———— (1966). *The Id and the Regulatory Principles of Mental Functioning.* New York: Int. Univ. Press.

———— (1968a). Affects and cognitions. Int. J. Psychoanal., 50: 647–53.

———— (1968b). Introduction to the colloquium on affect and cognition. Delivered at the meeting of the American Psychoanalytic Society, Boston.

Schwartz, A. (1987). Drives, affects, behavior—and learning: Approaches to a psychobiology of emotion and to an integration of psychoanalytic and neurobiologic thought. J. Amer. Psychoanal. Assn., 35: 467–506.

Scott, J. P. (1981). The function of emotions in behavioral systems: A systems theory analysis. In *Emotion: Theory, Research and Experience*, ed. R. Plutchik & H. Kellerman. New York: Academic Press, pp. 35–56.

Searles, H. F. (1955). *Collected Papers on Schizophrenia and Related Subjects.* New York: Int. Univ. Press.

———— (1979). *Countertransference and Related Subjects.* New York: Int. Univ. Press.

Segal, H. (1964). *Introduction to the Work of Melanie Klein.* London: Heineman.

———— (1973). *Introduction to the Work of Melanie Klein*, 2nd ed. London: Hogarth Press.

———— (1979). *Klein.* Brighton, Sussex: Harvester Press.

Shaver, P. R., ed. (1984). *Emotions, Relationships, and Mental Health.* Beverly Hills: Sage.

Sherwood, M. (1969). *The Logic of Explanation in Psychoanalysis.* New York: Academic Press.

Shevrin, H. (1978). Semblances of feeling: The imagery of affect in empathy, dreams, and unconscious processes—A revision of Freud's several affect theories. In *The Human Mind Revisited*, ed. S. Smith, pp. 263–94.

Sifneos, P. E. (1975). The prevalence of "alexithymic" characteristics in psychosomatic patients. Psychother. & Psychosom., 26: 65–70.

Smith, J. H. & Kerrigan, W., eds. (1983). *Interpreting Lacan.* New Haven: Yale Univ. Press.

Socarides, C. W., ed. (1977). *The World of Emotions.* New York: Int. Univ. Press.

Solomon, R. C. (1976). *The Passions: The Myth and Nature of Human Emotion.* New York: Doubleday.

———— (1980). Emotions and choice. In *Explaining Emotions*, ed. A. O. Rorty. Berkeley: Univ. of Calif. Press, pp. 251–82.

Solomon, R. L. & Corbit, J. D. (1974). An opponent-process theory of motivation. I: Temporal dynamics of affect. Psychol. Rev., 81: 119–45.

Solyom, A. E. (1987). New research on affect regulation: Developmental, clinical and theoretical considerations. Psychoanal. Inq., 7: 331–47.

Spiegel, L. A. (1966). Affects in relation to self and object. Psychoanal. Study Child, 21: 69–92.

Spitz, R. A. (1950). Anxiety in infancy. Int. J. Psychoanal., 31: 138–43.

——— (1957). No and Yes: On the Genesis of Human Communication. New York: Int. Univ. Press.

——— (1965). The First Year of Life. New York: Int. Univ. Press.

——— (1972). Bridges: On anticipation, duration and meaning. J. Amer. Psychoanal. Assn., 20: 721–35.

Stein, R. (1980). Differential responsiveness in different states of attention as measured by voluntary and by autonomic indicators. Master's thesis, Hebrew Univ. of Jerusalem.

Stern, D. (1985). The Interpersonal World of the Infant. New York: Basic Books.

Stern, R., ed. (1987). Theories of the Unconscious and Theories of the Self. Hillsdale, NJ: Analytic Press.

Stewart, W. A. (1967). Psychoanalysis: The First Ten Years. New York: Macmillan.

Stolorow, R. & Atwood, G. (1979). Faces in a Cloud: Subjectivity in Personality. New York: Aronson.

Stolorow, R., Brandschaft, B., & Atwood, G. E. (1987). Psychoanalytic Treatment: An Intersubjective Approach. Hillsdale, NJ: Analytic Press.

Stolorow, R. & Lachman, F. (1980). Psychoanalysis of Developmental Arrests: Theory and Treatment. New York: Int. Univ. Press.

Symposium on Cognition (1981). Carnegie-Mellon Univ., no. 17.

Tavris, C. (1984). On the wisdom of counting to ten: Personal and social dangers of anger expression. In Emotions, Relationships, and Mental Health, ed. P. Shaver. Beverly Hills: Sage.

Taylor, C. (1985). Human Agency and Language. Philosophical Papers, I. Cambridge: Cambridge Univ. Press.

Taylor, G. J. (1987). Psychosomatic Medicine and Contemporary Psychoanalysis. New York: Int. Univ. Press.

Thoits, P. A. (1984). Coping, social support, and psychological out comes: The central role of emotion. In Emotions, Relationships, and Mental Health, ed. P. Shaver. Beverly Hills: Sage.

Thompson, A. E. (1985). The nature of emotion and its development. In Event-Theory: A Piaget-Freud Integration. ed. I. Fast. Hillsdale, NJ: Lawrence Erlbaum.

Thorner, H. A. (1981). Notes on the desire for knowledge. Int. J. Psychoanal., 62: 73–80.

Tomkins, S. S. (1962–1963). Affect, Imagery, Consciousness. 2 vols. New York: Springer.

——— (1970). Affect as the primary motivational system. In Feelings and Emotions, ed. M. B. Arnold. New York: Academic Press.

——— (1979). Script Theory: Differential Magnification of Affects. In The Nebraska Symposium on Motivation, ed. R. A. Dienstbier. Lincoln: Univ. of Nebraska Press.

——— (1980). Affect as amplification: Some modifications in theory. In Emotion: The-

ory, Research and Experience, ed. R. Plutchik & H. Kellerman. New York: Academic Press, pp. 141–64.

——— (1981). The quest for primary motives: Biography and autobiography of an idea. J. Pers. Soc. Psychol., 41: 306–29.

——— (1984). Affect theory. In *Approaches to Emotion*, ed. K. R. Scherer & P. Ekman. Hillsdale, NJ: Lawrence Erlbaum, pp. 163–96.

Trevarthen, C. (1984). Emotions in infancy: Regulators of contacts and relationships with persons. In *Approaches to Emotion*, ed. K. R. Scherer & P. Ekman. Hillsdale, NJ: Lawrence Erlbaum, pp. 129–61.

Wallerstein, R. (1977). Psychic energy reconsidered: Introduction. J. Amer. Psychoanal. Assn., 25: 529–35.

Weiner, W. B., Russell, D. & Lerman, D. (1978). Affective consequences of causal ascriptions. In *New Direction in Attribution Research*, Vol. 2, ed. J. H. Harvey, W. Ickes & R. F. Kidd. Hillsdale, NJ: Lawrence Erlbaum, pp. 59–90.

Weinshel, E. M. (1970). Some psychoanalytic considerations on moods. Int. J. Psychoanal., 51: 313–20.

White, R. W. (1963). *Ego and Reality in Psychoanalytic Theory: A Proposal regarding Independent Drive Energies*. Psychol. Issues, no. 11. New York: Int. Univ. Press.

Whybrow, P. (1984). Contributions from neuroendocrinology. In *Approaches to Emotion*, ed. K. R. Scherer & P. Ekman. Hillsdale, NJ: Lawrence Erlbaum, pp. 59–75.

Winnicott, D. (1947). Hate in the countertransference. In *Collected Papers: Through Pediatrics to Psychoanalysis*. London: Tavistock, 1958, pp. 194–203.

——— (1960). Ego distortion in terms of true and false self. In *The Maturational Processes and the Facilitating Environment*. New York: Int. Univ. Press, 1977, pp. 140–52.

——— (1963). The development of the capacity for concern. In *The Maturational Processes and the Facilitating Environment*. New York: Int. Univ. Press, 1977, pp. 73–82.

Wittgenstein, L. (1953). *Philosophische Untersuchungen*. Frankfurt: Suhrkamp Verlag, 1975.

Young, P. T. (1961). *Motivation and Emotion*. New York: Wiley.

——— (1967). Affective arousal: Some implications. Amer. Psychologist, 22: 32–40.

Zajonc, R. B. (1980). Feeling and thinking: Preferences need no inferences. Amer. Psychologist, 35: 151–75.

——— (1984a). The interaction of affect and cognition. In *Approaches to Emotion*, ed. K. R. Scherer & P. Ekman. Hillsdale, NJ: Lawrence Erlbaum, pp. 239–46.

——— (1984b). On the primacy of affect. Amer. Psychologist, 39: 117–23.

———, Pietromonaco, P., & Bargh, J. (1982). Independence of interaction of affects and cognition. In *Affect and Cognition*, ed. M. S. Clark & S. T. Fiske. Hillsdale, NJ: Lawrence Erlbaum, pp. 211–27.

Zetzel, E. R. (1949). Anxiety and the capacity to bear it. In *The Capacity for Emotional Growth*, ed. E. R. Zetzel. New York: Int. Univ. Press, 1965.

——— (1965). Depression and the incapacity to bear it. In *Drives, Affects, Behavior*, Vol. 2, ed. M. Schur. New York: Int. Univ. Press, pp. 243–77.

Author Index

Subject Index

About the Author

RUTH STEIN is a lecturer at Tel Aviv University and a senior candidate at the Israeli Psychoanalytic Institute. She completed her M. A. in experimental psychology and received her Ph.D. in psychoanalysis at the Hebrew University of Jerusalem. She also works as a psychotherapist in private practice and has published several articles in psychotherapy journals, including the *International Journal of Psychoanalysis* and *Sichot/Dialogues*.